CONSIDERING THE CURRICULUM
DURING STUDENT TEACHING

CONSIDERING *the* CURRICULUM DURING STUDENT TEACHING

John Heywood

Kogan Page, London
Nichols Publishing Company, New York

First published in Great Britain in 1984
by Kogan Page Limited, 120 Pentonville Road, London N1 9JN

British Library Cataloguing in Publication Data
Heywood, John, *1930*
Considering the curriculum during student
teaching.
1. Education — Curricula
I. Title
375   LB1570
ISBN 0-85038-718-3

First published in the USA by Nichols Publishing Company,
PO Box 96, New York, NY 10024

Library of Congress Cataloguing in Publication Data
Heywood, John, 1930
Considering the curriculum during student teaching.
1. Student teaching.   2. Curriculum change.
I. Title.
LB2157.A3H49 1984   370'.7'33   83-6251
ISBN 0-89397-164-2

Contents

Acknowledgements

I am greatly indebted to R Derricott of the University of Liverpool, to Dr P Hogan of St Patrick's College, Maynooth (National University of Ireland), P J McGuinness and Dr D J Murphy of the University of Dublin, Trinity College, for their considerable help and advice in the preparation of the manuscript, although the responsibility for its final content rests squarely with me. I am also most grateful to Mr J Vaughan and his colleagues in the School of Education Library of the University of Liverpool especially during the summer vacation of 1982 when the first draft of this manuscript was completed within their walls.

The following students on my 1982 course allowed me to use extracts from their examination questions but cautioned me to remind the reader that they would have done much better in a coursework assessment exercise. In any event I am most grateful to them for the rapport which they developed with me on the course. I am also grateful to their colleagues from whom no quotations have been extracted. The contributors included: P M Bolger; G Brady; E T Butler; J Campbell; R Cheasty; C Colmey; A F Dack; M Delahanty; R E Donohoe; B M Donnelly; G Duffy; V Duggan; G M P Dunne; E G Feely; J S Foley; F Galway; M Gilroy; T G Halton; C G Hamill; G E Humphrey; H Hynes; A M Kearly; B M Kelly; S Kingston; M Lewis;   C Llewellyn;   J M McNamara;   K McBain;   G V McCooey; A McDermott; C McDonagh; P J McKenna; J McKennedy; J M McMahon; T McPhillips; M R McQuaid; E J Maquire; R P M Mallon; C M Nolan; O L-Allmhurait; C P O'Brien; K M O'Donnell; J O'Driscoll; B G O'Mordha; E P O'Nuanain; C B O'Reilly; K O'Sullivan; S M O'Sullivan; J Pawley; K Redmond; D P Ryan; F Savino; T F Sheridan; C M Somers; A J Trappe; M T Waldron; B N Walsh; C B Walsh; J C Walsh; J Williams.

Three years ago Ms Nancy Bates undertook a special project in the curriculum in religious education. It is of the kind that all students should undertake during their initial training. I am very grateful to her for allowing me to publish it as an appendix to this book.

I am deeply indebted to Loulou Brown of Kogan Page for her advice and help in preparing the manuscript. Last and by no means least I am grateful to David Heywood who typed the original manuscript, and to Janet Monaghan and Elizabeth Fleeton, who undertood the revisions, for their care and patience.

Those authorities who have given me permission to quote from their works are specifically acknowledged in the text.

Preface

This book seeks to demonstrate, through the ideas of student teachers, the value and importance of curriculum studies during initial training. For the most part, graduate student teachers are preoccupied with the problems of instruction and classroom management during their initial training. Trainers have endeavoured to make their courses relevant to the problems which the trainees face in the classroom. Courses are often problem-orientated and based on the methodology of the subject which the trainees intend to teach.

This preoccupation with the immediate and the relevant takes the student's eyes away from the horizon of the professional activity which will encompass his or her working life for many years. In contrast to *Pitfalls and Planning in Student Teaching*, which was concerned with the immediate needs of student teachers, this book is concerned with their 'vote', that is, with the wider context of the curriculum in which they teach their subject.

Everyone has views about what should be taught in schools and these are often forcibly expressed by politicians who claim to represent certain sectors of the community. Teachers might be expected to have a more informed view than either parents or politicians although it might be argued that if politicians and parents wish to debate content and method they should be as well informed as teachers.

This book invites the student teacher, the parent and the politician to consider the practice and problems in curriculum design, development and evaluation and more generally the role of the subject in the curriculum and the curriculum in society. Like *Pitfalls and Planning in Student Teaching* it is based on work with postgraduate students on the Irish Higher Diploma (Postgraduate Certificate) course and, as in that book, many of the illustrations are drawn from their examination scripts and projects. The reader should remember that these examples were written under the pressure of formal examinations and the time constraints that they impose. For this reason no attempt has been made to edit the examples.

John Heywood

Introduction

In *Pitfalls and Planning in Student Teaching* I borrowed the idea of advanced organization from the American educationalist Ausubel (1960). Each chapter was introduced with a set of illustrations which were intended to convey the purpose of the chapter. These illustrations consisted of examination questions and extracts from answers to them by graduate students training to be secondary teachers. Their purpose was to create an impression of the material to be covered in each chapter and more especially to show how student teachers relate theory to practice in the classroom. The examples, or organizing responses as I sometimes call them, are not meant to provide a programme for the chapter or section and are not therefore considered in sequence. For example, some of my colleagues who have read Chapter 1 found that they did not immediately see the relevance of the first quotation on p 11 from Newman's *Idea of a University* until they had arrived at the end of the chapter. But most of the examples are from examination scripts and the chapter contents relate to the examination questions from which they were obtained. No attempt has been made to correct the responses, neither are references in them footnoted, since the notes at the end of each chapter cover the principal references mentioned.

The publication of a book on curriculum studies presents a much greater challenge than one on instruction since trainee teachers can have little influence on the curriculum, especially in second-level education. Their concern is with the 'next' lesson and its planning and implementation — with survival. Yet, as the examples in this text show, they are able to go beyond lesson planning and implementation to consider theory and practice in relation to the curriculum. A typical student project on the curriculum is given in full in the Appendix. As might be expected, some of the more interesting illustrations are about those aspects of the curriculum that easily relate to their work in the classroom such as the hidden curriculum which is the subject of Chapter 1.

These examination questions were repeated in one disguise or another over a period of three years. On each occasion similar kinds of answers were obtained, a fact which has considerable significance, for the responses show that many ideas which have belonged to the macro theory of the curriculum may also be translated to the micro theory of the classroom and the topic presented. Examples of this point are shown in the received, reflexive and restructuring paradigms of the curriculum given in Chapter 2, and the responses on screening in Chapter 9 which relate to lesson planning and which are also used to introduce the more general idea of curriculum design in this chapter.

If a teacher is to be truly professional he or she has got to get to grips with such documents as *The Black Papers* (Cox and Dyson, 1971), for they represent a particular view about the curriculum. For many teachers the postgraduate course will be the only time that they have for formal study of the factors influencing the curriculum. Even so, they will have formed ideas about the content of the curriculum and often these will be dominated by the traditions of the subjects which they teach, and these ideas are likely to persist throughout their careers. So it is important that they should be faced with some of the issues which dominate thinking about the curriculum in the latter part of the twentieth century. Our version of curriculum studies is introduced toward the end of our course and we class it under the heading of professional study for within it we deal with the problem of accountability.

References

Ausubel, P (1960) Use of advance organizers in the learning and retention of meaningful verbal material *Journal of Educational Psychology* 51, pp 267-72

Heywood, J (1982) *Pitfalls and Planning in Student Teaching* Kogan Page: London

Cox, C B and Dyson, A (eds) (1971) *The Black Papers on Education* Davis-Poynter: London

Chapter 1

The Hidden Curriculum and the Aims of Education

Introduction

There is no better introduction to the idea that the curriculum is more than a syllabus or a collection of subjects than through the concept of the hidden curriculum which in this chapter is discussed in relation to its influence on the pursuit of the aims of education, whatever those might be. For this reason the organizing responses which follow immediately below begin with one of the best known statements of aims in educational literature, namely those in Newman's *Idea of a University*.

Organizing responses

Newman's aims of education

'A university training is the great ordinary means to a great but ordinary end; it aims at raising the intellectual tone of society, at cultivating the public mind, at purifying the national taste, at supplying true principles to popular enthusiasm and fixed aims to popular aspiration, at giving enlargement and sobriety to the ideas of the age, at facilitating the exercise of popular power, and refining the intercourse of private life. It is the education which gives a man a clear conscious view of his own opinions and judgements, a truth in developing them, an eloquence in expressing them, and a force in urging them. It teaches him to see things as they are, to go right to the point, to disentangle a skein of thought, to detect what is sophistical, and to discard what is irrelevant. It prepares him to fill any post with credit, and to master any subject with facility. It shows him how to accommodate himself to others, how to throw himself into their frame of mind, how to bring before them his own, how to influence them, how to come to an understanding with them, how to bear with them. He is at home in any society, he knows when to speak and when to be silent; he is able to converse, he is able to listen, he can ask a question pertinently, and gain a lesson seasonably, when he has nothing to impart himself; he is ever ready, yet never in the way; he is a pleasant companion, and a comrade you can depend upon; he knows when to be serious and when to trifle, and he has a sure tract which enables him to trifle with gracefulness and to be serious with effect. He has the repose of a mind which lives in itself, and which has resources for its happiness at home when it cannot go abroad (we think here of all that is said today about "education for leisure"). He has a gift which serves him in public, and supports him in retirement, without which good fortune is but vulgar and with which failure and disappointment have a charm. The art which tends to make a man all this, is in the object which it pursues as useful as the art of wealth or the art of health, though it is less susceptible of method, and less tangible, less certain, less complete in its result.'

(Newman, 1947)

An examination question about the hidden curriculum

Many educators use the phrase *hidden curriculum* to refer to what is actually taught in the result sense, implying that it can be significantly different from what everyone involved intends:

'Kohlberg speaks of the influence of the "hidden curriculum" — all the ways the teachers and other authorities transmit, usually unwittingly, moral lessons to children. Most students, for example, must compete for grades with their classmates; helping another person may be defined as cheating. Most kids go to schools in which rules are laid down by authority; children never have a chance to participate in formulating, revising or enforcing moral requirements, and they're expected to obey without question the adult in charge.

I recently came across [a story] about an incident in which a student called the teacher an obscene name . . . A second grade boy called his teacher a "son-of-a-bitchin' whore". The teacher marched the boy down to the principal's office and demanded that the child be expelled, which he was. The lesson that student learned was almost surely: the only reason to respect others is to avoid punishment.' (Thomas Lickona, How to encourage moral development, *Learning*, March 1977, p 42)

Identify two cases in your own work in which something was taught in the result sense but not identified. Why is it important for teachers to be aware of the "hidden curriculum" they may be teaching? (Set in this form from Fitzgibbons, 1981.)

Student responses to the question concerning the hidden curriculum, above

RELATING TO IRISH

'I realized the pupils had perceived that I had a "soft-spot" for the Irish language and so if they were late or misbehaved they thought (and sometimes did, I admit) they would get away with it if they apologized or made their excuse through Irish.

In this instance I realized that I taught or transferred a different "end-product" than I had intended as instead of getting to like and appreciate the language they simply used it as a "way-out" mechanism.'

RELATING TO PHYSICAL EDUCATION

'In the Gym the class was dispersed, some to basketball, some to boxing (Queensbury Type), some to Gymnastics. X and Y (X being a highly disturbed boy) indulged in some playful kicking (strictly forbidden by me — even in play serious accidents can occur) while my attention was diverted. One hard kick too many by Y hunted and ignited X and it was all-in from there on, boot, head, elbow, flushed faces. This had happened a hundred times before. My opening tactic was usually to take them outside, separate, allow to cool down, no talking (so each would not say "he started it"). First target was to make them feel sheepish for settling a difference with violence then carefully, detailedly explain why violence would only beget more violence and the peace it would achieve would be a falsely based one that differences were better solved by analysis of each other's actions, intent and *real* desire for not having hostilities. Firstly though I used the tactic to induce sheepishness, ie to let them see and feel the stupidity of humans deliberately inflicting pain on each other so I said "Right lads you want to fight? Go ahead, I won't stop you". Y replies: "No sir I don't want to fight, someone would get hurt". Turning to X "Now do you see how stupid it was". "No", he replied "You've just encouraged us to fight" (not my real intention but note the perception based on what he looked at and the state of his frames of reference for perception). The result intended was to make him see the foolishness of fighting, the actual result and one I couldn't shake him out of (a function of sociological, psychological and emotional conditions outside my control) was "fighting is OK he actually encourages it".'

RELATING TO RELIGIOUS EDUCATION
'In my own case, I have found that I sometimes end up teaching something not only unintended but not worthy of being taught. Last term my second form RE group asked if they might have five minutes at the end of my lesson in which to tidy their classroom. I said "Yes" but went on to say that I would expect the same amount of work, effort, etc to be done in 30 minutes as in 35. This they did. A week later they asked for five minutes to finish their prep for the next teacher. I said "No" and proceeded to tell them why, ending up with "RE is not the place to do prep". One pupil answered "But we thought RE didn't matter. Last week you let us clean the classroom and that isn't as important as doing our prep". I had unintentionally taught that RE was not to be highly regarded.'

RELATING TO FRENCH
'One example was in my first year class during a fairly straightforward French lesson. I asked one of the less-able pupils an easy question (as I saw it) and he completely muddled his answer. I tried to encourage him that it was almost correct and to try again. Eventually he refused to answer and said "How can I answer it, I'm worst at French". In this, I realized that Gerry had "learned" two things. Firstly, he had learned that he could *not* learn French and secondly that, despite school policy on avoidance of class positions, he was painfully aware of his position and hence, merit, in relation to his peers. It is not simply the weakest who learn their positions. According to Nash even within unstreamed primary classes the children's perception of their positions and those of the teacher had a very high positive correlation. The other point, the "I'm no use at French", is also taught to children who then see that others can learn the subject while they cannot.'

RELATING TO MIXED ABILITY TEACHING
'After two to three weeks in my class, it became evident that good marks and performance were the standard of the class. However, it was not only that high marks were valued, but low marks were held in contempt and the weaker pupils looked down upon. Pupils at this age (girls, 11 to 13 of mixed ability) can be unnecessarily very cruel, and some rather hurtful remarks were passed regarding the weaker pupils. I did my best to discourage this without actually drawing attention to the fact. In the beginning it was totally unheard of for one of the better pupils to help one of the weaker ones. In my approach to teaching, I tried to show I valued the weaker pupils as much (if not more) as the others. I did not make any great change in attitude and eventually what had been a major consideration in my teaching fell from my mind. At Christmas, however, we came to do projects. I decided to allow pupils to select their own groups (four to six pupils per group) and they were to tell me next day the names in each group.
Next day on scanning the list of names I was extremely surprised to find how mixed-ability each group was, and certain particularities arose which I would not have thought possible. During the course of the project work, bright pupils helped weaker pupils an awful lot.
The whole attitude of the class had changed and academic ability was not now seen as the only status symbol. Pupils were valued for other characteristics.'

RELATING TO ECONOMICS
'During a fourth-year economics class this year, I caught one of my students throwing a piece of chalk at another. I reprimanded him and asked him to go and explain his action to the headmaster. I was concerned lest the boy at whom the chalk was thrown would suffer injury, and was also concerned about the fact

that this action was rendering learning impossible. This I explained to the offender before he left the room. When he had departed, I warned the rest of the class that anybody else who threw chalk around the class would be similarly treated. Immediately one boy pointed out that this was not so — nobody would be sent out for throwing chalk, rather they would be sent out for *getting caught* throwing chalk. The lesson learned seemed to be that, if one could get away with it, throwing chalk around the class was perfectly legitimate — the crime was to get caught in the act. I had intended that the pupils should learn not to throw chalk because it was dangerous and interrupted the learning process. In fact, they surmized that the only reason for not engaging in such action was to avoid being caught and dismissed from the classroom.'

RELATING TO GEOGRAPHY
'An aspect of the hidden curriculum which I came across was the way in which kids learn to distract a teacher and try and get him off the point of the lesson. For example, I remember three weeks ago telling them about their summer exam and I had decided to spend 10 minutes talking about it, but in fact spent the whole class, because I was answering questions like "Where are we doing it?", "What book will we have next year?" etc.'

RELATING TO THE HAWTHORNE EFFECT
'[an] aspect I saw is the work which Eggleston quotes by Rist who shows how kids and teachers co-operate together to reach an acceptable rate of production. I found this happening, for if we finished a topic before the end of class due to the fact that they had given me their co-operation and not messed I would then let them read their magazines, etc.'

RELATING TO THE TEACHER
'Thus the hidden curriculum is really a misnomer. The only person from whom it is hidden is the teacher.'

Curriculum and society

Most student teachers latch on to the idea of the hidden curriculum quickly. It fascinates them! I am not sure whether every reader will agree that all these examples are illustrations of the hidden curriculum. In my collection of responses, many seem to be examples of unintended outcomes of the educational process. Before examining this concept in a little more detail it is useful to look more generally at both the role of education in society and the interaction between society and the educational institutions which it creates.

The education system is a social sub-system. It is one of the many sub-systems which contribute to maintenance and development of society. Within this system there are sub-systems of primary, secondary and tertiary education. In many countries at the tertiary level there are public (financed and controlled), private and independent (government-financed but independently controlled) sectors. In America there are the privately funded Ivy League universities and State funded colleges. In England there are the publicly financed and controlled polytechnics and government-financed but independent universities. The latter have, like the Ivy League universities in the United States, higher status and like them there is a pecking order beginning with Oxbridge.

Because governments contribute so much money to universities there is a continuing debate about accountability in terms of its 'nature' and the extent to which institutions should be controlled by the State. Some institutions of higher education have deliberately sought programmes which would involve them in the local community and, by so doing, create the image that they are committed to the goals of the community.

The degree and methods of control of education vary from nation to nation. In England school examinations are set by independent examination boards. Five of those which are used for university entrance are controlled by universities. The other three are independent. By contrast, the examinations for the intermediate and leaving certificate examinations in the Republic of Ireland are statutorily controlled by the Minister for Education who vests their setting and marking in the Inspectorate and their administration with the civil servants.

An important effect of the system is the influence that one system has over the other. In the British Isles it is a downward force, for the universities use school examinations as a means of selection and through these examinations exert an influence on both curricula and method (see also Chapter 6). The fact that children and students have to change from one sub-system to another creates discontinuities for them, some of which may impede learning. Although the problems of transition are not dealt with in this text they have an important bearing on both curriculum and method. Key transitions take place between infant and junior school, primary school and second level, and second level to further or higher education. Of these, the most discussed is the transition between primary and second level where it is noticed that there is often an absolute fall in achievement during the first year of second-level education. It is not without significance that the maximum wastage from university courses occurs in the first year. It has become part of the rhetoric that transition between primary and secondary is difficult if not harmful, although there is an argument that the effect is soon overcome. It is argued that there should be much greater liaison between school and that methods of appraisal and assessment should be improved. Derricott, who has edited a book of papers describing developments in England, argues for a 'planned discontinuity' (Derricott, 1983).

All this is to show that educational institutions are not completely autonomous of the society in which they exist. However conservative they may be, they are not entirely closed systems and respond to their environment, even though changes within them take place at a relatively slow pace. Change is inevitable! Thus any study of the curriculum which is the *raison d'être* of an educational institution has to begin with a recognition that it is a mechanism which is created for a social purpose notwithstanding the possibility of an innate desire for ordered knowledge.

In this sense *The Concise Oxford Dictionary* definition of the curriculum as 'a course of study' will not do. Eggleston (1977) suggests 'that the curriculum is concerned with the presentation of knowledge, and involves a pattern of learning experiences, both instrumental and expressive,

15

designed to enable it to be received by students' within the educational institution. It is a formal arrangement for the pursuit of education. We usually associate it with the subjects taught at second and third level. Sometimes we apply it to the syllabus of a subject; sometimes we use it in respect of the collection of subjects taught. In either case we are more often than not seeing the curriculum as a course of study. In the subsequent sections of this chapter an attempt is made to show that there is a much wider context in which the curriculum should be viewed if, on the one hand, we are to understand its effects on learning and, on the other hand, the way in which knowledge is controlled in society.

The formal and informal acquisition of knowledge

It is self-evident that we learn all the time both consciously and unconsciously. We are forced to store and extract information from that store and sometimes our learning is self-directed. Sometimes it is imposed on us in apparently inconsequential situations as, for example, when we are idly watching television or reading a newspaper. The range of learning which encompasses the everyday activities of an individual is enormous. We learn as much about people and their behaviour as we do about things. For many children informal learning is of more consequence than the formal learning in a course of study. But this informal learning takes place as much in school as it does at home and is a powerful influence on behaviour for there is some learning in everything we do. It is all our informal learning which has been called 'the hidden curriculum' by the present author. It is a major control of learning and behaviour.

P W Jackson (1968) is often quoted as the person who gave formal definition to the hidden curriculum although it is clearly understood by such authorities as Dewey, Newman and Whitehead. Jackson showed how the hidden curriculum is of value to both teachers and pupils. For example, if pupils do not help each other with their homework (notwithstanding the value of peer-group learning) teachers may have more correcting to do than they can handle if there is to be adequate feedback. Nevertheless, teachers are often unaware of the perceptions that students have of them, or for that matter just how perceptive their pupils are. Figure 1.1 (see p 17) shows some of the responses which pupils made to a question set by a student teacher some 20 minutes into the class which asked them to write down what they had learnt. Look in particular at the last response (I was in the class at the time)!

The student teacher examples illustrate many of the points made by Jackson and one or two deserve comment. First, there is the search to determine what is acceptable to the teacher, a point which is illustrated time and again in the answers; the attempt to give the teacher what the teacher wants. Second, the pupils have to live with their peers. Sometimes high marks are valued; sometimes they are despised. The high flier is called a 'swot'. Some intelligent children find that they have to behave unintelligently. Means for coping with interpersonal relationships are learnt.

Third, classes can co-operate almost unconsciously with their teacher to produce an acceptable rate of production which has its parallel in industrial organization.

---

1. I have learnt how a contra entry works.
2. I have learnt that if you take your time everything will be correct.
3. I have learnt to keep my work tidy.
4. Neatness.
5. I have learnt how to balance the cash book properly.
6. In the last 20 minutes I have become faster and neater.
7. Discount and balancing.
8. I learnt to look more closely at the question.
9. I have learnt to be neat and fast.
10. Neatness, speed, correct rules.
11. I have learnt how to balance my accounts.
12. I have learnt that the teachers get nervous when there is an inspector in the class. And I have learnt a bit more about balancing the accounts.

The teacher's lesson plan included the following statement.
Aim: To introduce the students to bookkeeping.
Objective: To lead the class in improving their bookkeeping skills of speed, neatness and accuracy.

Figure 1.1 *Some responses by students (13 to 14 years) to the question What have you learnt so far in this lesson?'* (The question was put 20 minutes after the class had started on a double-entry bookkeeping exercise.)

In the late 1920s a group of investigators from Harvard University were able to observe a group of 14 people at work over a long period of time (Roethlisberger and Dickson, 1939). They were engaged in wiring and soldering banks of equipment in the Westinghouse Electrical Company's works in Chicago. Those who wired, it was ruled, should not solder and *vice versa*. It was found however that jobs were traded as a means of relieving boredom and that the supervisors acquiesced in this practice.

However the observers found that the men divided themselves into two groups — one at the front of the room, the other at the back. Those at the front thought they were superior to those at the back and believed they got the more complicated jobs. There was much competition between the two groups. Although their output varied considerably from day to day they always reported more or less the same output each day. They under-reported rather than over-reported and it seemed that they had set themselves a 'norm' of what was fair. While this was evidently acceptable to management it was well below what could have been achieved. That it was deliberate was confirmed by the fact that pressures were exerted to prevent individuals from either 'chiseling' (working below the rate) or 'rate-busting'. Much the same goes on in classrooms for the same view of the worker-supervisor relationship is to be found. As one student said: 'those in authority (eg teachers) must not act officious or take advantage of their authority position' (see also the student example on p 13.

The industrial situation is a learning situation providing the same type of environment as the classroom and is a powerful influence on motivation. The Hawthorne studies led to the view that work, productivity, and quality of work are related to the nature of the social relationships between the workers themselves and between the workers and their supervisors. This is no different from the classroom although, as has been found in industry, the situation is much more complex (Lupton, 1964; Hargreaves, 1972).

While the concept of formal and informal organization was found to be of considerable use in studies of organizational behaviour its value has to a large extent been modified by other perspectives.

Institutions as social-technical systems

Shortly after the nationalization of the coal industry in Britain the Tavistock Institute was asked to investigate problems arising from mechanization of cutting of coal. Productivity had gone down and absenteeism had increased. In their report the investigators contrasted the traditional form of mining with new techniques and subsequently modified the new with some success (Trist and Bamforth, 1969).

In brief, they found that traditionally coal was hewn by small teams of between two to eight men. Each team cut a small section of the coal face. There would be one skilled worker, a mate and several labourers whose task was to remove the coal in tubs. The members of the group were picked by the team-leader and they came to form a social unit both above and below the ground. Thus if there was an accident (even death) involving one of the members, the rest of the group would look after that miner's family. There was much competition, to the point of aggression, between the groups for the best parts of the coal face.

The mechanized method changed this system. Instead of the small teams, 50 or so men were spread out over 200 yards in a very small tunnel. They did single or part tasks. At the same time a high degree of co-ordination was required but not achieved and output was consequently reduced. The small groups created by the technology were undermined by the fact that different jobs had different levels of prestige. Relationships between those who 'cut' the coal and those who removed it were particularly sensitive. The opportunities for the release of tension provided by the traditional system were not present and so work lost its meaning. The investigators redesigned the system so that there was a meaningful informal organization and whole tasks rather than part tasks were done.

These results suggest that social organization is not something that is merely informal. Rather, it is something created by the technology of production. It is easy to see that a school is both a social and a technical system, with similar tensions to those found in the industrial context (Rice, 1970). But so is a classroom and the arrangements employed by teachers influence the effectiveness of learning in the classroom. We can see at once how classroom organization may indirectly be a preparation for work, as for example, when it is rearranged for group activities or projects are carried out which require a contribution from each member of the class.

That the hidden curriculum is important seems self-evident. The implications of the last three sections on organizational effectiveness in normal and innovating circumstances lead to the view that structures in the school and classroom can have a profound effect on the characteristics of the hidden curriculum in the school. Over and above the school, the differential position of schools within the education system is likely to influence the perception that pupils have of themselves, their performance and their career potential. The goals that a school sets itself within the education system, combined with parental aspirations, have a profound influence on students (see also Chapter 3).

The aims of education and the hidden curriculum

This chapter began with a statement of the aims of university education from John Henry Cardinal Newman's *Idea of a University*. Most people would tend to agree with these ideals. The reader is invited to consider them while asking the question — 'Does the teaching of subjects (and the specialization in subjects) in school and university achieve these goals?' Then consider the examples in the student responses. Might it not be the case that the hidden curriculum achieves more of these goals than the formal curriculum?

> 'How is this to be explained? I suppose as follows: when a multitude of young
> men, keen, open-hearted, sympathetic and observant, as young men are,
> come together and freely mix with each other, they are sure to learn one
> from another, even if there be no one to teach them; the conversation of all
> is a series of lectures to each, and they gain for themselves new ideas and views,
> fresh matter of thought, and distinct principles for judging and acting, day by
> day ... For the pupils or students come from very different places, and with
> widely different notions, and there is much to generalize, much to adjust, much
> to eliminate, there are interrelations to be defined, and conventional rules to be
> established, in the process, by which the whole assemblage is moulded together,
> and gains one tone and one character.'
>
> (Newman, 1947)

Cognitive and moral development

References are made in this book to Piaget's theory of cognitive development and Kohlberg's theory of moral development. The latter is derivative of the former. Piaget's theories have had a major influence on the curriculum and his work has been the subject of much simplistic interpretation. The general theory of psychological development presented by Piaget contains four elements, the first three of which are to be found in other theories of development. They are:

1. Biological maturation.
2. Experience with the physical environment.

3. Experience with the social environment.
4. Equilibration.

With regard to the physical environment Piaget (1973) suggested that in addition to exercise and physical experience, there is a logico-mathematical experience which depends on the way the subject and the object interact. Hilgard and Bower (1975) considering this idea describe it as a 'cognitive know-how which Piaget calls structure'. Piaget's theories therefore are in the Platonic tradition of theories of knowledge and this perspective is well illustrated by Shulman (1970) in an article which any teacher can read in spite of the fact that it is in a book on mathematics education.

Much interest has been focused on this theory by those concerned with the development of the new mathematics; they have argued that the structures of the new mathematics relate to the logico-mathematical structures of the mind. If this is the case then children should obtain a better mathematical understanding from study through the conceptual structure provided by the new mathematics curriculum. Needless to say such arguments are controversial and there is much disenchantment with the new mathematics.

In regard to the social environment Piaget assigns most importance to language since it is the basis of our experience of socialization. However, he argues that the development of logical operations is prior to that of language. This is consistent with his concept of logico-mathematical structures and the notion that there are in-built structures in the mind which have to be brought out. Language aids this development: it is a servant of the intelligence which evolves in stages.

The fourth element — equilibration — co-ordinates the influences of the other three factors. Piaget suggests there are *schemes* or *structures* which enable the child to *assimilate* the external environment. But the *assimilation* of new information also requires a change in the existing structures so that there is congruence between external reality and the child's mental structures. This process is called *accommodation. Equilibration* is the adjustive process required for assimilation and accommodation.

An interesting feature of Piaget's theory is the attempt to relate it to the epistemological processes which go on in the child's mind as he or she learns by solving problems. Piaget's often quoted example is of the way a child uses clay. From experimenting with clay rolled into a sausage shape, the child learns that:

1. there is less clay in a thin sausage and more in a long sausage;
2. a sausage can be long and thin;
3. if a sausage can become longer, it can become shorter;
4. length and thickness can compensate for each other.

The transition between 2 (configuration) and 3 (transformation) is an example of equilibration: the children learn by their actions on their environment. Level 5 is called *conservation* by Piaget because a transformation does not change the quality of matter.

Textbooks often illustrate this point with an illustration of two beakers of different diameter. Each has the same volume of water, but the level of the water is different in each. At first a child may think there is more water in the beaker with the smaller diameter since it is at a higher level. Several deductions have to be made to arrive at the conclusion that there is the same amount of water in both beakers.

Piaget argues that children move through orderly stages of development. The first stage is from birth to about one-and-a-half years. This is the development of sensorimotor intelligence. Within this stage, there are six sub-stages. Each of these is a problem-solving activity involving its own logic. Thus after about 18 months the child is able to solve a detour problem by going round a barrier even if this means departing from the original goal for a short time. The child can infer causes from the observation of effects and begins to predict effects from observing causes; the child also begins to invent applications of something previously learned.

The second major stage of development is called the period of representative intelligence and concrete operations. This takes the child up to 11 or 12 years. The first part of this period is between two and seven years and is called the pre-operational phase. The second phase is that of concrete operations. It is in this period that the child learns *conservation*. For example, the size-weight illusion described above is resolved. Children tackle this problem in relation to matter, weight and volume. Piaget claims that the order of such learning is invariable. Learning by doing is the essence of concrete operations. In this period children learn to seriate, classify and establish correspondence.

The final period, when the child moves from middle childhood to adolescence, is that of formal operations. Now the child is able to undertake abstract thinking, to hypothesize and deduct, experiment and theorize. It is the stage of in-built maturity.

This summary does less than justice to the descriptive material offered by Piaget and his supporters to substantiate their view that intellectual development takes place in invariable stages. Its attraction to teachers will be obvious since the experiments (observations) which led to the theory provide teaching material appropriate to the supposed level of development in the child. Moreover, it is easy (rightly or wrongly), as the student responses illustrate, for teachers to make judgements about children in terms of these stages. They see that a child cannot handle certain concepts in their own subject and may wrongly conclude that the child is at the stage of concrete operations.

Piaget's experimental work has been much criticized. The reader is referred to Brown and Desforges (1979) for a recent and substantial evaluation of his work. The idea that children are not capable of philosophical puzzlement early in their lives has been challenged by G B Matthews (1980) in a book which ought to be compulsory reading for student teachers. Nevertheless it is a common observation of teachers that there is a sequence in the child's development toward the understanding of conservation. Teachers have shown how Piaget's theory can contribute to the development of teaching programmes in the secondary school as, for example, Shayer's work on the science curriculum (1980).

Some of Piaget's notions are of immense significance to the teacher. First is the idea that we learn by doing, which suggests there is likely to be some value in discovery learning. Despite the Western philosophical tradition and its influence on university education, there is much to suggest that we arrive at theories as a result of the need to solve practical problems (MacMurray, 1957). It is therefore clear that a concrete illustration is often necessary if we are to understand an abstraction. This suggests that we solve problems through stages similar to those marked out by Piaget for long period development. It also seems evident that some people never arrive at the level of formal operations. We learn from the respondents that individual pupils within the same class perform at different levels if different kinds of teaching are used. Developmental theories of intelligence force us to consider where a person is and how modifiable he or she is at that time. At the very least Piaget provides us with important insights into the way in which individuals learn. That the application of Piaget's theory to education is difficult (Kuhn, 1979) is no better illustrated than by the title of a paper which reads 'Either we're too early and they can't learn it or we're too late and they know it already: the dilemma of "applying" Piaget' (Duckworth, 1979). This is not true of Bruner's approach to development.

Jerome Bruner whose curriculum on man has been so influential (see Chapter 7) is a learning theorist whose work begins with an alternative theory of learning and instruction. It is discussed in *The Process of Education* and subsequent publications. The three features of his writings which are of special interest to student teachers relate to the teaching of advanced concepts, the sequence of development, and the need to account for the ways in which children actually solve problems. Bruner more than anyone else fostered the practice of discovery learning in the school curriculum, an idea also found in the work of John Dewey (1930) and strongly supported by Piaget. But Bruner differs from Piaget in that he believes learning situations should be structured to enable children to learn on their own.

Bruner outlines four characteristics of a theory of instruction:

1. *Predisposition to learn.* A theory of instruction must be concerned with the experiences and contexts that will tend to make the child willing and able to learn when he or she enters school.
2. *Structure of knowledge.* A theory of instruction must specify ways in which a body of knowledge should be structured so that it can be most readily grasped by the learner.
3. *Sequence.* A theory of instruction should specify the most effective sequences in which to present the materials.
4. *Reinforcement.* A theory of instruction should specify the nature and pacing of rewards, moving from extrinsic rewards to intrinsic ones. (Bruner, 1966)

These have to take into account individual differences as well as the differences between the structure of knowledge in different fields. Bruner argued in 1960 that 'Any subject can be taught effectively in some intellectually honest form to any child at any stage of development', a position which is markedly different from that of Piaget. I attempted to demonstrate this idea (1960) through the publication of a work on Einstein's scientific contribution aimed at the 12-year-old. It does not imply that a child will be able to do exercises in the theory of relativity, but my view is akin to that of Whitehead (1932), who suggested that learning took place in three stages: romance, grammar and generalization. Romance is the stage of curiosity; it is not a stage of analysis. We need the stage of romance to stimulate interest.

In Bruner's theory of cognitive development the three modes of representation follow in sequence. The first is called *enactive*. Bruner notes that conditioning and stimulus-response learning are appropriate to this mode; it is learning through action without words. The second stage, which is one of mental representation, is called *ikonic*. In this stage the child uses concrete visual imagery. It may be related to Gestalt psychology. The final stage of representation is the *symbolic*. Because children are able to translate experience into language and think with language, they are able to develop abstract images.

Bruner holds the belief that children can be helped to learn at the level of the most advanced kind of thinking in which they engage. That is, a teacher can help a child develop more sophisticated kinds of thought process. Thus Bruner would argue that we should *teach* readiness; we do not have to wait for it. In contrast, Piaget believes that children have to develop at their own pace and should not be subject to training for higher levels of thought. Bruner (1972) has subjected his earlier work to constructive criticism which does not deny the case for discovery learning but explores the conditions in which it is likely to be successful.

In keeping with such approaches to cognitive development, Kohlberg (1966) has suggested that moral attitudes are not acquired relativistically as a function of a person's cultural dimension, but that individuals advance through stages of moral development. In contrast with Piaget these stages are not age-related and not every individual develops through all of them. Stage 0 is called the premoral stage. At the pre-conventional level there are two stages. Stage 1 has a punishment and obedience orientation which changes into Stage 2 when right action is that which instrumentally satisfies a person's needs. At the conventional level Stage 3 is characterized by good behaviour which is designed to help or please others; in Stage 4 it develops into behaviours relating to doing one's duty, respect for authority and the maintenance of the social order. The post-conventional or autonomous level is achieved in two stages. Stage 5 is a level where individuals define right action in terms of individual rights and standards which have been critically evaluated by society. The final stage of moral maturity occurs when right is defined by a decision of one's conscience in accord with self-selected ethical principles appealing to logical comprehensiveness, universality and consistency. Such theories are of course not without their critics (Gibbs, 1977).

Studies of female and male children and adolescents have led Lyons (1983) to challenge this theory as applying to both female and male. Men and women respond in different ways to the same moral question. Lyons argues that in contrast to man's notion of morality as 'having a reason', the woman's sense of morality is a type of 'consciousness', which produces a sensitivity toward others. Caring predominates. These distinctive ways of making moral choices lie on a continuum and are not dichotomous.

Theories of intellectual development have also been applied to student development in higher education. Perry's (1966) model, based on work at Harvard University, is of special interest: it combines both intellectual and ethical development. For a recent study of its implications for the curriculum see Culver and Hackos (1982).

References

Brown, G and Desforges, C (1979) *Piaget's Theory. A Psychological Critique* Routledge and Kegan Paul: London

Bruner, J (1960) *The Process of Education* Harvard University Press: Cambridge: Massachusetts

Bruner, J (1960) *Towards a Theory of Instruction* Harvard University Press: Cambridge: Massachusetts

Bruner, J (1972) *The Relevance of Education* Penguin: Harmondsworth

Culver, R S and Hackos, J T (1982) Perry's model of intellectual development *Journal of Engineering Education* 73 (3) pp 221-6

Derricott, R (ed) (1983) *Across the Great Divide: Curricular Continuity Between Primary and Secondary Schools* The Schools Council: London

Dewey, J (1930) *The Quest for Certainty* Allen and Unwin: London

Duckworth, E (1979) Either we're too early and they can't learn it or we're too late and they know it already: the dilemma of 'applying' Piaget *Harvard Educational Review* 49, pp 297-312

Eggleston, J (1977) *The Sociology of the School Curriculum* Routledge and Kegan Paul: London

Fitzgibbons, R E (1981) *Making Educational Decisions. An Introduction to the Philosophy of Education* Harcourt Brace Jovanovich: New York

Gibbs, J C (1977) Kohlberg's stages of moral development: a constructive critique *Harvard Educational Review* 47, pp 43-61

Hargreaves, D H (1972) *Interpersonal Relations and Education* Routledge and Kegan Paul: London

Heywood, J (1960) *Albert Einstein* Mullers Children's Series: London

Hilgard, E E and Bower, G (1975) *Theories of Learning* (4th edition) Prentice Hall: Englewood Cliffs: New Jersey

Jackson, P W (1968) *Life in Classrooms* Holt, Rinehart and Winston: New York

Kohlberg, L (1966) Moral education in schools: a developmental view *School Review* 74, pp 1-30

Kuhn, D (1979) The application of Piaget's theory of cognitive development to education *Harvard Educational Review* 49, pp 340-60

Lupton, T (1964) *On the Shop Floor* Pergamon: London

Lyons, N P (1983) Two perspectives on self, relationships and morality *Harvard Educational Review* 53, (2) pp 125-45

MacMurray, J (1957) *The Self as Agent* Faber and Faber: London

Matthews, G B (1980) *Philosophy and the Young Child* Harvard University Press: Cambridge: Massachusetts

Newman, J H (1947 edition) *The Idea of a University* Longmans Green: London

Perry, W O (1966) *Intellectual and Ethical Development in the College Years: A Scheme* Holt, Rinehart and Winston: New York

Piaget, J (1973) Comments on mathematical education *in* Howson, A G *Developments in Mathematical Education* Cambridge University Press: Cambridge

Rice, A K (1970) *The Modern University* Tavistock Publications: London

Roethlisberger, F J and Dickson, W J (1939) *Management and the Worker* Harvard University Press: Cambridge: Massachusetts

Shayer, M and Adey, P (1980) *Towards a Science of Science Teaching: Cognitive Development and Curriculum Demand* Heinemann: London

Shulman, L S (1970) Psychology and mathematics education *in* Begle, E G (ed) *Mathematics Education* 69th Year Book of the National Society for the Study of Education) Chicago University Press: Chicago

Trist, E L and Bamforth, K (1969) Some social and psychological consequences of the Longwall method of coal getting *in* Emery, F E (ed) *Systems Thinking* Penguin: Harmondsworth

Whitehead, A N (1932) *The Aims of Education* Benn Brothers: London

Chapter 2

The Teacher and the Curriculum

Introduction

This chapter begins with a description of three curriculum perspectives: received, reflexive and restructuring. Although most curricula are received, teachers change their content and approach but this kind of reflexive thinking does not have the dynamic criticism called for by those who take a completely relativist view of knowledge as being socially constructed. Some curricula and examinations in both second- and third-level education allow students to construct their own course of studies. Eggleston's (1977) restructuring paradigm brings together both the received and reflexive perspectives, and it is concluded that restructuring is a continuous process in which teachers continually come to terms with their identity in the subjects they teach.

These perspectives may be related to learning theory, for the reality we perceive depends on our powers of perception and it is the factors which influence our perception that limit our learning. Perceptual learning theory leads to a view of liberal education as the process which provides a person with the widest possible range of internal schema together with the learning skills necessary for problem-solving at the highest levels of mental and moral development.

Organizing question

'No curriculum is entirely received. Teachers, of necessity, have to "restructure" within the subject they teach.' Discuss this statement with reference to the subject you teach.

Examples from student responses to this question

1. RELATING TO THE TEACHER RESTRUCTURING THE CURRICULUM
'Finally, with all aspects taken into consideration the teacher begins to teach his/her subject in the way she thinks is best. In other words, the school and the teacher take the curriculum study it and stamp their own interpretation on it, this is what I would consider as restructuring or at least there are elements of the restructuring process contained in the schools and teacher interpretation of the curriculum.'

2. RELATING TO THE REFLEXIVE CURRICULUM AND GEOGRAPHY
'I used the reflexive curriculum in geography where I was told to use X books, but with the class and with my own preferences we decided on the topics we would do, the order in which we would do them, etc. So there was dialogue, compromise, etc and we constructed the course as we saw fit and didn't take it as being given.'

3. RELATING TO FRENCH
'For example, when I began teaching French, I was given a certain book on which I was to base my classes. I found that my interpretation was very different from hers and discovered her teaching strategies were totally different although we were supposedly using the same method.'

4. RELATING TO SCIENCE IN A PRE-EMPLOYMENT CLASS
'One example was with my pre-employment class which I taught for science. When I arrived at the school I was told that I was to teach this class physics. One third of the class had not taken science for Intermediate or group Certificate and by and large the ability level of the majority of the pupils was below average. The first decision I made for the class was that physics, despite the high regard as a discipline in which it is held, was unsuitable for these students. I discussed this with the students and we decided to do general science. However, the important restructuring came when I actually came to teach some physics. I was teaching electricity. The purists would argue that the physics approach is: V=IR, lots of circuit diagrams, get students to work out the resistance of parallel and series arrangements, etc. Although these are very much at the heart of physics as a discipline, they were largely irrelevant and to a degree useless to my students. I had to forego the cognitive development that might have been (?) achieved if I had somehow managed to teach the pupils how to mathematically analyse circuits. Instead I spent two weeks with the pupils discussing domestic electricity, plugs, fuses, etc. The students may have learnt little of physics – the discipline, but they did learn.'

5. RELATING TO ECOLOGY
'In the area of ecology the syllabus outlined by the department indicated by its total lack of emphasis on this area that it was a relatively unimportant area of the curriculum at Intermediate Level. With this in mind I proceeded to introduce the concept to the children with a view to spending as little time as possible on the topic. However the enthusiasm with which it was given by students indicated that this indeed was an area of interest for the pupils as many of them came from the Clontarf area and could directly relate this area of the course to issues discussed in the course, relating to the preservation of Bull Island. Having initially intended to spend a 90-minute period on this topic, it transpired that it took me three weeks to cover it, including an interesting outing to the site in question.'

6. RELATING TO LITERATURE AND THE CHOICE OF TEXTS
'The received element in the literature syllabus is very strong and it is difficult to see how it can be restructured when the students have been taught (as I think they have from what I see) to rely on notes on the novel, notes on the plays and notes on the poems. Teaching a class to make personal responses to a list of works chosen by someone else and adults at that can be a very discouraging experience. Many of the poems for example are very unsuitable for the age groups they are prescribed for. There is no choice at all. The novels offer some choice but include books written by local authors whose study may be of interest to teenagers but whose work is not even near first class. How does one restructure in a situation like this? . . .'

7. RELATING TO THE MEDIA
'The ability to examine academically is a very important skill as regards the input of the media. Children are not taught to cope with the media. I believe history can be used to develop the skill of critical thinking. In "restructuring" the subject, the teacher can use the body of knowledge to teach skills.'

8. RELATING TO HISTORY
'As regards to my own subject – history, which I have taught to Leaving Certificate

level – my experience has been one of persistent mediation between the (somewhat over-eccentric) nature of the syllabus in the Irish School model and the learning and instruction processes within my 6L group. Because my group was in a repeat Leaving Certificate situation, it was evident at the beginning of the year that to cover the course was going to be an insurmountable situation, despite the stipulation of school principal. As these were mature students the class took on in many respects, the format of a tutor, where we formulated (negotiated *à la* reflexive theory terminology) to plan to cover a "reasonable" amount of the course through a project system based on a series of interlocking themes. Therefore the theme structure was as follows:

1. Nationalism (both Irish and European)
2. Imperialism
3. Social and culture change
4. Communication and technology.

These four themes we felt covered the Irish and European units adequately. The first two months were given to classes which dealt with the meaning and significance of the themes. The end of the first term and all the second term was then spent on project work, as the class divided up into four project groups. The school library facilities were excellent and according as each project was completed (they were organized on a dead-line basis), each project (diagrams and Key-fact packs) was preoccupied and distributed to each member of the class. This restructuring enterprise, which was done on a completely recognizable basis, proved to be extremely successful and improved the motivation level and conceptual development of the class as a whole. (NB Each project sub-group had a leader who reported to me on work progress at regular intervals and we arranged to have the group project presented – lecture, discussion and comments – to the class).'

9. RELATING TO IRISH

'I took a received syllabus and turned it upside down, restructuring it to my own objectives. The objective of the received syllabus was an ability to write good Irish. My objective was an ability to speak good Irish and I felt in most cases the writing would take care of itself. Hence I had to discard certain books which did not answer my objectives. I found the more they mastered spoken Irish, the more ability and interest they had in written work. But speech must come first.'

The received perspective of the curriculum and the status of subjects

The received perspective arises from the belief that there is a fixed body of knowledge which has to be handed down from generation to generation. It is structured by disciplines which we call subjects. In societies certain subjects acquire more prestige than others. For example in Britain and Ireland, countries which were both profoundly influenced by the liberal education movement of the nineteenth century, 'pure' is to be preferred to 'applied', 'theoretical' to 'practical' and 'university' to 'technical college', the latter being the institutional reflection of the academic versus vocational dichotomy in the hierarchy of subjects. Many secondary schools (as opposed to technical schools) in Ireland do not have practical subjects in their curriculum and in England woodwork and metalwork have low status in schools.

In the 1956 white paper on *Technical Education* (Cmnd 9703) the

Department of Education and Science in Britain created 10 institutions to offer a degree level subject in engineering for industry. But these colleges were not allowed to award a degree. It had to be a diploma in technology. It was to be specially geared to the needs of industry and to operate on the sandwich principle (ie six months in industry and six months in college for four years). In contrast to most university degrees the colleges included substantial projects and compulsory liberal studies. Their fourth years tended to be directed toward technologically oriented problems. Despite all this there were many complaints from industrialists that these courses were not meeting the needs of industry (Bosworth, 1963). These complaints related as much to the attitudes of students as they did to their knowledge. The majority, 40 per cent or more of the diplomates wanted to go into research and, surprisingly, there were only two departments of production engineering in these colleges. But this was as much industry's fault as it was the colleges' for production engineering is a low status job in Britain (Burns and Stalker, 1961) in contrast to Germany (Lawrence, Hutton and Smith, 1980). Given the equation diploma equals degree it is not surprising in a society in which social class, according to Mant (1979) is an 'Art Form', that many teachers in these colleges should demand the facility to award degrees. Many of them reinforced this view in practice by ensuring that their syllabuses and examinations were similar to those offered by universities. This 'curriculum drift' was widespread (Heywood, 1969). These 10 colleges had their endeavours rewarded by attaining university status (which when the history of the period up to 2,000 is written may not be seen to have been the best thing for them, since most of them suffered more severely than other similar institutions in the university cuts of the 1970s).

This undervaluing of technical skills is a cultural phenomenon for as several writers have shown from Ashby (1958) onwards, Germany in particular highly values its engineers and the *Technische Hochschulen* have high prestige, which will be discussed further in the next chapter. At the present time Australia, Ireland and Norway also operate binary systems but with the pressures for open-access to the prestige institutions, it would not be surprising to find in 50 years' time that these divisions have disappeared (Heywood, 1974). Moves in this direction can already be seen in Britain. The pressures for change in any society are against the established order and the received perspective of the curriculum is very much part of the social order. Educational institutions like examination boards reinforce that perspective.

Secondary examinations, grades and status

In Ireland secondary school examinations are set by the Inspectorate and in England by examination boards which are independent of Government influence. In England one group of boards set the Certificate of Secondary Education (CSE) which was originally intended for those leaving school at the age of 15. The examination was intended for most of those in the upper quartiles of the age group. For the top of the ability range, those staying in school to 16 and beyond, an Ordinary level (O level) of the General Certificate of Education (GCE) is provided. At around 18 an Advanced level (A level) of the General Certificate of Education is set. This is a highly specialized examination. Because the school leaving age has been raised to 16 it has been proposed that there should be a common entrance examination (16+) for the so-called top 60 per cent of the ability range. Students may take a single subject or a range of subjects in these examinations. In Ireland a group certificate examination may be taken at around 14. This is usually regarded as an examination for the weaker pupils. Sometimes it is used as a preparation for the Intermediate Certificate examination which is taken at around 15. This certificate is equivalent to the CSE except that most students, and this is about 80 per cent of the age range, take around seven subjects. Three of these, Irish, English and mathematics have pass and honours syllabuses. Two years after this examination students take the Leaving Certificate in five or more subjects. There are honours and pass syllabuses and good grades at the honours level are essential for university entrance. The GCE (General Certificate of Education) boards provide the examinations which universities use as exemption from matriculation, the university entrance qualification. Because university faculties value some subjects more than others they exercise considerable influence over the curriculum in school and the subjects children take. Grades in England and points in Ireland become all important, the high prestige subjects like medicine requiring the largest number of points. In England some children make choices related to careers as early as 13 or 14 (see also Chapter 6).

It is most remarkable how these structures have persisted over a long period of time. One might expect there to have been a response to the perceived needs of technology in post-industrial society, but attempts to persuade high-grade attaining students into engineering in England have failed. For example engineering science offered as an alternative to physics at the Advanced level of the GCE has only ever been able to attract 300 or so students per annum since 1969 (Carter, Heywood and Kelly, 1984).

The influence of the received curriculum
on teaching and learning

In Ireland, at the primary level, the Inspectorate worked out a new curriculum for primary schools which came into operation in 1970 that is printed in two substantial curriculum guides (Government Publications, 1970). In contrast the curriculum offered in primary schools in England is very much in the hands of the principal of the school. There can be considerable variations between primary schools in the same district which can cause problems for children in their secondary schools if it is assumed they have reached a certain level of performance in certain subjects like English and mathematics when they have not in fact attained that standard.

At secondary level in the Irish examination system, syllabuses dominate teaching and cause teachers to believe that there is no room for anything but the syllabus even when they demonstrate themselves that pupils can quite happily do, for instance, projects in history just prior to their examinations (Heywood, McGuinness and Murphy, 1980). Student teachers argue that they cannot experiment with discovery methods or utilize accepted principles of learning because they have to cover the syllabus and in this way relevant teacher training becomes irrelevant. Experimentally derived evidence suggests however that this view cannot be sustained.

The disciplines of knowledge

In supporting the received perspective teachers use such terms as discipline (subject), and standards for the disciplines legitimate the curriculum for them as they are considered fundamental to human learning. Those who advocate this kind of curriculum can find support from both philosophers and psychologists. Common to both is the idea (with its origins in Plato) that there are common structures of knowledge in the mind of the learner which can be drawn out. So for Bruner (for example) they need to be discovered by the learner if he or she is to be educated, and discovery learning in consequence is an important technique for learning.

Hirst (1975) argues that there are distinguishable clusters of specific concepts and modes of thought which make up seven cognitive systems (the empirical, the mathematical, the philosophical, the moral, the aesthetic, the religious and the historical/sociological), although he seems to have doubts about the last grouping.

In *Knowledge and the Curriculum* Hirst argues that each category or system is a unique form of knowledge characterized as follows:

(a) Each category consists of a network of interrelated concepts, which is logically independent of the network of each other form.
(b) Each category has distinctive tests for truth, by means of which its distinctive concepts are substantiated and its distinctive propositions validated.
(c) Each distinctive test for truth involves skill as well as knowledge, with the result that the forms have to be learned by contact with practitioners on the job.

The appeal of Hirst's axioms to those concerned with teacher training is self-evident. In my view certain forms of philsophy, psychology and sociology are prerequisites to the study of the curriculum and this point is examined in some detail in Chapter 10. Teachers seem to be unable to distinguish between their subject and the forms of knowledge, but would find support from Hirst who argues that all the subjects of the curriculum which he calls 'fields of knowledge' reduce to the forms of knowledge listed above. Brent (1978) has illustrated the differences between subjects and the forms of knowledge in a more substantial discussion elsewhere.

Hirst argues that the forms of knowledge necessarily arise because of the need to communicate:

31

'Whatever private forms of awareness there may be, it is by means of symbols, particularly in language, that conceptual articulation becomes objectified, for the symbols give public embodiment to the concepts. The result of this is that men are able to come to understand both the external world and their own private states of mind in common ways, sharing the same conceptual schema by learning to use symbols in the same manner.' (Hirst, 1975)

The disciplines of knowledge and the common core curriculum

Clearly if this is the case, the theory not only provides a basis for a common core curriculum, that is, a common set of concepts which everyone should learn, but a means of evaluating the changes in the fields of knowledge brought about by new 'knowledge' (see also Chapters 6 and 7). This seems to predicate fundamental internal structures in the mind which respond to these forms of knowledge, or problem-solving mechanisms which store information and which can be drawn on if stimulated by the problem to be solved. Whether or not this provides the support that traditionalists (subject specialists) require for their curriculum scheme seems open to doubt, for men and women come to understand the world through the solution of practical problems. It is for this reason that they develop theories to help them solve these problems. Most problems require information from more than one category of knowledge for their solution.

If the student examples which provide the advanced organization for this chapter are inspected closely, it will be seen that despite the fact that the curriculum is received, there is nevertheless much experimentation at the micro-level of the lesson. This confirms the view that no curriculum at this level can be totally received since that would imply authorized programmed instruction only, and allow for no intervention by the teacher.

Most changes are relatively small and occasionally society feels it necessary to countenance large changes within subjects. The launching of the first artificial earth satellite by Soviet Russia in 1957 undoubtedly shook many establishments in America and England. Curriculum developments in science and mathematics, which were already in process, were suddenly supported by massive infusions of funds. However, they were subject *developments*. The subject *structure* persisted, despite attempts to introduce new integrations of knowledge between physics and chemistry or within the applications of science as an engineering science (see also Chapter 7).

The reflexive perspective

The reflexive perspective in contrast to the received perspective finds a base in the work of such theorists as Berger and Luckman (1966) who argue that knowledge is socially constructed and depends on our experience and environment. In this situation teachers and students should define a curriculum which is real to them in their social context. In this sense the curriculum should be negotiable and worked out to meet the individual needs of pupils. The authorities who espouse this view believe that the review of the curriculum, which this perspective recommends, should be thoroughly critical. Whether the examples of teacher negotiations in the examples above (eg 2.) would satisfy the theorists is a matter of conjecture. Certainly the student author of the fourth illustration (see p 27) would not agree that the curriculum was reflexive.

Ruthven (1978) in a short paper has examined the practical implications of the disciplines thesis for curriculum design in mathematics with some surprising conclusions, for it would seem at first sight that mathematics is a subject in which the disciplines thesis is clear cut. On the contrary, Ruthven argues in his paper (which can be read with ease by non-mathematicians) that commonsense and social conceptions of the disciplines are in conflict with logical conceptions. 'It is', he writes, 'a contingent social fact, rather than a logical necessity, that has led to the tradition of enquiry commonly known as "mathematics" . . .' Ruthven's perspective is *cultural*. The reinterpretation of mathematics in strictly logical terms is to ignore the plausibility of the socio-historical context in which it has been taught and developed. The essential question for curriculum design for Ruthven is 'How can we reinterpret "mathematics" so that it will contribute to the development of a rational perspective on the lives and affairs of men?' This seems to be the approach being taken by curriculum designers in mathematics at the present time (see also Chapter 5), and is certainly consistent with Lawton's idea of a common culture curriculum (Lawton, 1975).

Sociologists are the prime supporters of this paradigm which derives from their particular view of knowledge. For example Mannheim wrote that:

> 'The sociology of knowledge is concerned not so much with distortions due to a deliberate effort to deceive, as with varying ways in which objects present themselves to the subject according to the differences in social settings.
> Thus mental structures are differently formed in different social and historical settings.' (Mannheim, 1936).

The contrast with Piaget and those who, like him, are in the Platonic tradition is marked, for knowledge is relative, except perhaps in mathematics and some sciences, and these relative perceptions account for most of our knowledge.

Eggleston (1977) who discusses this paradigm suggested that neither Mannheim nor Marx advocated a totally relativist perspective. Indeed the mainstream of Marxist educational thought as represented by, say, Simon (1974) and Williams (1961) claims that not only is every child educable but that children should be subject to a core curriculum. This view is in contrast to the speculative Marxism of Young (1971) which is relativist and in the tradition of the philosophy of Sartre. It is Young's interpretative paradigm which has been debated so much (White and Young, 1976). Young and his collaborators challenged many conventional assumptions about high and low status groups in society, in particular the fact that we insist on continuing to provide a more or less common curriculum for all pupils to the detriment of many pupils from the working class. Neither is he alone in this criticism; the conservative educationalist Bantock (1971) thinks that an alternative curriculum should be provided for these children. In contrast to Young, however, he argues that the curriculum should be received.

Lawton (1975) suggests that there are five levels of development to be found in the papers which make up Young's (1971) book. At the first level the concern is for the social distribution of knowledge because society tends to preserve the status quo. At the second level the content of education becomes problematic, that is, it is open to critical examination, and curriculum content should not be taken for granted. The third stage in the argument, which cuts right across the received perspective, is that the subject barriers are arbitrary and artificial and mainly used for the convenience of those in control of education. It is then argued at the fourth level that knowledge is socially constructed, and finally that rationality as well as knowledge is a convention.

It seems to the author that if this is the case then communication between groups is impossible. The examples provided by the students seem to belong to the second level and were undoubtedly influenced by the need to cope with working class groups. It seems unlikely for example that Catholic students in Ireland would go so far as to accept the totality of levels four or five, although it seems to the author that it is equally possible to relate the idea of the social construction of reality to the theory of perceptual learning that is found in the writings of Aquinas (Pieper, 1963; Singer and Ramsden, 1969). But that must be the subject of another discourse (see the section below on perceptual learning theory).

The student examples suggest that at the level of the lesson there is some reflexive thinking within subjects, and that while it is not of the critical kind called for by the theorists it is nevertheless independent. The most popular approach to such independent study is the substantive project in which students are allowed to choose and pursue their own investigations. The aims of such investigations are illustrated by Figure 2.1 (see p 34) which shows instructions on the project outline for engineering science at A level (JMB, 1984). Projects have been completed in history with considerable success with younger pupils. These can be critical in the sense used by Young, as various examples throughout this text in relation to the teaching of Irish history show. Such projects allow for independent study. For example, at the University of Lancaster and the North East London Polytechnic courses for independent study are offered at diploma and degree level. Figure 2.2 (see p 36) shows the introductory statement to the *Guide for Intending Students in Independent Study* at the University of Lancaster. There are many forms of school-based developed curriculum assessment available to schools and colleges.

School-based curriculum development is based on the premise that the school and the school teacher should have primary responsibility for the curriculum and its content (Skilbeck, 1975). It is a more limited view of the reflexive paradigm since it is based on the premise that the teacher

---

Advice to candidates on the submission of project outlines

Project outlines are submitted to the external moderators for three reasons:

   (i) to encourage the preparation of the project plan at an early stage;
  (ii) to encourage the planning of the project through the stimulus of impartial comment by the moderator;
 (iii) to provide an independent check on the likelihood of the success of the project in developing abilities and providing a sense of achievement.

The importance of the initial planning of the project cannot be over-stressed. It is not assumed that in all cases you will stick to your original proposals; indeed in some cases two or three sets of proposals might have to be considered. It will be only on the basis of the initial thought demanded at the planning stage that you will be able to arrive at an acceptable outline. As each stage in the planning process is completed the nature of the project will become clearer and your commitment to it greater.

The contents suggested on page 2 are not essential to all outlines and their presentation will vary from project to project. It is however important that all the main contents listed should be considered and, where they are relevant to your particular project, a careful analysis of them should be made. Your outline should be kept short, consistent with making a clear statement of your proposals.

Figure 2.1 *Introductory paragraphs to the project outlines submitted prior to commencement of the project in engineering science at A level of the General Certificate of Education, Joint Matriculation Board* (Reproduced by kind permission of the Joint Matriculation Board, Manchester.)

and the learner should enjoy the freedom to form educative relationships which do not necessarily imply that the learner will be involved in the critical evaluation of his or her programme. It also differs from the reflexive paradigm in that its proponents see it as combining the advantages of national policy making and research and development with local needs for flexibility and adaptability. It can be argued with some force that the majority of teachers when faced with such freedom would be constrained by their subject norms, and that in any event there is no great desire for substantial change. This argument is supported by the fact that in those examination boards which provide both for external examinations and school-based syllabuses the majority of teachers follow the more traditional procedures. It is the combination of external examination and coursework assessment which seems to best meet the needs of both pupils and teachers in terms of each individual's adaptability and flexibility.

It seems clear from the student examples that there are received and reflexive (negotiable) elements in every curriculum. Indeed the latter are more likely to occur in lesson and coursework activities than they are at the macroscopic level of curriculum enquiry. Eggleston's paradigms are generalizable to the micro-level but often have different meaning for teachers. The examination boards allow for an element of independent choice and in certain cases teachers may set and assess their own examinations. Those teaching subjects traditionally held to be difficult, as for

35

The nature of the beast

Independent studies offers you a different way of making use of the resources available in the University — principally (a) a range of people (the academic staff) with a mastery of their particular subject area, (b) books, lab facilities, etc and (c) other students. The orthodox way is to package these up into courses, and then to allow a student a structure choice amongst them. The independent student does not choose amongst packages, but constructs his or her scheme of studies directly out of the raw materials out of which the packages themselves are made. So the challenging but liberating question an intending student faces is: how can I draw on the resources represented by the University in order to get the most out of my two Part II years?

The school invites prospective students to design a scheme of activities with this basic question in mind, and takes the student on if it finds the proposals acceptable.

To stand a good chance of being accepted, proposals have to be 'academic' in character, though for good or bad it is often difficult to say what this test rules out. The best guidance is to say that those activities that already figure in established courses in the University are the sort of activities that are likely to be acceptable in an independent studies scheme. The overwhelmingly predominant activity in past schemes has been *reading*, followed by critical *writing*, and indeed many schemes have been defined by students simply specifying what reading they planned and under what headings they intend to write in response to what they read. But other activities have also figured: making sculptures, conducting architectural surveys, writing short stories, magazine editing, doing formal logic, play producing, digging (archaeologically), taking photographs, painting pictures, conducting sociological and anthropological fieldwork, etc.

Figure 2.2 *Guide for intending students in independent study at the University of Lancaster. Introductory paragraphs* (Reproduced by kind permission of W Fuge.)

example Latin, have found that elements of coursework assessment are of considerable value (Wilson, 1982). The report of the Intermediate Certificate Examination Committee in Ireland (Government Publications, 1974) recommended a structure in which every teacher would be involved in the marking of scripts as well as in subject development, and it is this kind of approach which is used by the Southern Regional Examinations Board in England (Heywood, 1977).

A restructuring perspective

These latter views of reflexiveness do not derive from the concept of reality as a social construct, but from the value attached to learning skills of autonomous learning. Similarly the ability to negotiate a curriculum with children who are not interested in school work derives from the desire to motivate these children rather than from any other critical factor, as well as from despair with the traditional curriculum. More generally it seems that the student teachers in the illustrations are, to use

Eggleston's term, restructuring the curriculum. According to him, the restructuring perspective brings together the other two paradigms — the received and reflexive perspectives — 'as two related modes of understanding both the realities of knowledge in the school curriculum and the possibilities of change therein' (Eggleston, 1977). Eggleston shows (Figure 2.3, below) how these different perspectives may contribute to our understanding of the curriculum in which three explanations are presented for curriculum achievement. The reflexive perspective develops from the received and the restructuring from the reflexive. 'In particular, it shows one of the central tenets of the received perspective; the dominance of teacher perceptions and the way in which in the restructuring perspective these perceptions are augmented by new evidence from the children and teachers.'

Sociological perspectives of the curriculum and perceptual learning theory

But is this really the explanation? The idea that the objects of knowledge do not have a reality outside their social construction is nonsense and neither would Berger and Luckman expect us to take that view.

'The reality of everyday life is organized around the "here" of my body and the "now" of my present. This "here and now" is the focus of my attention to the reality of everyday life. What is "here and now" presented to me in

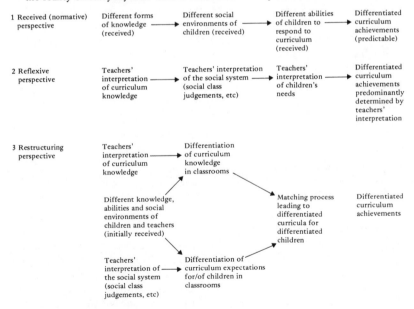

Figure 2.3 *Eggleston's (1977) explanations for curriculum achievement using the received, reflexive and restructuring paradigms*
(Reprinted by kind permission of the author.)

37

everyday life is the realissimum of my consciousness. The reality of everyday life is not, however, exhausted by these immediate presences, but embraces phenomena that are not present "here and now". This means that I experience everyday life in terms of different degrees of closeness and remoteness, both spatially and temporally.' (Berger and Luckman, 1966)

The explanation must surely lie in the nature of knowledge and learning. Knowledge has two components: *knowledge acquisition* and *knowledge making* and learning is the skill (or skills) required for both. Human beings learn and therefore acquire and make knowledge. This is self-evident, for knowledge continues to grow and from this growth there is no escape. We necessarily have to learn that there must be both reflexive and received components in our thinking. The latter relates to our need for security and the former to our search for an identity which we hope will be unique. But because we are only able to proceed to, and internalize, new understandings in small steps for fear of upsetting our equilibrium, both change and development are slow and so it is that we continually restructure knowledge.

The reality that we perceive depends on our powers of perception, and it is the factors which influence perception that limit the control we have over learning. What we perceive depends not only on what is to be perceived but on the state of the perceiver. This means that the perceiver is internally organized to perceive. There is an internal structure which we use to impose meaning on the objects of knowledge by reference to previously acquired information. Psychologists have termed the 'bits' of this information variously as schemata, schema, categories or frames of reference. Abercrombie (1960) says that these 'bits' may be regarded as tools which help us to 'see, evaluate and respond'.

Hesseling (1966) wrote:

'The working of these schemata can be indirectly observed in everyday experience. For example when we instructed a group of chargehands during a residential course to observe accurately and in detail some charwoman cleaning up the house, they reported individually the observed behaviour in terms of work, methods, tools, performance and similar categories. They used these categories in their daily work and they expected to be asked for such observations in this training situation. They did not observe this behaviour. Much socio-psychological research demonstrates an inner consistency among an individual's perceptions and his needs, his values, his cognitive style and way of looking at life.'

We can argue that the life styles associated with the different economic groups provide different internal structures and frames of reference, and that these differences lead to differences in perception which create communication barriers between the groups. Often highly specialized and highly qualified persons working on the same problem cannot understand each other because they do not comprehend the language of each other's specialization. For instance, the ways in which lawyers and engineers look at an aircraft which has crashed due to metal fatigue are totally different, and the two may well have difficulty in communicating with each other as well as with laymen. Clearly the acquisition of such different perceptions has within it the seeds of conflict. I have argued in *Analysing Jobs* (Youngman, Oxtoby, Monk and Heywood, 1978) that too much experience can be harmful to innovation for we tend to rely on experience and this prevents us from going outside the realms of the familiar.

It should be evident that we cannot cope with all the information available to us for necessarily we have to be selective. This selectivity will be influenced by our internal structure including our intelligence, aptitudes and interests. However, as we collect information from our particular environment it provides its own sampling mechanism. Some environments are very limiting and this is yet another way of accounting for the learning differences between the socio-economic classes.

Also influencing the acquisition of information is bias (prejudice) which is a conditioned tendency to favour and support a certain point of view or conclusion despite the absence of adequate or even any evidence. The influences of home, school and work on our prejudices are considerable. It is often very difficult to reject a prejudicial frame of reference, to get used to new attitudes and values, and often prejudice is compounded by the disposition of personality. An authoritarian personality is much more likely to be 'closed' to new experiences than a more democratic personality (Adorno *et al*, 1950).

All this leads to the conclusion that we will not always see things as the next person sees them, a fact which can be demonstrated by very simple experiments (Heywood, 1982).

> 'We can find in common experience many examples of the different meaning attached to specific behaviour. A student had to make a sampling study of chargehands in a fairly confined factory, without complete introduction.
> He started on a Monday morning. A new product was now assembled and production was under time stress. Because he often spoke to the chargehands and was continually making notes, he appeared to most of the young assembly workers as a controller of their bosses. His appearance near their assembly lines was welcomed with some satisfaction: they became bolder towards the chargehands, made jokes and nudged each other when he was approaching. To the chargehands he seemed a menace: they became uncertain and nervous and they concerned themselves more with the production process itself than with their group of workers. To the departmental manager he became a scapegoat: he blamed several production faults on this work sampling study and he walked about in the factory more than usual.' (Hesseling, 1966)

Combine all this with the fact that we impose *meaning* on the objects and events which surround us and the complexity and significance of perceptual learning becomes apparent. It can account for the difficulties that people have in reconciling different beliefs, for few people are aware of the factors which influence their learning. This is why an understanding of how we learn should be an important component of moral education. With regard to the curriculum in general, I have argued that perceptual learning theory leads to a view of liberal education as the process which provides a person with the widest possible range of frames of reference (schemata), together with the learning skills necessary for problem-solving at the highest levels of mental and moral development.

In a society such as England which makes an art of its social structure, the implementation of a separate curriculum for the children of those who are unskilled such as that proposed by Bantock (1971) must surely perpetuate 'bias' and prevent understanding between social groups. All social groups need to comprehend each other and no group is free from its own limitations. But changing the reality that individuals perceive inevitably means changing their environment, for it is in the environment that learning begins. This view is supported by Lawton (1975) who argues for a common culture curriculum, for the 'school curriculum (in the wider sense) is essentially a selection from the culture of a society. Certain aspects of our way of life, certain kinds of knowledge, certain attitudes and values are regarded as so important that their transmission to the next generation is not left to chance in our society but is entrusted to specially-trained professionals (teachers) in elaborate and expensive institutions (schools)' (Mant, 1979).

Cognate structures

It does not seem that the mind has a framework which enables it to match the order found in the universe. The central activity in enabling the mind to know the universe is learning. To simply see it in bands of knowledge, as Hirst (1975) does, is to see it in a passive form. Similarly to argue, as Eggleston (1977) does, that the reflexive derives from the received is only partially true. Both views derive from a Western view of how man thinks. Taken out of its 'control' frame, the reflexive may be seen to be describing humanity's capability to 'make things'. It is this 'active component' which is missing from Hirst's cognitive domains. Yet it is clear that the cognitive and the affective cannot be separated in this way. One has to allow for 'Technik', for theory derives only as a function of the necessity to solve practical problems, and the self is the agent in that process (MacMurray, 1957). The reflexive leads to the received. It is in the received that our identity is confirmed but the need to solve problems continually brings about the need to restructure in small increments, for large increments are not psychologically tenable. They lie outside 'plausibility' to use Berger and Luckman's (1966) own term.

Thus it is that teachers continually restructure as part of their search for identity within the subjects they teach, and the student illustrations support this view. It is for this reason as much as any other that great projects are soon forgotten, particularly in a world that bristles with new ideas. The great curriculum projects in the 1950s and 1960s in the USA are not mentioned in the major reports on education for Americans during the next 20 years (Armbruster, 1977; NCE, 1983; NSB, 1983). There is a need to improve literacy and numeracy skills, although the substantial data on which beliefs about declining achievement levels are based need to be treated with caution. The same is true in England where recently there has been much concern with standards. Change it seems takes place in waves or cycles and what was the vogue in one cycle becomes forgotten in the next. It was not the sputniks which started it all: all they did was to come at a convenient time in educational thinking (McGuinness, 1984).

The lesson of the big curriculum projects to central direction was that it was extremely difficult to disseminate information and, as Murphy (1976) has shown, it is essential that teachers internalize the objectives so that they act in accordance with a changed value system. So the emphasis swings to the individual and the school as the ordinands of change but all within broad national guidelines. Within the scope of most individual thought there is plenty of room for change. The problem is reflexive insofar as people are critically aware of needs, and it seems to be a major criticism of the teaching profession that it is not.

Inspection of the syllabuses as between, say, 1951 and the present, in any subject, at any level of education, in any country, will show considerable change. Overall, however, the remarkable thing is that in general curriculum structure persists. However, when examined country by country it is clear that there are cultural differences which cause the interaction between the curriculum and society to have different outcomes, as for example in the education and training of technologists. Why this should be so is a matter of considerable interest and the subject of the next chapter.

References

Abercrombie, M L J (1960) *The Anatomy of Judgement. An Investigation into the Processes of Perception and Reasoning* Penguin: Harmondsworth

Adorno, T W, Frenkel-Brunswick, E, Levinson, D J and Sanford, R N (1950) *The Authoritarian Personality* Harper Row: New York

Armbruster, F E (1977) *Our Children's Crippled Future: How American Education Has Failed* New York Times Book Co: New York

Ashby, E (1958) *Technology and the Academics* MacMillan: London

Bantock, G H (1971) Towards a theory of popular education *in* Hooper, R (ed) *The Curriculum Context, Design and Development* Oliver and Boyd: Edinburgh

Berger, P L and Luckman, T (1966) *The Social Construction of Reality* Allen Lane: London

Bosworth, G (1963) Towards creative activity in engineering *Universities Quarterly* 17, p 286

Brent, A (1978) *Philosophical Foundations for the Curriculum* Routledge and Kegan Paul: London

Burns, T and Stalker, G H (1961) *The Management of Innovation* Tavistock: London

Carter, G, Heywood, J and Kelly, D T (1984) On the development of engineering science at A level. A report for the Joint Matriculation Board: Manchester (in press

CMND 9703 (1956) *Technical Education* Her Majesty's Stationery Office: London

Eggleston, J (1977) *The Sociology of the School Curriculum* Routledge and Kegan Paul: London

Government Publications (1970) *Curriculum Bunscoile* (Two volumes) Dublin

Government Publications (1974) *Final Report of the Committee on the Form and Function of the Intermediate Certificate Examination*

Hesseling, P (1966) *A Strategy for Evaluation Research* Van Gorcum: Aassen: Netherlands

Heywood, J (1969) An evaluation of certain developments in higher technological education, thesis (Two volumes) University of Lancaster Library: Lancaster

Heywood, J (1974) *New Degrees and Courses* Council of Europe Report for the Committee on Higher Education: Strasbourg

Heywood, J (1977) *Examining in Second Level Education* Association of Secondary Teachers: Ireland

Heywood, J (1982) *Pitfalls and Planning in Student Teaching* Kogan Page: London

Heywood, J, McGuinness, S and Murphy, D (1980) *The Final Report of the Public Examinations Evaluation Project to the Minister for Education* The School of Education, The University of Dublin: Dublin

Hirst, P (1975) *Knowledge and the Curriculum* Routledge and Kegan Paul: London

Joint Matriculation Board (1984) *Project Outline for Engineering Science at the Advanced Level of the General Certificate of Education* Joint Matriculation Board: Manchester

Lawrence, P, Hutton, S P and Smith, J H (1980) *The Recruitment, Deployment and Status of the Mechanical Engineer in the German Federal Republic* University of Southampton for the Department of Industry: Southampton

Lawton, D (1975) *Class, Culture and the Curriculum* Routledge and Kegan Paul: London

MacMurray, J (1957) *The Self as Agent* Faber and Faber: London

Mannheim, K (1936) *Ideology and Utopia: An Introduction to the Sociology of Knowledge* Routledge and Kegan Paul: London

Mant, A (1979) *The Rise and Fall of the British Manager* Pan: London

McGuinness, S (1984) Unpublished work for PhD thesis, School of Education, University of Dublin

Murphy, D E (1976) Problems associated with the development of a new national scheme of assessment in Ireland MEd thesis School of Education, University of Dublin: Dublin

National Commission on Excellence (1983) *A Nation at Risk* NCE: Washington, DC

National Science Board (1983) *Educating Americans for the 21st Century* The NSB Commission on pre-college education on mathematics, science and technology: Washington, DC

Peiper, J (1963) *Introduction to St Thomas Aquinas* Faber and Faber: London

Ruthven, K (1978) The disciplines thesis and the curriculum: a case study *British Journal of Educational Studies* 26, pp 163-76

Simon, B (1974) *Intelligence, Psychology and Education* Routledge and Kegan Paul: London

Singer, E J and Ramsden, J (1969) *The Practical Approach to Skills Analysis* McGraw Hill: London

Skilbeck, M (1975) School based curriculum development *in* Lee, V and Seldin, D (eds) *Planning in the Curriculum* Hodder and Stoughton: London

White, J and Young, M F D (1976) A dialogue *Education for Teaching* 98, p 4

Williams, R (1961) *The Long Revolution* Penguin: Harmondsworth

Wilson, D J (1982) Problems of assessment at 16+ (in classics) *Hesperiam* 5, pp 15-21

Young, M F D (ed) (1971) *Knowledge and Control* Collier-Macmillan: London

Youngman, M, Oxtoby, R, Monk, J D and Heywood, J (1978) *Analysing Jobs* Gower Press: Farnborough

Chapter 3

Societal Pressures

'There is, of course, much more that is "hidden". It could be argued that the purpose of the mathematics curriculum is not only to enable pupils to learn mathematics but also to allow some to understand that they cannot learn mathematics, and to acquire a suitable respect for those who can (the teachers and the more able pupils destined for superior occupational status). If this is the case, of course, the unstreamed class or the comprehensive school may provide a more suitable arena for such learning.'   J Eggleston (1977)

Introduction

It appears that it is self-evident that the hidden curriculum goes beyond the classroom. When children begin to make career selections they see that without certain examinations they will not be able to pursue certain careers, so they make adaptations to their curriculum. The influence of the home environment will be very important in such choices and often parents do not perceive their child's potential. A pupil who is bright can be made to feel that he or she is not bright and therefore does not try. This can happen at any social level although it is clear that the effects of the environment on the children of unskilled workers is particularly depressing.

Societies differ considerably in the type of social mechanisms used for selection, which is why it is difficult to compare one country with another. Yet we do try to compare, and there is no doubt that our ideas are sometimes influenced by the ideas of other systems (Mallinson, 1949). For example, British engineering educators have brought substantial pressure on the system to introduce five-year courses since a five-year pattern is to be found in Germany and, as a result, there are now many more four-year courses in British universities than there were a few years ago.

In this chapter the influence of the British professions and sub-professions on the educational structure and in particular on career choices is considered. It is concluded that the complexity of the system leads to inflexibility and adaptability in later life is thereby impeded (see pp 47 - 59). The values which underpin the meritocratic structure are discussed in the light of studies by Mant (1979) and McClelland (1961).

The development of professional associations

The form which professionalism has taken in England relates very much to class structure. Many authors refer to its uniqueness and, while there is seen to be much of value in the system, it seems to be not only the cause of poor industrial relations (Heywood, 1984) but also the cause of the poor technological performance of the English as well (Lilley, 1973). To the question 'What factors make one society eager to innovate and leave another content with what it has inherited?', Lilley responds that, 'Much of the answer would seem to lie in the class structure of society . . .' (Lilley, 1973). Writing of German success in the nineteenth century he says: 'The roots of this chemical pre-eminence were not economic. Its origins are to be found in German national pride trying to re-assert itself after the ignominies of Napoleonic defeat'. Mant (1979) writes that the 'British have made social class an art form'. Thus it is that coping with class, and it is much more than coping, is as much a part of the hidden curriculum as the peer-group and teacher interactions in the classroom. It is with this underlying societal pressure that this chapter is primarily concerned. Its focus will be a peculiarly Anglo-Saxon phenomenon: the professions.

The professions and the education system

If the question is asked 'Who makes policy?', and the answer is given 'Parliament', and if it is also asked 'Who in Parliament?' it will be appreciated that parliamentarians are a different group of people from the professionals — even though some of them may be professional people — mainly lawyers. There is a marked contrast in attitudes between the working class representatives and those from the upper middle and moneyed classes in the British parliament. It will also be found that there is a considerable link between the upper middle classes and the financial institutions of the City of London.

'Behind' the Government are the civil servants who are often called professionals and by and large this administrative cadre is drawn from the universities of Oxford and Cambridge. Again it is a mix of the classes, for the meritocratic system enables very bright and motivated children from the lower middle and working classes to work their way through grammar school to Oxbridge. However the public schools (private, independent and requiring substantial fees) feed many individuals into important sectors in the world of business and finance without the requirement of the 'Oxbridge' tag. It is family money which is necessary for their entry into the system. But it is still possible to make money and jump the system as can be seen in the world of banking and finance. The children of such parents necessarily benefit from these advances.

Added to these complexities is an aristocracy that is independent of the upper middle classes and which shares in the government of the country. Both Mant (1979) and Turner (1969) have drawn attention to the fact that many senior men in industry seem to be more concerned with the award of honours from the Queen than with the pursuit of business. Thus, in Mant's view, management in Britain is more about holding court than it is about driving industry forward.

For most people the main route for advancement is along meritocratic lines and, as we have seen, subjects acquire status just as the professions do. Since 1945 (the end of the Second World War) there has been a massive search for professional status in which the educational system has played a major role for the ability to control entry to the professions via educational qualifications is one of their major features. It is one of the major restrictive practices and it helps the professions create closed shops.

The search for professional status

A profession may be distinguished by the following characteristics:

1. The specific knowledge thought to be necessary for performance in a given task, measured by tests of competency.
2. The ability to regulate practitioners' behaviour and the possession of a code of conduct.
3. A special relationship between the professional person and the client.
4. Support by legislation.

Not all those organizations which call themselves professional have all these characteristics. Nevertheless, as will be shown in the paragraphs which follow, there is a considerable search for what is perceived to be professional status. In consequence, society in its response to this development differentiates between one professional society and another, assigning more status to some and less to others. This influences pupil attitudes to the subjects they study at school if they are thinking of pursuing a particular career.

Traditionally the three professions were the Church, the Army and the Law. Very often official forms such as applications for passports required the witness to be from one of these professions. However, the term 'profession' is now used by a wide variety of persons and organizations. Actors commonly speak of the 'acting profession', engineers of the 'engineering profession' and so on. Attempts have been made to distinguish between the professions, and numerous sub- or semi-professions have been identified (Lees, 1966). There has been a huge increase in the number of organizations which describe themselves as professional. It is a way of obtaining status in society. Some organizations, particularly those in engineering in Britain, have been preoccupied with the problem of status.

Status as a value ascribed to British society depends in a 'peculiar' way on the relationship that the professional person has with individuals. The more direct this relationship and the more the individual depends on the knowledge of a particular professional person, the more society is likely to value this profession. Thus it is that society puts high value on the doctor and less on the nurse since it is the doctor who is ascribed the diagnostic, planning and operational skills. A nurse is regarded both as the servant of and as having less knowledge than the doctor (Becker et al, 1958).

45

In this way education and, by inference, examinations acquire importance. A person who acquired all these skills but did not possess an approved qualification would not be allowed to practise. Thus it is that education is seen as a means of acquiring professional status (Marshall, 1939).

Marxist commentators on the emergence of the professions argue that the particular prestige and power of medicine and law can, to an extent, be seen as a product of the law's involvement in establishing the exact nature of property arrangements and its crucial role in contract law as bourgeois society replaced the feudal system. Similarly medicine, co-opted to ensure the health and well-being of the wealthy, also stood in close proximity to those who are able to confer a certain prestige and power to its most useful lieutenants. The semi-professions cannot aspire to this prestige because the sort of things that teachers, social workers and engineers (in non-technocratic societies) do are not absolutely necessary to the maintenance of the dominant elites. In Britain the liberal professions supply the key personnel to the administrative cadres and use 'Oxbridge' as a vehicle for maintaining their status.

There is of course some validity in both the more traditional and Marxist explanations. Even so the picture is confused. We do not speak of the professional scientist, yet the scientific institution The Royal Society clearly has the highest status among the engineering, medical and scientific learned and professional institutions, but it would not regard itself as a professional institution. Entry to it is restricted to about 32 persons annually. Scientists do not need to think of themselves as professionals and are clearly distinguished from the technicians in the field. Engineers need to think of themselves as professionals in order to separate themselves from the technicians and mechanics who call themselves engineers. Physicists do not need to call themselves chartered physicists whereas to secure this separation engineers seek to call themselves chartered engineers. The British Academy, equally severe with its entry requirements, does not have the same prestige as The Royal Society.

A distinction may also be made between employed and self-employed professional people. There seems to be a crude relationship between self-employment — particular relationship with client — earnings, and the status of the professional. In this respect doctors have higher status than architects and, more interestingly, dentists. Private chiropodists and physiotherapists do not have much status and their earnings are much less than those of doctors; engineers by and large are employees. Although the majority of doctors are employed by the National Health Service in Britain, they are regarded and probably regard themselves as self-employed. There is therefore a 'master' element in the status which society ascribes to professionals.

Finally, the professional-individual relationship necessitates codes of conduct, and the degree of specificity in relation to control over membership also distinguishes the professions. The greater the control, it seems, the higher the status, as for example in the regulation of doctors and lawyers. There is therefore a more general search for codes of conduct among the lower status professions. But for those who are employed three conflicts are created. The first relates to the use of codes of conduct by employees and the exercise of social responsibility. For example, most engineers and scientists are employees and as such could be brought into conflict with their employer as regards practice, say, in the specification of equipment (Engineers Council, 1972). Most recently the engineer's role in the design of nuclear power plant has been questioned. Professional values would imply recognition of, and working to, certain standards of safety. The engineering professions in both America and England have been much concerned with the development of codes of conduct. In the medical unions in Britain there has been equal concern about the possible misuse of private records by the police.

There seems to be a good correlation between the relative status of professions in given areas, and earnings, and this relationship seems to be more generally applied with the outstanding exception of nursing. Until recently, the fees charged by solicitors for conveyancing, for example, were controlled by the Law Society. Although the law seems to prevent persons other than solicitors from setting up as conveyancers, the fixing of fees is now legally regarded as a restrictive practice in Britain.

Professional values can also be in conflict with trade union values. During the last 10 years there has been a trend toward the unionization of professional people who have become more militant and prepared to strike. The significant area of trade union growth is among white collar workers including doctors which has also brought questions about the role of the professional institutions in trade unionism.

For example, the British Association of Social Workers has promoted a parallel trade union, the British Union of Social Workers, as its negotiating wing. It continues to be seen as a specifically professional association. This is an interesting instance of the way in which professional organizations try to adjust to the simultaneous problem of 'standards' and negotiating rights. In the British Medical Association this is done discreetly. Some members of the engineering profession would welcome an increasingly union-based professional association as is seen from the foundation of the United Kingdom Association of Scientific and Professional Engineers. But this Association has found itself opposed on numerous occasions by both the Amalgamated Union of Engineering Workers and the Association of Scientific and Managerial Staff. This exemplifies the worries that professionals perceive in relation to the decline in their status and power at the expense of unionized workers.

Mant suggests that this has had a profound effect on the *raison d'être* of the professions.

'. . . in recent years the old professions have swung alarmingly away from the work end of the work/survival continuum into survival type behaviour. The most obvious manifestation is the increasing tendency of professionals to behave like the more unregenerate elements of the trade union movement. It is an understandable shift; pay differentials have been eroded and a growing number of professionals such as doctors and teachers are nowadays simply salaried employees of large bureaucratic organizations. In such circumstances, the client, the *raison d'être* of the "professional" structure, begins to merge into the shadows.' (Mant, 1979)

and

'. . . so many new entrants to the most prestigious "professional" jobs are there for personal gain and status (what you take out) rather than the intrinsic purpose of the work (what you have put in).' (Mant, 1979)

All in all the professional organizations play a major role in British working life because they are qualifying agencies and their bearing on the educational structure is of considerable importance.

Professionalism and the educational structure

Writing as long ago as 1939, T H Marshall described the changing professional structure thus:

'. . . At the lower social level the picture is different. Here the remarkable thing is the rapid spread of the forms of professional organization among occupational groups which are not professions in the full meaning of the term. The forms which such groups can adopt are recognized courses of training in a specialized technique, a means of testing efficiency in that technique, the admission of those duly qualified into an association, the building up of the prestige of the association as against non-members, the imposition of certain standards of honourable dealing and the rudiments of a code of ethics. The foundation of the whole structure is the specialized technique, and it is the multiplication of these techniques that has made possible the spread of these organizations.' (Marshall, 1939)

The educational system acquires its importance because it provides the specialized technique, but this has not always been the case, and it is important that the reasons for this should be understood.

In the nineteenth century the universities of Oxford and Cambridge were concerned with liberal education. Although they educated scientists they were not in the business of training for the practical arts. Training for the practical arts began in mechanics institutes and eventually, by about 1920, a system of training while at work, with evening and sometimes day release, had come about at technical colleges. It was a system of apprenticeship in the tradition of the medieval guilds. Trainee solicitors and architects 'articled' themselves to firms and studied primarily in their offices. The system of part-time release became hallowed but the qualifications which these students sought were the qualifications of a professional organization. The technical colleges provided a service for this purpose. Thus students took examinations which, with the approval of the professional body, would exempt them from the educational requirements of that professional organization. The largest number of such awards was made by the engineering institutions which maintained standards generally accepted as being of pass degree level.

In 1945 a Government Report on Technological Education recommended that new diplomas in manufacturing technology should be established, resulting from substantially more time in college study. This should be achieved by sandwich (co-operative) courses which would consist of consecutive six-month periods of training for industry and college over a four-year period. The diploma would be equivalent to a degree.

No action was taken on this recommendation until 1955/56 when the Government created a National Council for Technological Awards to award such a diploma. In the same period it reorganized 10 technological colleges so that they would only do advanced level work. Of these 10 Colleges of Advanced Technology, the three in London also prepared substantial numbers of students for degrees from the University of London in science and technology. It was subsequently argued by many people from these colleges that if a diploma was equal to a degree it ought to be called a degree and that because these institutions operated at degree level, they ought to become universities. This they did in the period 1966-68.

In the meantime, as part of their search for professional status, the engineering institutions changed their regulations so that by and large individuals training in the part-time route would no longer be able to obtain exemption. That there was mutual support between the Government and these particular institutions was evident from the 1961 White Paper on *Better Opportunities in Technical Education* (CMND 1254). This document proposed a rather more rigid stratification between technologist, technician, craft and operative qualifications. Formerly the national certificates had been a means of exemption into professional organizations but now the standards of these certificates were to be lowered with the object of providing technician qualifications only.

When the 10 colleges of advanced technology became universities, the Government established a Council for National Academic Awards (CNAA) to replace the National Council of Technological Awards. It was to award degrees, not diplomas, in any subject, not just technology. These degrees would be awarded in the public sector. Since then (*circa* 1966):

'It is important to notice the effects of these changes on social mobility. An organized profession admits recruits by means of an impartial test of their knowledge and ability. In theory they are selected on merit, but it is merit of a particular kind which usually must be developed and displayed in a particular, prescribed way. A narrow road leads into the profession through certain educational institutions. How far this favours social mobility depends on whether those institutions are open to the masses, so that merit can win recognition in all classes. Granted that broadening of the educational ladder typical of modern democracies, the system of the official examination is more favourable to mobility than one of arbitrary appointment or casual promotion. But the chance to move comes early, during school days. Once it has been missed and a career has been started at a non-professional level, the whole system of formal qualifications makes movement at a later stage well-nigh impossible.

There is another point. In the church or the army, in law or medicine, a man at the head of his profession is on top of the world. He admits no superiors. But many of these new semi-professions are really subordinate grades placed in the middle of the hierarchy of modern business organization. The educational ladder leads into them but there is no ladder leading out.

The grade above is entered by a different road starting at a different level of the educational system. Social structure, insofar as it reflects occupational structure, is frozen as soon as it emerges from the fluid preparatory stage of schooling. Mobility between generations is increased, but mobility during the working life of one generation is diminished. That appears to be the direction in which things are moving today, towards the transfer of individual competitiveness from the economic to the educational world, from the office and workshop to the school and university.' (Marshall, 1939)

This transfer of competitiveness continues unabated. The period spent in the education system is being lengthened, and unemployment is causing many pupils considerable changes in attitude. It raises considerable problems for the fixing of the school leaving age (see also Chapter 6). At the same time it seems clear that if society is to become more adaptable, early stratification within the education system would only lead to inflexibility. The need for a reappraisal of the structure of education to be provided for our post-industrial society is great. That the interaction between qualification and structure relating to the labour market is self-evident, and that for too many individuals this relationship is formed too early, surely creates structures which inhibit flexibility and adaptability. As Thomas and Madigan (1974) show, a job search after redundancy is in part a normatively structured process in which people attempt to maintain their expectations of the situation against the action and expectations of the other groups with an interest in the outcome. The more qualifications operate to prevent people from changing jobs the less flexible and adaptable the system on the one hand, and on the other, the greater the need to provide for continuing education. Unfortunately, roles are implicit in job titles and often employers and employees do not see that the skills which they use in one job may be transferred to another. We need to think more in terms of 'skill areas' than in training for specific jobs (Youngman et al, 1978). In all these respects the recent proposals of the Engineering Industries Training Board for a single system of training from the Youth Training Scheme recruits to graduate engineers, similar in many respects to the proposals for Gesampthochschulen in Germany in the 1960s, is of interest. The idea is shown diagrammatically in Figure 3.1 (see p 51).

More generally these professional structures are part of the hidden curriculum with which pupils and staff cope in their everyday life. The influence of social values on staff is profound and not always recognized as it affects us all in whatever field of human endeavour. It is with these hidden values as they relate to the economy and education that the next section is concerned.

Professionalism, the economy and education

Three authorities at least have suggested that the poor performance of the British economy is due to negative national attitudes toward growth; that is to say there is a relationship between economic growth and psychology (Reynaud, 1981). Sir Alec Cairncross in his presidential address to the

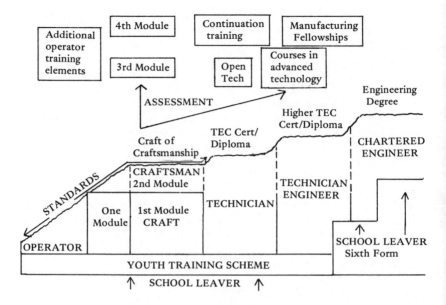

Figure 3.1 *The Engineering Industries Training Board's proposals for a single system of engineering training.* (Adapted from the *Times Educational Supplement* 15:4:83.)

economic section of the British Association said that he could not help suspecting 'that interest in growth is fainter than we pretend' (Cairncross, 1970). Both Mant and McClelland believe that the high regard for professionals in Britain and America is conducive to slow economic growth. Both are concerned with the character of nations rather than with the character of individuals.

Mant argues, among other things, that the British live in a culture of dependence, 'a drawn-in, reflective, unambitious place, revering the female gods of existence rather than the masculine gods of action' (Mant, 1979). His idea of dependence stems from the work of Bion of the Tavistock Institute who had studied the factors contributing to the display of power and leadership among small groups of people. Mant (1979) argued that underneath what we observe of the tasks performed by individuals in working groups, is an emotional structure belonging to the group itself, and that it is that structure rather than the individuals themselves which directs the action of the group. In other words just as there is a psychology of the individual so there is a psychology of the group and it applies equally to large aggregates of people. A nation or culture, therefore, has its own inner dynamic. In this theory dependence is the reliance of a group on super-leadership, and is to be seen in, for example, the creation of a Minister for Drought (as happened in the UK in 1976).

The opposite parameter expresses the willingness of a group to stand

and fight or run away from whatever is troubling its members. If industry is to succeed then fight/flight behaviour is essential in competition. Fight/flight behaviour influences both Germans and Japanese, for they in particular had to rebuild themselves after the Second World War. However, this was not the case with the victors of this war. Britain, who no longer wanted to fight, and with the memory of the Great Depression, set about creating a welfare state which embraced major industries as well as health and education. Recent approaches by the Conservative and Labour parties (since 1979) have, for the first time since the Second World War, brought the fight/flight and dependence assumptions into public display, although the issue is almost certainly not understood by the public. The Falkland Islands' battle is a recent example of fight at the national level as is the tendency to stand firm in industrial relations. Whether these acts signify a substantial change in disposition remains to be seen and will be tested in elections now that the major political parties have moved away from concensus at the centre.

> 'Britain, as a whole, had become uncannily like the kind of family that becomes a casualty of the welfare state – dependent upon others, riven by habitual patterns of internal conflict, but stubbornly keeping alive an idealized, wildly inaccurate self-image.' (Mant, 1979)

Within the family there are fights between the 'bosses' and the 'workers', the 'lower classes' and the 'upper classes', etc and all the energies which should be put into the fight for trade go into fighting within it. There are plenty of illustrations of working class dependence, and deprived families not only depend heavily on the State but learn how to play the dependence game. They do not fight to improve their position, but only fight within the confines of the family. In contrast, the middle class family is knit together by dependence while the fight to improve the family's status takes place in the outside world. If the working class view about the family in relation to the State is transferred to the company, then the company is the family and it is a matter of who to fight within the company. Paternalism and respect for paternalism (as opposed to loyalty) are deeply embedded in the thinking of the social classes in Britain. No wonder, Mant argues,

> 'the British big company board, in a strange parody of Court, frequently contains a collection of otherwise harmless, but bemused peers of the realm who roll up to board meetings, ask some silly question to justify their fees and listen in bewilderment as the executive directors push through all manner of nefarious schemes. How can one possibly explain the presence of the non-executive peers except that they represent the bridge between the fell purposes of trade on the one hand, and the Queen on the other. The full board therefore is a pure expression of dependence, in the sense that it helps to legitimize, to connect up the firm with society as a whole. Beneath that level, the fights break out, usually at the key discontinuities in the organizational structure – divisional directors, plant or branch managers, foremen, but most of all with the unions.' (Mant, 1979)

Mant refers to a generally accepted view of British society that to be in industry is to be dirty in the sense of 'tainted'; it is not quite nice to be associated with the practical, so an important fight is to avoid going into industry or, if one trains to be an engineer or a scientist, it is important to do research and not produce. The social press is toward the professions and so those who could fight for industry fight for their professions, 'Here, they are likely to fight successfully for . . . the creation of a ludicrously inflated professional sector.

As Illich has pointed out, the number of "professionals" in parasitic occupations such as law and medicine governs the number of clients, rather than vice versa' (Mant, 1979) and this point is underwritten by the discussion in the preceding section of this chapter.

There would seem to be much truth in this polemic for it is generally agreed that the education systems in the British Isles do not value the practical, neither do they encourage risk. One of the earliest studies to point this out was due to McClelland (1961), some of whose points are considered in more detail in the section which follows.

The hidden curriculum and economic development

Organizing questions

'The values in a society have an important bearing on the level of that society's achievement motivation, so McClelland argues. How are these values thought to be reflected in the curriculum, and how might the curriculum change such attitudes?'

Commentary

McClelland (1961) suggested that families may be typified by the way in which parents influence their children toward bureaucratic or entrepreneurial values. Bureaucratically-oriented parents will try to teach their children to value patience and conformity. Children will learn to trust their environment, not how to manipulate it. They will be advised to look for secure jobs in the professions for example and particularly in the Civil Service. Risk-taking will not be part of their life. In contrast, entrepreneurially-oriented parents will try to help the child develop self-control, self-denial and independence. The world will be their oyster: it is there for the taking. Simple observation suggests that there is more than an element of truth in this theory.

We can safely argue that child rearing and socialization patterns both at home and school are powerful moulding influences on the development of values. They in their turn will influence the career motivations of youngsters just as much as the conscious or unconscious recognition of employment patterns in the outside world.

McClelland argues that the values which predominate in a society are reflected in economic growth. In a fascinating thesis he argued that the prevailing values in a society at any particular point in time could be derived from an analysis of children's literature. When popular literature becomes achievement-oriented the rate of economic growth speeds up.

More controversially he suggested that in individuals there is a psychological need for achievment which he labelled (N.ach). He argued that not only could (N.ach) be measured but that it could be developed through training. Other psychologists would argue that there is no such thing (Butcher and Cattell, 1968; Kunkel, 1969). Even so every teacher is familiar with the 'success breeds success' dictum and also with the characteristics of high achievers. Thus even if there is no need to posit 'need for achievement' as a factor, some individuals remain achievement-oriented and others are not. The general thesis in relation to growth would remain. If that is the case then, independently of (N.ach), McClelland's finding that Britain's (N.ach) level (estimated from children's textbooks) which was relatively high around 1925 (ranked fifth out of 25 countries studied) had dropped to twenty-sixth out of 39 countries studied by 1950, is relevant. McClelland was able to relate such information to indices of economic growth, concluding that 'Britain today is suffering from a shortage of aggressive entrepreneurs, at least as compared to a generation ago at home or to other countries today' (McClelland, 1969). However much we may criticize the technique, it does suggest that the polemics of Cairncross and Mant are open to experimental investigation. Not only does the original thesis support Mant's view about professionals and professionalism but so do some of his later studies. In an example from engineering McClelland also draws attention to the problem of State involvement in industry through individuals who are bureaucratically-oriented.

The three illustrations from his 1969 paper are self-explanatory:

'. . . these findings tend to support the conclusion that the general level of achievement orientation of a people determines whether they focus primarily on rapid transfer of technology to improve efficiency, or on pursuing other goals such as those wrapped up in professional pursuits like law and education . . . individuals and firms exist within a total society which may or may not emphasize achievement at a particular moment in history. Such an overall climate is bound to affect them. Can it be changed by conscious planning and intervention? No one knows for sure because it has never been tried. In the past major events have changed the value orientation of a people, just as the world-wide responsibilities of the United States at the present time appear to be increasing the power orientation of the American people at the cost of their earlier strong achievement orientation. It might not be possible to reverse such a major reorientation (and would we want to?) but it should certainly be possible to develop an achievement mystique in more limited areas such as the war on poverty or the moon shot.' (McClelland, 1969)

'The original businessman was a generalist. He knew something about production, finance and sales and he knew about them as a means to the end of maximizing business achievement, not as ends in themselves. But as industry grows more complex, it has had to acquire more specialists — more chemists, metallurgists, engineers, psychologists, accountants — many of whom develop a professional identity and point of view rather than a business identity. That is, the other values of the professions begin to assume importance along with achievement values . . . In a project which studied the rate at which small companies producing shoes in New England adopted innovations like plastic lasting, the investigator found to his surprise that the greater the technical capability of the company — the more industrial engineers it employed — the sooner it learned of the innovation, but the later it adopted the technique. . .

one could guess that the engineers felt responsible enough to their profession to be cautious, to insist on evidence a non-professional would not be so likely to demand, to want to approve only what they could really understand.' (McClelland, 1969)

'Civil servants are paid on a salary basis, just as professionals are and for the same reason, to keep the powerful representatives of government from exploiting their position by seeking rewards proportionate to the services they provide. Bureaucrats must be impartial, disinterested; they must treat all applicants for service universalistically, without regard to race, creed, or colour; they must not get personally involved with the clients they serve. Since these values are primary, bureaucrats also tend to become defensively orientated. They must worry, above all, not about achievement in the sense of performance results, but about the defensibility of what they have done in terms of such criteria as universalism, lack of personal prejudice, general political consensus as to what is "sensible", etc. . . Does the contract involve any risk? Here the contrast with business is very great. Businessmen accept the fact that continued growth in achievement terms involves innovating, taking moderate risks. But a bureaucrat can no more take a conscious risk with people's money than a doctor can with a patient's well-being or a teacher with a student's future.
Just as in the professions, this leads to an excessive concern with correct procedures as contrasted with the excellence of results. . . Researchers living on government money tend also to learn in time that it is more important to do the right (ie defensible) thing than it is to get results in the same sense that a businessman means "results" when he is thinking of profitability.' (McClelland, 1969)

The comparison with Mant's view seems obvious and it is interesting also to compare it with Dahrendorf's theory of the British *malaise* put forward on television early in 1983 (Dahrendorf, 1983). They both provide different perspectives on the problem. Both Mant and McClelland draw attention to the need for aggressive entrepreneurs if a society is to grow economically. Both point to the concept of national (aggregate) character expressed through the views of society. Both indicate the importance of the family and, by implication, the teacher and the curriculum. In my own polemic (published at about the same time as Mant's) I drew on McClelland's work to argue that, if Britain's economic growth was a reflection of its management, and since its management (establishment) was mostly educated at Oxbridge, if there was a relationship between education and economic performance, not much could be said for the effectiveness of the Oxbridge model (Heywood, 1978).

The management of learning

Learning is something much more than the acquisition of facts, yet most of the arguments are about standards and the cognitive domain. They are not, with rare exceptions, about the way school organization or teachers influence values. Do some schools emphasize survival skills through their curriculum, formal and hidden? Do others emphasize the team spirit? Does the mode of thinking associated with study at Oxbridge lead to a particular style of analysis which is not conducive to the skills required for decision-making and leadership in industry? How do teachers, families and society act to influence the value dispositions of the young? We know very little about these matters except by implication.

Even if teachers do not create long-term value dispositions there is no doubt that either consciously or unconsciously pupils associate such dispositions with them. There is far too little discussion of this aspect of the curriculum process in teacher training courses (Degenhardt, 1976).

Recently when I suggested a curriculum in teacher education, I put forward a course with the title 'Management of Learning' to embrace recent thinking about the role of the teacher in getting pupils to learn in the classroom (ie you cannot teach anyone anything, you can only help them learn). I was surprised to be told that this title should not be used because in this society it appeared to be manipulative. But this is surely what happens. For example, pupils are very often placed in circumstances where they do not learn. In this case, they are deprived of knowledge. Over and above the situation in the classroom, and relevant to the curriculum, is the fact that a teacher can make choices about the content of the curricula taught in his or her classes. Moreover in those classes he or she may well be conveying a particular set of values and these student-teacher answers to an examination question illustrate this point.

'However, the less bright pupil (as I perceived) was quite annoyed when she sometimes did not do as well as her friend and thought she should get an A also. She was also annoyed if she did not receive the same homework. So here was I having to justify my decisions to a precocious 12-year-old along with everybody else. But it made me think, what values am I trying to transmit to these children? What choices can I make in my teaching? How do I serve their needs?

The school I was in was full of rich well-to-do children, with a few *nouveaux riche* scattered here and there. Their values were going to be essentially different than the values I and my friends had in school. It was an inter-denominational school which in one way made the teaching of the Reformation easier and in another way more difficult. Often I had to step in among arguments among Jews, Catholics, Protestants and Presbyterians. The values of each of these religions is different especially between Christians and Jews. If I had been teaching in a purely Protestant school I would have had to teach the Reformation in a much different light. However, I realized that a teacher cannot just take the curriculum as it is, it does have to be restructured according to the needs of the children.'

'I was working on the period from 1918 to 1921 talking about the war of independence. I made a statement of comparison between the situation then and the present situation in Northern Ireland. The statement was to the effect that Britain saw the IRA then as a terrorist group much in the same way as they now see it. I went to great lengths afterwards to explain all the differences between the two movements, their motives, methods and the situation. However, I later gave an essay on the war of independence and at least half the class gave me back the statement that the war of independence was fought by terrorists and they then proceeded to write beautiful accounts of what the situation was like based on the news reports from Northern Ireland.'

I chose these two examples because several years ago two Ministers of Higher Education in Britain said that the teaching of history in Irish schools was a cause of the troubles. The Public Examinations Evaluation

Project did not find any evidence of this in its history project. It would not, however, be surprising if the attitudes of teachers in general reflected those prevailing in society, a point which has already been considered. But any independent observer who lived in Ireland through that period will testify there was no such naive attitude toward the troubles which would support the thesis of those particular Ministers.

'All teachers, and, to some degree, even all students are propagandists as well as scholars, in the sense that their general outlook on culture and life itself must of necessity communicate itself in some degree to the academic community to which they form a part. As we have seen, one of the greatest dangers of today is that so many propagandists are found in every university, and often the most effective are those who are at least conscious of their power. Even the teachers who disclaim all propaganda, and hold that it is the sole business of each member of the academic body to stick to his own job, are the propagandists of one of the most dangerous of all philosophies, *laissez-faire*.' (McGrath, 1962)

As Häring has pointed out, 'education is the marketplace of various ideologies and of those who put their trust chiefly in manipulating others' (Häring, 1975). Television, for example, does not treat individuals as partners in the process of growth in which both teacher and learner can develop together. 'The manipulative — or quasi-manipulative — elements that seem to be integral to the educational process receive, however, a totally new meaning if, in the decisive dynamics, they are oriented towards growth in sight, motivation according to a scale of values, intuition, interiorization, personal convictions and free assent to values' (Häring, 1975). It is for this reason that training in the application of philosophy to educational decision-making is important in the training of teachers. Like Newman, I see such training as the development of a philosophical habit of mind.

'A habit of mind informed which tests through life, of which the attributes are freedom, equitableness, calmness, moderation, and wisdom; or what in a former discourse I have ventured to call a philosophical habit.' (Newman, 1947)

But this does not mean that a traditional course is required, for it is possible, as Fitzgibbons (1981) has shown, to learn this habit through the evaluation of educational problems, for example, the relevance of education and, more generally, its aims. His book attempts in a quite unique way to show how the method of philosophy can make a major contribution to our thinking about educational problems.

The management of the curriculum

This chapter has presented two perspectives on the hidden curriculum. It began with the study of the role of the professions in English society and suggested that, while they existed to protect the public, they also existed to protect themselves. This protection was achieved in part by qualification, the net effect of which was to create an educational system which was stratified at too early an age in terms of society's needs for adaptability and flexibility. It was then suggested that national values and attitudes also influence economic growth. It is the desire or otherwise for growth which can influence the direction of the economy.

By implication it was suggested that education, both formal and informal at the level of society and in the classroom, can influence dispositions in one direction or another. Not every school, nor every classroom, is orientated toward achievement. Many teachers abhor the idea of competition in the classroom and there is a strong anti-examination movement. Teachers do convey their values in the classroom in all sorts of ways; sometimes unconsciously and sometimes deliberately, they apply themselves to the teaching of attitudes. And this is not the special province of the humanities.

The teaching strategies we use may influence our attitudes to authority, help us to work in teams (group work) and inspire divergent thinking (individual project work). It also seems clear that we have relatively little understanding of the influence of teaching strategies on personal development, except in the area of discipline. Nevertheless, in the evaluation of aims and objectives and the subsequent design of the overall curriculum or the development of the subject we teach, we need to take the role of teaching strategies into account. This demands a wider perception of the role of the subject we teach within the framework of the overall curriculum than too often seems to be the case. It is with this aspect of the secondary school curriculum that the next chapter is concerned, especially as it relates to language development.

References

Becker, H S, Geer, B and Merton, R K (1958) *Boys in White* USA
Butcher, J and Cattell, R (1968) *The Prediction and Assessment of Creativity* Bobs Merril: USA
Cairncross, A (1970) Presidential address to the economics section. Report of the Annual Meeting of the British Association, The British Association: London
CMND 1254 (1961) *Better Opportunities in Technical Education* Her Majesty's Stationery Office: London
Dahrendorf, R (1983) *On Britain* BBC Publications: London
Degenhardt, M A B (1976) On indoctrination *in* Lloyd, D I (ed) *Philosophy and the Teacher* Routledge and Kegan Paul: London
Eggleston, J (1977) *The Sociology of the School Curriculum* Routledge and Kegan Paul: London
Engineers Council (1972) The newspaper of the Engineers Council: USA
Fitzgibbons, R E (1981) *Educational Decision. An Introduction to the Philosophy of Education* Harcourt Brace Jovanovich Inc: New York
Häring, B (1975) *Manipulation, Ethical Boundaries of Medical Behavioural and Benetic Manipulation* St Paul Publications: Slough
Heywood, J (1978) Factors influencing attitudes to technology *British Journal of Educational Studies* 26, pp 137-49
Heywood, J (1984) *Men, Industry and Society. Men and Institutions as Learning Systems* (in press)
Kunkel, J H (1969) Some behavioural aspects of social change and economic development *in* Burgess, R L and Bushel, D (eds) *Behavioural Sociology: The Experimental Analysis of Social Process* Colombia University Press: New York
Lees, D (1966) *The Economic Consequences of the Professions* Institute of Economic Affairs: London

Lilley, S (1973) *Technological Progress and the Industrial Revolution* Fontana Economic History of Europe, Collins: London
McClelland, D C (1961) *The Achieving Society* Free Press: New York
McClelland, D C (1969) The role of achievement orientation in the transfer of technology *in* Gruber, W H and Marquis, D B (eds) *Factors in the Transfer of Technology* MIT Press: Cambridge, Massachusetts
McGrath, F (1962) *The Consecration of Learning* Gill: Dublin
Mallinson, V (1949) *An Introduction to the Study of Comparative Education* Oxford University Press: Oxford
Mant, A (1979) *The Rise and Fall of the British Manager* Pan: London
Marshall, T H (1939) Professionalism in relation to social structure and policy reprinted *in* Marshall, T H (1963) *Sociology at the Crossroads and Other Essays* Heinemann: London
Newman, J H (1947 edition) *The Idea of a University* Longmans Green: London
Reynaud, P L (1981) *Economic Psychology* Praeger: New York
Thomas, B and Madigan, C (1974) Strategy and job choice after redundancy: a case study in the aircraft industry *Sociological Review* 22, pp 83-102
Turner, G (1969) *Business in Britain* Penguin: Harmondsworth
Youngman, M B, Oxtoby, R, Monk, J D and Heywood, J (1978) *Analysing Jobs* Gower Press: Farnborough

Chapter 4

Language for Life: English for Meaning

Introduction

Despite the fact that language is fundamental to communication and thus to the curriculum and teaching, it appears that the development of language and communication skills are not easily achieved. Recent reports from America (Adler, 1982; ASCD Update, 1983; NCE, 1983; NSB, 1983) and England (Bullock, 1974; Cockroft, 1981) are highly critical of the way in which literary and numeracy skills are developed in schools. Such skills, it is argued, are the bases for all learning.

Nevertheless, throughout the 1960s and 1970s there has been continuing research and debate not only on language as a communication skill but on the factors influencing language acquisition, and in turn the role of language in emotional development. Some of this work has had a great influence on teachers even if their interpretations have been simplistic. But as the examples show this simplistic approach toward rather complex theories is helpful to beginning teachers in developing communication skills.

This does not mean that these students do not appreciate the complexity of the issue as anyone listening to a discussion among English teachers will know. They reject much of what is said for they are much concerned with the moral dimension of literature as well as its contribution to emotional development. For this reason this discussion centres around the contrasting positions of the American, Labov, and the British sociologist, Bernstein, on the one hand, and the Bullock Report on language development in England and Holbrook, a well-known British teacher of English on the other.

Central to the views of all these authorities is the idea that every teacher has a role to play in the development of language regardless of his or her subject. Therefore in training, all teachers should begin by observing and interpreting the way in which language is transacted in the classroom, and it is with this dimension that this chapter begins through examples of student responses to an examination question on this topic.

Language within the classroom

Organizing question

'There is also a need for more direct attention to the student teachers' understanding of language transactions in the classroom and the way they influence the quality of their teaching.' (*Teacher Training and the Secondary School*, (DES, 1981.)

Critically discuss with reference to the subject you teach.

Organizing responses from student answers to the question

1. RELATING TO COMMUNICATION

'Initially when I started teaching I wrongly assumed that the language transaction between myself and the students was a given one. In fact with the pressures I was undergoing in my first days of teaching it never occurred to me that a language barrier might exist between myself and the pupils influencing the quality and effectiveness of my teaching.

Having given the first test at the end of the second week I realized that while most of the pupils had understood the language used several had not.'

2. RELATING TO THE CORRECTION OF MISTAKES

'One student told me that when a report which I had written on a written exam reached her parents, she had a terrible time. I had written among my comments that her "language needed improvement" meaning her grasp of language structure. However her parents immediately assumed she had behaved badly in my class and used obscene language. This was a case of semantic breakdown. To me "bad language" means problems connected with structure, syntax, spelling, and the components of language but to Vereena's parents it could only mean "four-letter words". Although when she told me about it, it drove home to me a problem which I'd encountered in this class.'

3. RELATING TO THE ROLE OF HISTORY IN THE DEVELOPMENT OF LANGUAGE

'History highly motivates children and this, I've found, is half the battle in achieving our goals — one of these must, of necessity, be the cultivation of articulate, argumental minds which are capable of making informed judgements of events and people while drawing on evidence to support these judgements. This requires a solid understanding of language itself and it remains an important job of the history teacher.'

4. RELATING TO UNDERSTANDING IN BIOLOGY

'Student teachers also need to understand that words used by the teacher do not always have the same meaning for the pupils. This can lead to a communication gap and confusion on the part of the student. For example, the phases of photosynthesis cryptically called "light" and "dark". My pupils have great difficulty in understanding that "dark" in this case meant that light was not necessary. Many of the pupils still write about the "dark" phase taking part in the dark despite many explanations of this point.'

5. RELATING TO THE CORRECTION OF MISTAKES

'I have often considered the much debated questions of whether or not to correct mistakes in grammar made by my students. The method of correction will be important too. Personally I am inclined to see the point of correction in a relatively unobtrusive manner, eg when a student says "I brang a game to school" I might add "You brought what game to school?" I feel that it is the student's right to have a clear understanding of what society will be expecting of him.'

John Vaughan, the librarian of the School of Education in the University of Liverpool, when asked about recent studies in language transaction in the classroom remarked that 'it's a growth industry'. Every now and again some idea hits the educational scene and creates a vogue, as for example the publication of *The Taxonomy of Educational Objectives* (Bloom, 1964) or the debate about theory and practice in the training of teachers. The major stimuli to this outburst of literature on language in the classroom was the publication of the Bullock Report on *Language for Life* (Bullock, 1975).

Holbrook's *English for Maturity* (1967) had considerable influence on the teaching of English and it may be claimed that he re-oriented the teaching of English toward the imaginative while at the same time embracing the cognitive. It is a work that may be compared with Guilford's attempt to relate creativity and intelligence in psychology (Guilford, 1967). Given the influence of *English for Maturity*, it is surprising that neither the Bullock Committee nor its exponents (eg Elliott-Kemp, 1981; Hutchcroft, 1981) refer to Holbrook. The Committee makes little reference to the development of creativity and imagination, and surprisingly it makes no reference to Bernstein. As the literature shows there is much concern about the same matters in the United States (Grayson, 1983; Oreo Vicz, 1983; Starr and Bruce, 1983).

Clearly, there are many dimensions to 'language' in the classroom ranging from the simple to the complex, from reading, writing, talking and listening, to the imaginative. I doubt in these circumstances whether we can afford to ignore any of these authorities for, as I have argued elsewhere, education is an eclectic subject (Heywood, 1977). We do not have a global theory on which to base our methods but we have a lot of ideas and research which can provide important insights into teacher and pupil behaviour. We do not have to follow the particular Marxist line of Young (1971) or accept wholly either Bernstein's thesis (see pp 65 - 69) or the opposite stance taken by Labov (1973) to see that they all have some relevance both to the classroom and to life.

At the first level of classroom activity we have to examine the ways in which teachers and pupils interact through language. That this is a matter of general concern is well illustrated in the student examples in this chapter. At the second level we have to look at the role of language within the subject that is taught by the teacher, that is, the language necessary for understanding the subject. At the third level there is the specific problem of English and its teaching.

Most problems in the classroom require a multi-disciplinary approach for their solution. That is, there is a value judgement (philosophy) in the choice of learning strategy (psychology) for a particular social class (social factor). The teacher is expected to be aware of all these factors, and therefore thematic approaches have been developed for teacher training which try to solve classroom problems within the context of the teacher's subject specialization. But these often ignore the so-called bases or foundations of education and consequently there has been a continuing debate about the relevance of theory to practice in teacher education (Hartnett and Naish, 1976; Hirst, 1980).

No better example of the problems which this creates is to be found than in comments by Lawton (1978) on work by Barnes (1969; 1976). Lawton argues that Barnes should be read by all teachers and offers this interpretation of his findings:

'1. Many teachers use language which is unnecessarily remote and difficult.
2. Some teachers rebuff children who try to get to grips with complicated ideas by expressing themselves in their own natural language.
3. Children (and adults) learn by talking: talk of the right kind helps clarify thinking.
4. Most teachers talk too much.' (Lawton, 1978)

These axioms are to be found in textbooks of learning which deal with the ways in which children learn concepts and principles and the role of questioning and discussion in such learning. Microteaching has as one of its aims the development of clarity in trainee teachers. It is also evident from the student examples above that most, if not all, trainee teachers learn that some of their work is above their pupils' heads. The gaps between sociologists, psychologists and philosophers is further illustrated by contrasting and comparing the following statement:

'Pupils' behaviour, including language, is likely to be influenced by the way in which they perceive their subject-matter and their role as learners of that subject, by the audience to which they are expected to address speech and writing, by the immediate task which they have been given.' (Barnes, 1969)

with the findings of learning theory as it relates to discipline on the one hand and perception on the other hand (Heywood, 1982) or philosophy on saying and doing where for example we read that:

'In brief then: (1) concepts are forms of thought and therefore forms of life; (2) some concepts are basic to all culture and to all human thought since they belong to the definition of human thought and culture; (3) many concepts are, however, subject to cultural change.' (Brummer, 1981)

I labour this point because only at the level of initial training can an introduction to the problems of the curriculum be given. We have little difficulty with Lawton's summary for it is, as the illustrations show, part of the everyday experience of student teachers, and many teachers and students will have had similar experience in higher education. The difficulty arises when we are told that they lead to a communication of traditional (transmissive) teaching in favour of discussion (discovery) teaching. This conclusion depends on the definition which Barnes attaches to meaning and thus to knowledge and this is a major philosophical problem. It is a powerful illustration of the relationship of method to the curriculum. No teacher who claims to be a professional can ever be satisfied with the limited discussion of such issues which initial training courses offer. There is bound to be some distortion of points of view; hence the need for renewal at higher levels of learning should be evident. It is also apparent that it is through the study of the curriculum that integration between the discplines takes place, and theory is related to practice.

Of course, teachers of subjects other than English can help children and students with their English, not merely correcting for spelling and grammar, as each subject has its own language and literature forms (see below) which can contribute to the broadening of the child's or student's experience. Warren (1981), a teacher of English, has said that it was not until he had singing lessons that he realized 'that composition — writing at any level — is an art' and that in consequence it should be taught as an artistic process. Some subject teachers only operate at the pedantic level and this can only be to the detriment of the subject if it does not illustrate its imaginative scope.

Many pupils who study science perform badly in English and this is as true of the United States (Grayson, 1983; Krowne and Covington, 1982) as it is of Britain (Hewitt, 1967). My experience of assessing project reports suggests that with proper training in the writing associated with planning, specifying, analysing and evaluating, students would perform better in their scientific technological work; so often it is the poor report which shows that they do not understand the 'meaning' of what they are doing. This view would seem to be supported by the fact that books on writing are being bought by university students (Barrass, 1982) and by the hypothesis which pervades the work of the Soviet scientist Luria (introduced to this country by the language specialist J Britton). 'Speech', he says, is a

'means whereby he (the child) organizes his own experience and regulates his own actions so that the child's activity is medicated through words.' (Luria and Yudovitch, 1971).

In England, Austin (1962) drew attention to the fact that speaking is a form of intentional action and as such can be analysed into elements of the process. This points to a possible solution for the poor performance of students in written English examinations in that oral training in arguments might precede training in writing. Davis (1981), who teaches history, has argued that skills such as documentary analysis are better developed through both written and spoken dialogue.

Inspection of reports and essays suggests that pupils are often confused by the mass of information with which they are presented. Apart from the fact that this encourages memory skills at the expense of other high-order activities, it also serves to confuse learners. Students with learning difficulties often cannot distinguish between facts and concepts, concepts and principles, and principles and problems, to use Gagné's hierarchy (Gagné, 1976).

In project work the poor student is often characterized in the first instance by an inability to formulate the problem. Given an essay subject the same child is likely to have no idea as to how to go about writing a response, let alone presenting it in a coherent manner (Heywood, 1978). To mention the habit of discipline in study methods is to be old fashioned. Nevertheless, schools need to encourage discipline throughout the pupil's career. It is not merely the setting of homework, it is the setting of homework together with its marking which will enable the pupil to develop an organized approach to study (Heywood, 1960). There is evidence to suggest that study habits differentiate good from poor students even in higher education. Confidence, so necessary to effective performance, accompanies the development of such habits.

When in the 1950s I was faced with a class of day-release students who were preparing for a written examination, my first homework yielded the fact that none of them had ever attempted to write the kind of descriptive essay required for an answer to a scientific question. Neither had they the discipline required for homework. They had to be provided with learning experiences which would help them learn these skills. Those who acquired the discipline of organized work succeeded; those who did not failed. The majority succeeded.

There is much, therefore, that teachers are likely to be able to do in their own subject to develop the skills of language appropriate to that subject. But, in communicating with students (pupils) of this kind they may well have difficulty at the first level. Often there is a communication gulf between a teacher who has inhabited a middle class culture and pupils from the lower working class. This has been highlighted by Bernstein (1961) who has suggested that the different socio-economic classes employ different language codes, and that social structure is the primary force in their use.

The concept of restricted and elaborated language codes

As early as 1961 Bernstein had drawn attention to two types of language which he called 'public' and 'formal'. These were broadly related to language use in the different socio-economic groups. As his work in the sociology of knowledge developed, he redefined his terms. A restricted code was used by those in lower socio-economic status groups and an elaborated code by those in higher economic status groups. The restricted code limits both scope of expression and thought. It progressively orients the child to a lower level of conceptualization. It is through using the language of implicit meaning that it becomes difficult to make explicit, and to elaborate verbally, subjective intent.

The teacher who speaks with an elaborated code has, according to Bernstein, to make that code available without depriving the pupils of the dignity of their own restricted codes. Common characteristics of the restricted code are:

- short, grammatically simple, often unfinished sentences;
- simple and repetitive use of conjunctions;
- little or no use of subordinate clauses;
- rigid and limited use of adjectives and adverbs;
- frequent use of statements where the reasons and conclusion are confounded to produce a categoric statement.

As between the subjects of the curriculum it is self-evident that pupils from any social class may use a restricted code because of limitations in their understanding (eg second languages and science; see, for example, Champagne, Gunstone and Klopfer, 1983). It can be seen that the language usage of the tabloid daily newspapers and newspapers like *The Guardian* corresponds very much to this distinction, and it is clear from the student examples below that in general terms this conceptual frame is of considerable value to them in developing their communication skills with children.

From this theory it is possible to argue that some children from the lower working class (ie the socio-economic groups of children of unskilled and semi-skilled workers) are deprived, and that some form of compensatory education is required. In the past substantial funding has been given to compensatory education projects in both Britain and the United States. The Rutland Street Project in Dublin is another example of compensatory education (Holland, 1979).

Bantock (1968) in *Culture, Industrialization and Education* argues that subjects are for those who can cope with them. Mass education is a failure because it has attempted to force a literary culture on the masses whose tradition is primarily oral. In consequence they require a different kind of education from that of the middle classes. For Bantock, backwardness is endemic but it is a view that is considerably limited by its lack of forceful reference to psychological research. For example, he argues that media studies are more appropriate than Shakespeare and yet ignores the fact that TV undoubtedly popularizes great literature in a way that no other form of teaching can.

Organizing responses from student answers to the question on p 60

1. RELATING TO COMMUNICATION IN BIOLOGY
'I was not aware of the two codes of language at first as discussions in class moved freely. In the first few weeks of the term I was not familiar with the pupils as individuals and so found it difficult to monitor participation. Eventually I realized discussion was dominated by about 60 per cent of the class — some people never seemed to contribute. I encouraged their participation in class by questioning and they responded.

I did not become aware of the root of the problem until correcting homework that week. We had been studying the earthworm in class and constructing a wormery. I wanted to ensure all the children understood the importance of the habitat — its location, characteristics, etc — to the earthworm, and later, to all animals. I had set a question of habitat as part of their homework. Some of the responses I got back made no sense and I was forced to ask the pupils what they were trying to say. I discovered that many children did not understand the word "habitat" and thought I was referring to "habits"!

2. RELATING TO HISTORY
'I was teaching in a working class school where I encountered a "restricted" code quite often in the classroom. I was conscious that I did not want to appear

too "uppity" to the children which might discourage them from contributing to the class. When teaching history, I was anxious that they understood that history was not just a list of dates, facts and figures, that it was to some extent open to interpretation and that there were many ways of looking at the one thing. This was transmitted to them by the kind of language I used in class, the kind of questions I posed to them, and the form of written homework I gave, which ranged from questions like "You are Shane O'Reilly, you have to decide whether to surrender to Elizabeth I or not . . ." to usually factual recall ones.'

3. RELATING TO ENGLISH
'When one might wish to discuss imagery, similes and other aspects of poetry one may be met by blank looks. I have found that in order to explain the concept of images in a poem, the best way is to relate to something the children are familiar with. So I refer to television — in particular still shots when the camera freezes on a particular scene or event and everything stops still.'

4. RELATING TO IRISH
'In my lesson plans and teaching strategies throughout the year I made a conscious effort to bridge the gap between our codes. I felt this was important not to reduce their confidence in their verbal fluency (which according to Bernstein reflects a blockage between implicit meaning and explicit expression, which in turn influences conceptual development). However, I felt as I was getting to know them better, by Christmas I had begun to learn some of their slang. This presented me with an interesting opportunity of blending my elaborate code with their slang and restricted code without altering very much the quality of my teaching. For example it worked particularly well in regard to second language teaching, where textbooks (particularly Irish textbooks) are completely unsympathetic towards children within the restricted code domain. *Example* In Dublin slang the term to get "reefed" means "to get caught", therefore a typical language reconstruction with 2G7 would run like:

Irish	*English*	*Slang (R/C)*
Rug na gardai	The police caught me	The cops "reefed"
Ar na gardai	Robbers	the thief.'

However, Bernstein (1966) and Lawton (1968), who verified Bernstein's codes for the written word, would argue that this theory of socio-linguistic codes does not imply that working class children are linguistically deprived, or that programmes of compensatory education should be developed from simple generalizations about working class children. 'Linguistic difference', argues Lawton, 'is not the same as language competence', a point which has considerable implications for the teaching of language in the classroom.

Lawton's position is that while there have been two different kinds of selection of knowledge from culture, high status pertaining to public and grammar schools and low status pertaining to elementary practical skills and training, there is sufficient in common between them to merit a common culture curriculum. Some support for this approach (which has been criticized by Ozolins (1982) is to be found in a recent study by Corson (1982). He has argued that a major reason for the apparent language deficiency among some English speaking children is that there is a lexical bar in the English language which separates the users of some social dialects from a ready access to the lexis of semantic categories essential for success in education, and that this limitation is of words and meanings which are ultimately Graeco-Latin in origin. After showing how this arose historically he demonstrates his point empirically, and by reference to American research (Masciantonio, 1977) and by implication suggests that the teaching of Latin should be a key component in the curriculum. It would seem therefore that learning Latin may help children to move from a restricted to an elaborated code and successes have been reported in teaching Latin for all (Robertson, 1981).

Labov (1973), an American linguist who studied Negroes in New York, argues that the 'myth' of verbal deprivation is particularly dangerous because it diverts attention from real defects in our educational system to imaginary defects in the child. He distinguishes between standard dialects used by the middle classes and non-standard dialects used by the lower classes. He is critical of Bernstein (1966) whom, he argues, sees middle class language as logical in every respect. Labov in contrast sees much middle class language as verbose with no inherent logic and supports his argument with striking illustrations. The average middle class speaker is 'enmeshed in verbiage, the victim of socio-linguistic factors beyond his control'. Using syllogistic techniques, Labov demonstrates that there is also a logic in the non-standard dialect. The differences between the dialects are demonstrated thus:

	Standard English	*Non-standard Negro English*
Positive	He knows something.	He know something.
Negative	He doesn't know anything.	He don't know nothing
Double	He doesn't know nothing.	He don't know nothing.

Linguists argue that non-standard dialects are highly structured systems and that there is no reason to believe that any non-standard vernacular is in itself an obstacle to learning. Labov draws attention to the influence of peer-groups on linguistic development which is a more powerful influence than the family. At around nine or 10 the influence of the peer-group predominates.

Both Lawton and Bernstein argue that language development is closely related to the context situation and thus to the ways the school is organized, the pupils are grouped and how the teacher behaves in a classroom. Labov points out that the peer-group phenomenon is such that the school is dealing with children who are integrated into groups of their own, with rewards and value systems that oppose those of the school. Bernstein and Lawton also argue that teacher effectiveness (whatever that might mean) can be seen largely in terms of verbal interaction. The brackets are mine, for while it is easy to agree that verbal interaction is important, the factors which contribute to effective learning are many and varied.

In the event that both Lawton and Bernstein are adamant that teachers should be concerned with language difference and not language deficit, there would seem to be little difference in the outcomes of their work or Labov's for teaching. Teachers should learn the non-standard dialect and not see it as evidence of mental inferiority. If the American philosopher Matthews (1980) is correct and children do think philosophically at very young ages, then teachers should be trained to search for such understanding within the non-standard dialect.

Even if we argue that socio-linguistics are but one facet of the problem, it is clear that they have considerable significance in later life. Elsewhere (Heywood, 1984), it has been argued that some of the conflicts between management and workers arise in part because the two codes are at work in negotiations. To oversimplify, neither side understands the other. It also seems, in certain circumstances, that Kohlberg's theory of moral development can be applied to the same situation. Not only are two codes at work, but two moral levels (or systems); one side cannot understand the morality of the other because they are at different levels of moral understanding and under the influence of different pressures. This does not imply that the middle class manager is likely to be more moral than the working class negotiator. On the contrary, moral relativity is very much the prerogative of the middle class. Recent work in the United States complicates the issue by suggesting that female moral development differs from male (Lyons, 1983).

This view, however acceptable, does give us an idea of the kind of work which can be done in schools. For example in the joint training of shop stewards and managers it is possible to make a video-tape of their discussions and ask them on replay to rate the effectiveness of their performance (Heywood, 1984). Subsequent evaluation necessarily involves them in language learning. Activities of this kind are appropriate to fourth- and fifth-year activities for the group of pupils who do not do well academically and have been undertaken by the students on my course, but in my experience programmes for this group have to be both teacher- and equipment-intensive.

The less able/able debate continues to throw up problems of school organization as we saw above. It is not resolved in social terms by the simple comprehensivization of schools, or by mixed ability teaching, or by a common 16+ examination. It is still felt necessary to provide alternative programmes for some children in their fourth and fifth years or on leaving school. At present the organization of such programmes seems to be somewhat chaotic and to pay little attention to the concept of lifelong education which might in the long run hold out the best prospect for the organization of the curriculum.

At the other end of the spectrum questions have been asked about the age of transition from primary to secondary school. In England there are a variety of ages arising from the inclusion of middle schools (8 to 13 years) in some local authorities. The majority transfer at 11; those who go to the public (private) schools mainly transfer at 13. In Ireland the transfer takes place at 12. One question in particular has been the extent to which primary methods and primary curricula should be extended into the highly subject-structured and teacher-centred system at second level.

Communication and imagination

Some relevant responses to other questions in previous years by student teachers of foreign language learning

1. 'The emotional environment also needs consideration. The language will be completely strange to many of the pupils and will be difficult for them in many respects, for instance the acquiring of the accent. Therefore the teacher should seek to make the class relax and enjoy their new experience. One of the most effective ways of doing this is through the attitudes and expectations which she portrays. The pupils must be encouraged to speak the language at all times, to say whatever they can and so they must not be afraid to make mistakes. The teacher must not condemn them for their mistakes but praise them on their attempt to use the language. Factors such as the teacher's tone of voice, her willingness to incorporate humour so long as it does not go too far, and her techniques of control are important but most important is that she radiates an enthusiasm for the language and the culture and the civilization which it represents.'

2. 'If I decide I want my pupils to be able to speak and communicate effectively in the foreign language then my methods must be in line with this behavioural objective. I must emphasize the spoken word, give plenty of opportunity for practice to the pupils and use plenty of situations in which the pupils must use language in a meaningful way. My method must include situations where there is active pupil involvement. In teaching the verb "choisir" (to choose) I would ask them what library books they like to choose when they go there, what books they would choose from a list, etc. Although the method may appear contrived the pupils soon forget this in their participation . . . For passive comprehension I would teach grammar and syntax from a textbook and give them written practice of French language.'

3. 'Listening is the initial objective of the teacher. The pupil's ear must be trained to new sound patterns. He must learn to distinguish the native language from the target language and to distinguish sounds from one another within the target language. Perceptive listening without any repetition should be a priority: the initial stages of language learning. Tapes, native speakers and if possible a language laboratory are desirable "aids" in the acquisition of listening skills. Songs are also valuable, and help to contribute positively to the affective domain . . . The students may have to go through repetitious drills so as to learn sounds. The objective of the teacher here will be one of sheer pronunciation. It will involve repetition, listening, and eventually speaking in a less restricted fashion.

No stage stops where another one begins. These skills have to be practised throughout the period of language learning. Speaking will develop as our mastery of the language increases . . .'

RELATING TO THE TEACHING OF ENGLISH
4. 'With regard to the essays the teacher would design experiences for the children using tapes, music, stories, posters, prints, not only to motivate them but also to give them something to write about. Too often the titles on an essay paper are taken to be a reflection of what children ought to know something about and then there is resentment, dissatisfaction, improperly apportioned

blame when essays written in such conditions are judged weak in style and deficient in content. I myself never wrote an acceptable essay until my first year in university when I became fascinated by the Sutton Hoo ship burial. *One has to have something to say* and this is the teacher's responsibility to provide for.

One could encourage wider reading and attempts to write poems or short stories but as I have said students would see this as wasting precious time from examination work which they see is preparation by "notes". One could use a thematic approach to the poems for instance in an attempt to create meaningful learning. One could ensure children had experiences of art and music for example as alternative approaches to such a theme with the aim of widening experience in the arts and deepening personal response. But it would be a difficult task.'

Commentary

Holbrook, as long ago as 1964, called for a different approach to those who were then called C and D streamers. He argued that backwardness was due to emotional starvation which could be remedied by imaginative work centred on English.

'If I did learn nothing else, I did learn that for these children there is no point in thinking in terms of "subjects" — apart from games, art, crafts, dancing and music, everything else became English. Their most successful mathematics was related to stories about hire purchase or car rallies — the only sense of history they could gain was that given by imaginative accounts of, say, a medieval peasant's life. In geography they responded to what was really anthropology, much mixed with imaginative fantasy about modes of life in other lands. And in all these subjects by the time they were interpreted to 3C became virtually English and mostly imaginative English in the context of a close personal relationship with the teacher — closer than that in other kinds of teaching except perhaps in the infant classes of the primary school.' (Holbrook, 1964)

We have, argues Holbrook, to forget that we are English teachers when we relate to these children. Rather, we should educate them in such a way that their potentialities are realized and they can acquire both civilized powers and refinement. Holbrook's objections to the Bullock Report stem from this view. He argues that the teaching programme suggested by the report is based on a cybernetic model of language usage and that a false analogy is set up between computers and the human mind (Holbrook, 1979). Little space is given to poetry and literature, to creativity and imagination. A teacher of English brought up on the Leavis concept of the 'living principle', which is the intentional relationship between mind, symbol, language and reality would be forgiven for not reading the Bullock Report had he or she prior knowledge of Holbrook's work and his criticisms in America (Comstock, Rubenstein and Murray, 1972) and England. Although no single study unequivocally confirms the conclusion that television violence leads to aggressive behaviour, and no single study reflects that conclusion, the convergence of findings from many studies suggesting a positive relationship between television violence and later aggressive behaviour should be sufficient to cause concern. Thus some teachers were worried that the Bullock Report did not appear to be concerned about the effect of television on emotional development. It seems, for example, that

71

much more than aggressive behaviour is learnt. For example, a viewer can learn to be a victim and to identify with victims; while some viewers may be influenced toward aggressive behaviour others might exhibit fear and apprehension, and so on . . . (NIMH, 1982; Schmid and Graaf, 1982). This is what might be expected from a diverse population. Nevertheless, because television is an obvious influence on language usage it is perhaps surprising that there is still so little attention to the media in teacher training.

Some clue to the problem is to be found in the writings of Oakeshott (1962). In *The Study of Politics in a University* he makes a distinction between the language and literature of a subject.

> 'the distinction between a language (by which I mean manner of thinking) and a "literature" or a "text" (by which I mean what has been said from time to time in a language) . . . is the distinction between poetic imagination and a poem or a novel; or between the "language" or manner of thinking of a scientist and a textbook of geology or what may be called the current state of our geological knowledge. Now what is being studied in a "vocational education" is a "literature" or a "text" and not a "language". What is being acquired is a knowledge of what has been authoritavely said and not a familiarity with the manner of thinking which has generated what has been said. For example, in this sort of education what is learnt is not how to think in a scientific manner, how to recognize a scientific problem or proposition or how to use the "language" of science, but how to use those products of scientific thought which contribute to our current manner of living. Or, if this distinction seems to be too rigid, then it may be said that in a "vocational" education what is learnt is not a "living" language with a view to being able to speak in it, but a "dead" language; and it is learnt merely for the purpose of reading a "literature" or a "text" in order to acquire the information it contains. The skill acquired is the skill of using the information, not of speaking the "language".'
> (Oakeshott, 1962)

This seems to hold the same Platonic dualism which Brent (1978) draws attention to in Newman. It is that which marks out British education from, say, the German system: the practical/vocational is inferior. There is the same dualism inherent in the Bullock Report and among those who have suggested how its ideals might be implemented.

Holbrook (1979) contrasts the English taught in 'outward situations' which he takes the Bullock Committee to have in mind with the contribution which English can make to those powers which symbolize 'existential being'. He argues that the Bullock Committee failed to understand the point of *English for Maturity*. Although the Report says that 16-year-olds should have some understanding of the use of language, including its use in the development of creative imagination, he maintains the Committee does not give order of precedence to this creative imaginary discipline, or see the need, which he and others have seen, of defining it as a primary discipline.

If we regard the Bullock Committee as being concerned with communication and Holbrook with the creative use of the imagination, both have, surely, an equally important role in the emotional development of a person.

Education is eclectic. If emotional development is seen to be as equally important as cognitive development in the aims of education then Holbrook's approach can hardly be ignored. The difficulty with Holbrook's general thesis is that he does not realize that very many children have limited language codes, and that if literature is to be appreciated linguistic competence has to be developed. Similarly if 'confidence', which is an emotional attribute, depends on the ability to communicate, then the general findings of Bullock need to be taken into account. Courses in communication for technicians (business and technical) recognize this fact and realize that communication studies should embrace liberal components which recognize the emotional and intellectual needs of an adolescent's particular stage of development. The headings in Garland and Jones' (1981) book on *Communications and General Studies for Technician Students* read as follows:

Communication and Study Skills

Introduction:
1. What is communication?
   models − giving instructions − graphical
2. Listening and taking notes:
   note-taking − brainstorming − diagram techniques − revision
3. Using a library:
   Dewey − subject index − classified index − reference − layout − booklists
4. Information-finding:
   sources − alternatives
5. Giving a short talk:
   planning − delivery − observation
6. Technical writing:
   instructions − descriptions
7. Writing a report:
   layout − style − purpose
8. Formal letters:
   purpose − layout − style − tone − salutations − subscriptions
9. Punctuation
10. Spelling:
    problems − rules − techniques
11. Some aspects of language:
    persuasive − jargon − ambiguity − emotive − bias − selection of mode
12. Teamwork and decision-making:
    informal groups − observation − formal meetings
13. Statistics:
    surveys − polls − numerical presentation − tables − bar charts − graphs − histograms − cake diagrams − pictograms

General Studies

Introduction:
1. Identity:
   self-image − verbal behaviour − non-verbal behaviour − confidence − social activity
2. Relationships:
   intimate − informal − formal − conflicting − hostile
3. Transactional analysis:
   stroking − structure-and-stimulus-hunger − PAC model − analysis
4. Philosophy:
   knowledge − belief − logic − arguments − Venn diagrams − paradoxes

5. Sex:
   physiology — intercourse — conception — contraception — sexually
   transmitted diseases — abortion — problems
6. Sociology:
   class — mobility — education system — the home — language and learning —
   family — marriage — divorce
7. Economics:
   production — specialization — primary, secondary and tertiary sectors —
   fixed costs — variable costs — supply and demand — elasticity — national
   and international trade
8. Health and safety at work:
   hazards — accidents — prevention — law
9. Industrial relations:
   context — employees — management — trade unions — employers'
   associations — TUC — CBI — government agencies — disputes
10. Technology and the future:
    Industrial Revolution — technological revolution — environment —
    resources — pollution — forecasting — the future

One of our students wrote:

'The Bullock Report pointed out that many students are leaving school and
entering work. "We are able to do imaginative detailed composition — they were
not trained in the basic skills of being able to produce a written report." This
problem also exists in Ireland and while more and more of our young are
entering final management surely some training is needed. The reason that many
basic skills in English language are not emphasized in schools is because the
syllabus is too broad and complex and contains too many literary tests and the
teacher is faced with the problem of "covering" the course. There is too much
emphasis on literary skills in relation to poetry, drama, etc.
  The young are not trained in these skills of critical thinking in relation to
factual data. They don't know how to write a report. Since in Bloom's
taxonomy the basic skills are knowledge, comprehension, synthesis, application
and analysis they need definite practice in this. The Leaving Certificate syllabus
does not provide the means to do this and many teachers are not trained in this
area either . . .
  Because there is not much emphasis on our literary skills there is no time for
the teacher to develop the skills of argument (through debate) so necessary to
the world of work or to help the young clarify their use of language in
conversation to get across a point and to understand another's and reflect
another's point of view.'

None of the authorities discussed so briefly here would be entirely satisfied with this account of the debate. Yet, there is an obligation in initial
teacher training to draw the student's attention to these different
perspectives for each has much to offer the teacher regardless of the
subject taught. That every teacher has a responsibility for language as well
as being involved in preparation for life and work is the subject of the
next chapter.

References

Adler, M J (1982) *The Paedeia Proposal* MacMillan: New York
Association for Supervision and Curriculum Development Update (1983) Should
  there be a single curriculum for all, as the Paedeia group proposes? 25 (2) pp 4-5
Austin, J L (1962) *How to do Things with Words* Oxford University Press: Oxford

Bantock, G H (1968) *Culture Industrialization and Education* Routledge and Kegan Paul: London

Barnes, D (1969) *Language Learner and the School* Penguin: Harmondsworth

Barnes, D (1976) *From Communication to Curriculum* Penguin: Harmondsworth

Barrass, R (1982) *Students Must Write: A Guide to Better Writing in Coursework and Examinations* Methuen: London

Bernstein, B (1961) Social structure, language and learning *Educational Research* 3

Bernstein, B (1966) Elaborated and restricted codes: their social origins and consequences *in* Smith, A G (ed) *Communication and Culture* Holt, Rinehart and Winston: New York

Bloom, B (ed) (1964) The cognitive domain (Vol 1) *The Taxonomy of Educational Objectives* Longmans Green: London

Brent, A (ed) (1978) *Philosophical Foundations for the Curriculum* Unwin: London

Brummer, V (1981) *Theology and Philosophical Inquiry* Macmillan: London

Bullock, Sir Alan (1975) *A Language for Life* Her Majesty's Stationery Office: London Majesty's Stationery Office: London

Champagne, A B, Gunstone, R F and Klopfer, L E (1983) Naive knowledge and science learning *Research in Science and Technological Education* 1, pp 173-84

Cockroft, Sir Wilfred (1982) *Mathematics Counts* Her Majesty's Stationery Office: London

Comstock, G A, Rubinstein, E A and Murray, J P (eds) (1972) *TV and Social Behaviour* US Government Printing Office: Washington DC

Corson, D (1982) The Graeco-Latin lexical bar *Hesperiam* 5, pp 49-59

Davis, R (1981) A plea for student dialogues *Improving College and University Teaching* 29 (4) pp 155-9

Department of Education and Science (1981) *Teacher Training and the Secondary School* An HMI report DES: London

Elliott-Kemp, H (1981) Initiating a language development policy. A practical guide for post-holders in schools, Sheffield City Polytechnic: PAVIC Publication: Sheffield

Gagné, R N (1976) *The Conditions of Learning* Holt, Rinehart and Winston: New York

Garland, P and Jones, G (1981) *Communications and General Studies for Technician Students* McGraw Hill: London

Grayson, L P (1983) Leadership or stagnation. A role for technology in mathematics, science and engineering education *Journal of Engineering Education* 73 (5) pp 356-66

Guilford, J (1967) *The Nature of Human Intelligence* McGraw-Hill: London

Hartnett, A and Naish, M (1976) *Theory and Practice in Education* (2 vols) Heinemann: London

Hewitt, E A (1967) *The Reliability of GCE 'O' Level Examinations in English Language* The Joint Matriculation Board: Manchester

Heywood, J (1960) The training of first year students of radio servicing, LCP thesis, College of Preceptors: London

Heywood, J (1977) *Assessment in Higher Education* Wiley: London

Heywood, J (1978) *Examining in Second Level Education* Association of Secondary Teachers Ireland: Dublin

Heywood, J (1982) *Pitfalls and Planning in Student Teaching* Kogan Page: London

Heywood, J (1984) *Man, Industry and Society, Men and Institutions as Learning Systems* (in press)

Hirst, P H (1980) The PGCE course and the training of specialist teachers for secondary schools *British Journal of Teacher Education* 6 (i) pp 3-20

Holbrook, D (1964) *English for the Rejected* Cambridge University Press: Cambridge

Holbrook, D (1967) *English for Maturity* (2nd edition) Cambridge University Press: Cambridge

Holbrook, D (1979) *English for Meaning* National Foundation for Educational Research: Slough

Holland, S (1979) *The Rutland Street Project* Pergamon: Oxford

Hutchcroft, D M R (1981) *Making Language Work* McGraw-Hill: London

Krowne, C M and Covington, D H (1982) A survey of technical communication students *Journal of Engineering Education* 73 (3) pp 247-51

Labov, W (1973) The logic of non-standard English *in* Keddie, N *Tinker, Tailor. The Myth of Cultural Deprivation* Academic Press: New York

Lawton, D (1968) *Social Class, Language and Education* Routledge and Kegan Paul: London

Lawton, D (1978) Language and the curriculum *in* Lawton, D *et al Theory and Practice of Curriculum Studies* Routledge and Kegan Paul: London

Luria, A R and Yudovitch, I (1971) *Speech: The Development of Mental Processes in the Child* Penguin: Harmondsworth

Lyons, N P (1983) Two perspectives on self, relationship and morality *Harvard Educational Review* 53, pp 125-145

Masciantonio, R (1977) Tangible benefits of the study of Latin: a review of research *Foreign Language Annals* 10 (4)

Matthews, G B (1980) *Philosophy and the Young Child* Harvard University Press: Cambridge, Massachusetts

National Commission on Excellence (1983) *A Nation at Risk* NCE: Washington, DC

National Institute of Mental Health (1982) *TV and Behaviour: 10 Years of Scientific Progress and Implications for the Eighties Vol 1 Summary Report* NIMH: US Department of Health and Human Services, Rockville: Maryland

National Science Board (1983) *Educating Americans for the 21st Century* National Science Board Commission on precollege education in mathematics, science and technology NSB: Washington, DC

Oakeshott, M (1962) *Rationalism in Politics and Other Essays* Methuen: London

Oreo Vicz, F S (1983) A writing instructor's best friend: the word processor *Journal of Engineering Education* 73 (5) pp 376; 378

Ozolins, U (1982) Lawton's 'Refutation' of a working class *in* Horton, T and Raggatt, P *Challenge and Change in the Curriculum* Hodder and Stoughton: London

Robertston, G J (1981) Latin for all *Hesperiam* 4, pp 34-45

Schmid, A P and Graaf, D J (1982) *Violence as Communication. Insurgent Terrorism and the Western News Media* Sage: London

Starr, K and Bruce, B C (1983) Reading comprehension: more emphasis needed *ASCD Curriculum Update* Association for Supervision and Curriculum Development: Alexandria

Warren, L (1981) Singing and the art of writing *Improving College and University Teaching* 29 (9) pp 179-83

Woodcock, M (1979) *Team Development Manual* Gower Press: Aldershot

Young, M F D (1971) (ed) *Knowledge and Control* Collier-Macmillan: London

Chapter 5

Life and Work

Introduction

In this chapter the vexed question of the relationship between education and work is discussed. To this the parameter of 'life' is added. Student responses to examination questions, which illustrate their beliefs about the role of their subject in relation to life and work, introduce this chapter. It is argued that as things stand the curriculum is not an adequate preparation either for life or work. Some examples serve to illustrate the potential for development.

Some student responses on the role of their subject in development for life and work

1. RELATING TO THE IDEOLOGY OF EDUCATION

'The teacher that holds the academic ideology holds that school should be the place for producing the research workers of the future, the teachers of higher education and higher secondary school. The values portrayed by this approach lead to the view of the curriculum as consisting of distinct subjects. Barriers are raised between subjects and much of the material presented to the pupils would be divorced from human reality. This ideology would not have direct (discussions) of value questions. The second ideology, that of economic renewal, sees education as training the future managers and technical innovators. Here the application of science to problems would be encouraged by a teacher. The teacher holding this ideology is more likely to have a practical orientation to science teaching. The egalitarian ideologies' values are reflected directly in the curriculum in such matters as mixed ability classes, comprehensive schools, etc. This ideology is concerned with inequality of society and is likely to value in a curriculum such skills and ideas as hypothesis-making, social awareness, individuality, etc, geared toward producing a person with a questioning social conscience. The consensus ideology would consider the settling of disputes through a minimum of conflict and emphasize achieving the greatest common denominator of agreement. Proponents of this ideology would in a school place high value on co-operation between pupils through group work, etc . . . McClelland, I think, would believe that the extent to which the school/society values the ideology of economic renewal is a major factor in determining the achievement motivation of the pupils and hence eventually the society. The curriculum can have a great effect on the attitudes and values which the pupils obtain provided these values are not diametrically opposed to those of parents or society at large.'

2. RELATING TO THE TEACHING OF ENGLISH AND WORK

'One of the most interesting experiences occurred with my IV Extra English group. This group consisted of 12 pupils of decidedly mixed ability — some were slow learners with problems in English and had had extra English throughout their school career. Others had dropped out of French or Irish, etc

and were taking extra English instead. During a discussion with the class before the Easter vacation I discovered that 10 of the 12 were planning on leaving the school at the end of the year and hoped to be able to find employment in a variety of occupations including apprenticeship, shop assistants, etc.
Throughout the year we had studied short novels, drama and poetry and had spent quite a deal of time on basic English skills such as punctuation, sentence construction, letter and essay writing, etc. I decided to change tactics after Easter and began using a book called *Going Solo* (Parts I and II) compiled by the Dublin Vocational Education Committee's Curriculum Development Unit. The reaction of the class was most enthusiastic. The book contained practical exercises and information on moving from school to work and several extracts of prose and poetry which were interesting and provided useful organizers for discussion and debate. We were still doing basically the same things we had all year (ie practice of reading and writing skills) but pupils' performance showed a marked improvement which I believe to have been a direct result of the fact that pupils could see the relevance of what they were doing and why they were doing it.'

3. LITERATURE AND THE CULTIVATION OF SENSIBILITY
'Literature cultivates the sensibility. The insights desired from reading a poem or listening to a piece of music are not "useful" or directly applicable to any job. They may contribute indirectly to some task, because the response to a challenge comes from the resources of the whole character, intellectual and emotional, and the arts contribute enormously to development of individual character. This is the fundamental aim of teaching literature in school, and any way in which it contributes to the "requirements of work" is essentially incidental. Thus, if education is to be redefined, determined by the economic demands of a particular time, eg at the moment we need engineers, this would be a very limited and short-term view of the overall purpose of education.'

4. RELATING TO THE TEACHING OF HISTORY TO CULTURAL DEVELOPMENT
'Until about 1972 history courses in Irish schools tended to be overly concerned with Irish nationalism and leaders of rebellions tended to be treated as great folk heroes. Developments in Northern Ireland since 1968 have caused a re-appraisal of our attitudes down here. Out attitudes were identified as being unhelpful in relation to Northern Ireland. Our history teaching — syllabus — textbooks, etc were examined and, while it was agreed they reflected undesirable attitudes which were held by a large number of people down here, it was decided that it would be better if such attitudes were not to be promoted any more within the education system, especially within the history syllabus. We have now had a major change of the history syllabus.'

5. RELATING FOREIGN LANGUAGE TEACHING TO PREPARATION FOR LIFE
'An example from my own teaching experience of something being taught in the result sense but not intended would be the enormous range of benefits to be derived from travelling abroad and meeting people of different nationalities. . .
Wherever possible, I tried to relate it in some way to my experience of the living language by saying "When I was in France last year, I found that most people said it this way . . ." or whatever. I tried to make them anecdotal in nature if possible, since first-years will gladly welcome any sort of story.
Gradually I began to realize that for many of them, their imagination had been fired by the idea of someone going to live in a foreign country and spending, what seemed to them, the interminable period of a year. They questioned me on customs, habits, etc and I felt that they had learned something . . . it was a realization that Dublin 5 was not the centre of the universe.'

6. THE RELEVANCE OF COMMERCIAL SUBJECTS TO PRACTICE

'All learning is through experience. I would disagree fundamentally with the approach to this subject by the Department of Education. Their curriculum is in line with Dickensian-type ledgers with a page area of two feet by one foot and at least six inches thick. Part of the first-year syllabus is to teach the pupils how to write up the books of prime entry. One of these books is called the *Cash Book*. In my six years' practical work, I have *never* seen the *Cash Book* the way the Department of Education recommend it to be written up. Any pupils going from Leaving Certificate to work would have to be retrained in modern commercial methods.'

At the end of his essay this student wrote, 'All learning is based on experience not only of the student but of the teacher as well.'

Commentary

These examples have been selected to illustrate the many dimensions which any discussion on education and work must have. The student response in example 1. illustrates this point. Examples 2. and 3. show contrasting ideologies, while example 4. illustrates an important cultural aspect which relates more generally to the functioning of society and this (as example 1. shows) relates to the economy if the arguments put forward in Chapter 3 are acceptable. The other examples relate more generally to the contributions which subjects can make to work and, surprisingly, to the lack of relevance of the commerce curriculum in Irish schools!

An alternative title to this chapter might have been 'education and the economy' for there is no doubt that it is the economic advantages of higher education which have influenced educational policies in Britain (Heywood, 1981b) and Ireland (Government Publications, 1965). The 1956 White Paper in Britain set up a new system for the education of technologists (CMND 9703) and another White Paper in 1961 set out a new programme for the education of technicians, craftsmen and operatives (CMND 1254). The Robbins Report in 1963 (CMND 2154) led to an expansion of degree level education in all subjects but particularly in the public sector which, because of miscalculations of growth in the 1960s and 1970s, led to very severe cut-backs in both the public and university sectors in the early 1980s apart from technological subjects. It was particularly severe in teacher education. Several of the colleges of advanced technology created in 1956 which became universities seemed to be hit more than other universities, and some observers put this down to prejudice on the part of the University Grants Committee. Nevertheless, the science and technological departments of universities, particularly in the area of computing and information science, were those which received support in the belief that they would contribute most to the restoration of the economy. Ministers also believed that second-level education paid insufficient attention to the needs of industry.

Although the system of education is very different in Ireland there are some similarities. There is for example a legislated binary system. In the 1980 Irish White Paper (Government Publications, 1980) there was virtually no mention of the universities, although positive pressure was put on them to expand their faculties of engineering; the main emphasis was to be on the expansion of technical education in the public sector. One paper internally circulated in a university at the time of the White Paper suggested that similar mistakes were being made to those which were made in 1956 in Britain (Heywood, 1981a) about the relationship between technology and education. However while governments have the intention of exploiting education for economic purposes there are hidden mechanisms at work which may prevent the attainment of this goal and these relate to the overall ideology of education that a society has.

Educational ideologies and their significance in policy-making

K G Collier (1982) has drawn attention to four competing ideologies which are to be found in all Western societies. These are the academic, egalitarian, consensus and economic renewal paradigms. They work themselves out in different ways in different societies. The 'soft' egalitarian ideology is concerned with equality of opportunity and access to top positions and it creates a meritocracy. Its attainment has been a major goal of international organizations such as the Council of Europe and the Organization for Economic and Cultural Development (Council of Europe, 1972). Much discussion at this level has been about open access to higher education (OECD, 1974). In Ireland the drive in this direction was heralded by O'Connor's paper in the 1968 volume of *Studies* (O'Connor, 1968). In England there was a political consensus about comprehensivization for a decade and positive discrimination and compensatory programmes were introduced (Halsey, 1972), but this consensus broke down during the 1979-83 Conservative Government.

> '. . . underlying this outlook is a deep attachment to the freedom of action of the individual or the group: which is usually thought of as the heart of a "liberal" ideology.' (Collier, 1982)

Comprehensivization has undoubtedly had a great effect on the educational system but policy, particularly at third level, has been dominated by a conflict between the academic and economic renewal ideologies (Embling, 1974).

Binary systems help preserve the public sector from the academic ideology which is the main influence on educational thinking. But there is a drift toward the academic in the public sector institutions, and there is considerable consensus between the two sectors about what constitutes a degree. Thus while the British system finances developments in technological education there is a general drift toward 'Oxbridge' ideas which have the highest status and this reinforces the regard which these institutions have of themselves as 'strongholds of certain values in an irrational and often barbaric society' (Collier, 1982), even though in their teaching and curriculum 'there is very little explicit discussion of value questions, that is, questions of the nature, validity and relative priorities of moral values in specific areas of (for example) literature or history' (Collier, 1982). These institutions lend strong support to the maintenance and development of the established disciplines and, while emphasizing freedom for the individual academic, they undertake an 'authoritarian system of training testing' (Collier, 1982) based on an underlying social consensus about what is sacrosanct and what values are important (see also Chapter 3). If economic renewal were really regarded as important, the economic ideology would have succeeded. One effect is that Platonic dualism persists and the 'pure' maintains its status.

Teachers of traditional subjects do believe that without modification, their subjects contribute to the 'life needs' of children on a broad (liberal) basis (see example 3. p 78).

It is in the vocational/technical sectors, that is with those of lower academic ability, that governments are able to force the economic renewal ideology, and in this they are aided by increasing unemployment. In Britain in 1983-84 those 16-year-olds who refuse to join the Youth Training Schemes offered to them will be deprived of their right to social security. These schemes, according to the Manpower Services Commission which is charged with their development, are:

'to provide for what the economy needs, and what employers want — a better equipped, better qualified, better educated, and better motivated workforce.' (Davies, 1982)

But is this what is wanted? Should this be the response to social change brought about by the technological revolution? The numbers employed in manufacturing industry continue to decrease as capital-intensive high technology is increasingly used and high unemployment seems here to stay not only in inner city areas but in rural areas as well. Education is as much about life and unemployment as work — so the argument goes — but is there, should there be, any real distinction between them? Answers to such questions are about the aims of education. As Fitzgibbons (1981) puts it, 'When we ask what the individual outcomes of a person's education ought to be, we are essentially inquiring into what some characteristics of that person's life ought to be.'

Thus discussion of the role of education in work and life must begin with an evaluation of the aims of education and the following examples from student answers to examination questions fully illustrate this point.

1. RELATING GENERALLY TO THE AIMS OF EDUCATION
'If we have as an aim in education the formation of individuals who have (i) a basic numeracy adequate for life (must be capable of using a calculator); (ii) a basic literacy — must be capable of reading, writing and communicating his ideas, thoughts, either verbally or in writing, expressing himself accurately and precisely and following a logical argument; (iii) a wide frame of reference which enables them to see things objectively; (iv) the ability to make objective value judgements; (v) the basic skills in problem-solving; (vi) attitudes to others, to work, to his obligation to society and to himself that are in keeping with the norms of society. An articulate individual, with plenty of initiative, a high self-esteem and high regard for others. With these as an aim I cannot possibly see how there could be any difference between the aims of education and the requirements of work.'

2. RELATING THE AIMS OF EDUCATION TO THE SKILLS OF LEARNING
'One could begin on an abstract level and say that the aims of education
consist of:

1. transfer of training;
2. problem-solving;
3. critical thinking;
4. motivation; all these combining to produce
5. the ideal autonomous learner.

Few would argue with this although there might be different opinions on how
to achieve it. If we accept this, as I do, does this mean it must conflict with the
requirements of the economy? I don't think so. It has always been a source
of amazement to me that industrialists are obsessed with functional learning
and numeracy. They complain that students leave school with masses of
irrelevant knowledge and call for a more relevant curriculum.

They seem to me to just want to swap some of the "irrelevant" subjects
with subjects more amenable to their needs. Students would then leave school
with masses of knowledge in "relevant" subjects. While this might be an
improvement from their point of view it would still not be ideal. It would
still do nothing to develop qualities of initiative and entrepreneurship. The
present examination system does not measure these qualities nor does it
measure the so-called higher order intellectual or cognitive skills.'

3. AIMS AND ECONOMICS IN SECOND-LEVEL EDUCATION
'The following are some of the skills I would suggest are required in order to
pursue a career; they complement rather than conflict with my aims of the
economics course for last year. *1. Skills in interpersonal communication.*
David Whitehead in his book *Teaching Economics* suggests that the economics
teacher must try to develop interpersonal communication skills in pupils.
I have attempted to do this by dividing the class into groups of four, and each
group is given a certain amount of time to put forward solutions to a problem
which is written on a blackboard.
I have also noted if you go into the class and give pupils notes, you are
failing to allow pupils to learn independently of you.
Pupils will only understand and recall what they themselves have learnt.
I allowed pupils to play cards in my class following a discussion on the role
and function of the entrepreneur. I told the pupils that following the game of
cards we would discuss some of the main characteristics of the entrepreneur.
The pupils were playing cards for paper money. After 10 minutes they stopped
playing cards. I asked the question why did some pupils win more money than
others? Why did some people lose more money than others? Most pupils
answered because some pupils took more risks than others. This led the lesson
on to the major attributes/characteristics of an entrepreneur.'

4. AIMS AND HISTORY IN SECOND-LEVEL EDUCATION
'The aims and objectives for the Intermediate Certificate in history suggest
that there are a number of skills which can be learnt. For example, the ability
to handle historical material, ability to locate historical information and to
examine critically issues in their textbooks and in today's world. Bruner suggests
that improvement in transfer will occur when the information required is useful
in everyday living. In recent years the importance of the teaching of values
within one's subject has been labelled. In "restructuring" the curriculum the
teacher can help shape the pupils' values. Learning is a behaviour. We teach in
order to change the pupils' behaviour. History can be used very effectively to
develop skills within the child. The pupil can be taught to feel a responsibility
to be objective with material . . . It is important to note however that
examinations will have to examine this kind of skill. At the moment they

do not to any great degree. Examinations will become more effective when they are linked more effectively with the learning strategies.

One important affective skill which can also be learnt through history is the ability to empathize. Pupils can be taught to feel that each person has a right to be different and to hold different view points. Since history is involved with people this skill can be developed on any period of history.'

5. AIMS AND BIOLOGY IN SECOND-LEVEL EDUCATION
'The values, attitudes, interests and skills and needs of the pupils must be considered when forming aims and objectives and when teaching. For example, I was teaching biology to fifth-year students. The syllabus said that they should know the structure of the heart, the blood vessels, the composition of blood, the structure of the lungs . . . that is, they should know the basic human physiology. The syllabus did not say that I should teach the pupils how to take care of their bodies, how to avoid heart diseases, what causes leukaemia, heart attacks, strokes, ulcers, etc. The pupils I taught were fascinated by disease and I used this interest to motivate them how to, and why they should, care for their bodies which I believe they need to know.'

Inspection of the aims of education in example 2. shows that they relate to many aspects of life and work. Education is seen to be a preparation for life, and life is about more things than work as the illustrations show. Indeed in some cultures it may be thought necessary to emphasize value objectives at the expense of economic objectives as for example in the Anglo-Irish context, where there is continuing friction between Catholic and Protestant to the point of death. It could be argued that the teaching of history plays a critical role in the formation of values. If this is the case, then it is possible to argue that all students should take a history course which pursues the aims set out in Figure 5.1 (see p 84) which attempts to force pupils in Ireland to take a more objective view of events and that the time necessary for them to develop the skills necessary for this should be allowed. Too often aims are spelt out but no provision is made for the strategies and materials which will obtain them; to achieve these aims project work and evaluation exercises would be required which would certainly require more time than is allowed by the timetable when set against the syllabus requirement (Heywood *et al*, 1981).

Statements of aims therefore lead to competition between subjects not only for time but for inclusion within the total curriculum programme (this is discussed in detail in Chapter 7). In relation to policy it is therefore of some consequence to understand the significance of the ideologies referred to in the last section and to realize that, given appropriate instructional and assessment strategies, the subjects of the curriculum may contribute to the attainment of aims in each ideological area.

Suspicion of industrialists

Some of the student responses are clearly suspicious of the intentions of industrialists and for this there is some justification especially as they apply to the employment of those who normally leave school at 15 or 16. Teachers feel industrialists want fodder for particular jobs, people who will

Knowledge and Comprehension:
Pupils should be able to recall, recognize and understand the principal events, trends and issues of the periods of history set out in the syllabus. They should have some understanding of the recent evolution of the world in which they live.

Skills:
Pupils should be able to practise, at a level suitable to their stage of development, the skills used in history; more particularly:

   (i) the ability to locate, understand and record simple historical information; and
  (ii) the ability to examine critically and discuss statements on historical matters encountered in their textbooks and in everyday life.

Pupils should feel a responsibility:

    (i) to be objective in interpreting historical material;
   (ii) to find rational explanations for historical events and developments;
  (iii) to understand what it is like to be in someone else's position;
  (iv) to respect the right of others to be different and to hold different points of view.

Pupils should be encouraged to value their heritage from the past.

Figure 5.1 *Aims and objectives of the Irish Intermediate Certificate for the 1976 examination* (Government Publications, 1984)

fit into a disciplined and motivated workforce which will accomplish tasks that are boring and often distasteful without error and with satisfaction for the sake of profit. Historically, industrialists were able to call on a cheap labour force. 'Us' and 'them' attitudes were part of the system and there was no call for technological change to better working conditions and these 'us' and 'them' attitudes have persisted. But as society has encouraged everyone to be more articulate so it has shown the power available on the shop floor, and workers are able to sublimate the shortcomings of jobs with strikes, careless workmanship and so forth. They are reinforced by Employment Protection Acts which make it difficult for them to be sacked. This is an over-simplified stereotype of the average employment situation held by teachers who are also aware that industrialists are slow to change. By and large there is no meeting between educationalists and industrialists and in consequence, industrialists, who nevertheless have to respond to changes in the educational structure, are ill-informed about developments in education and *vice versa.*

An educationalist is bound to consider the total life span of an individual and the contribution which education can make to personal equanimity during that time. In the teacher's view, education should not be about training for jobs but about education for life, and it is unfortunate that just when a pupil may be capable of fundamental thinking about life and formal reasoning the same pupil wants to leave school and formal study.

Teachers will argue that high technology is reducing the number of jobs in manufacturing industry and that unemployment at a relatively high level is here to stay. Since those who are unemployed will require a philosophical disposition which can sustain them, education should be concerned as much with this as it is with work.

The influence of technology on social change is such that everyone will have to become increasingly adaptable and flexible. The major question is not whether education adequately prepares people for work, but whether it adequately prepares them for life in which work is included. It is a fair criticism of educationalists to say that they have not really come to grips with this issue in any detail except through pious platitude.

Meeting points

Nevertheless, there should be important meeting points between industry, education and society in the curriculum. For example, in Britain at the top level of academic performance, it seems that the most able do not wish to pursue careers in industry and commerce. At all levels of ability there is a shortage of individuals prepared to take risks, that is, to become entrepreneurs. In general we can argue that there is great need for economic and social understanding and that it is important to both life and work. At the present time a pupil can go through school and university without formal contact with economics, and some can escape formal discussion of moral issues. Despite all its protestations, the academic ideology is pragmatic and fosters subject specialization. But breadth in terms of the number of traditional subjects studied will not achieve either economic or social understanding. The ideas which teachers have about the contribution their own subjects can make to such understanding only touch upon the issue, as the illustrations show.

At the lower level of ability much of what is taught seems to be irrelevant. Several of the student-teacher responses touch on this issue and indicate that they had to change their courses to meet the needs of those who are not very able nor very well motivated. The changes which teachers of English made in their courses are clearly in a direction which will assist the young person both at work and life. But is that enough? If the arguments set out in the previous chapter are correct then more substantial changes are required and this also seems to be the view of these student teachers.

Very often industrialists make criticisms of mathematics education, saying that pupils are innumerate. Student teachers soon find that there is a group of teachers for whom mathematics (new or old) is an abstraction which they neither appreciate nor understand. Both the Cockcroft Report (Cockcroft, 1982) in Britain and the Final Report of the Public Examinations Evaluation Project (Heywood, McGuinness and Murphy, 1981) in Ireland call for 'streaming' in mathematics — the latter on the basis of experimental examinations which tried to test higher order skills. The research unit concluded that there is only a small group of pupils who benefit from the traditional academic approach to mathematics while the majority require something that is at once more practical and less abstract; a third group, the least able, are only capable of simple problem-solving and should be taught by mastery methods of learning for certificates of competency. The results of an enquiry by the Engineering Industries Training Board in England would generally support such conclusions (Matthews, 1977). The Cockcroft Committee commissioned two studies on the mathematical needs of various types of employment, one of which led to the Mathematics at Work project at the University of Bath (1981).

Fitzgerald, the senior research fellow on this project, said that teachers could not expect the general educational value to be apparent to their pupils without a conscious teaching effort to this end, and that it would require a radical change in teaching methods (Fitzgerald, 1983). Fitzgerald concluded that syllabuses could be considerably reduced without affecting the employment prospects of their pupils, and he argued for a more flexible approach to syllabus construction and grading which would assess the strengths of pupils. 'This was dramatically illustrated by a young clerical trainee I met during the MIE study, who had been unclassified in O level mathematics, but obtained Grade B in accounts' (Fitzgerald, 1983). Consider the girls or boys who take the cash in a supermarket. They require knowledge of the basic operations of a cash register if they are to check for machine errors. Little else is required, but for living they require a knowledge of simple accounting, rates of interest, etc.

The Manpower Services Commission (MSC, 1980) calls for basic skills training in the following areas — basic calculations, fractions, decimals, money, mental arithmetic, percentages, ratios and proportions (maps, cooking), rounding off, sequencing numbers (articles, prices), conversions (fraction, decimal, percentages), averages (wages, lengths, height), time (job versus wage rate), calculators, log tables, trigonometric calculations, powers and roots, using formulae, quadratics, skills of measurement and drawing, reading skills, units, conversions (weight, distance/length, area, volume), calculating perimeters, areas, volumes, angle calculations, estimating, drawing with instruments, freehand sketching or drawing, graphs or pictorial charts, scale drawings and drawings which show how one gets there, how the parts fit together, how a thing works, how a thing ought to be, and how it ought to be made.

The US National Science Board Commission's 1983 report recommended that all students should be able to recognize the basic algebraic forms and have knowledge of how to transform them into other forms. They should also understand the logic behind algebraic manipulations. All students should develop skills in solving linear equations and inequalities and quadratic equations. They should be able to use graphs of linear and quadratic functions in the interpretation and solution of problems. The Commission calls for familiarity with permutations, combinations and simple counting problems, and knowledge of relations and functions. There is also a recommendation for a syllabus in geometry and it is of interest to note that whereas the geometry syllabus begins with the ability to think logically, the algebra syllabus calls for a development of problem-solving abilities (NSB, 1983).

The Manpower Services Commission's statement has the advantage of simplicity of language whereas the report to the National Science Board is in the language of mathematicians. McGuinness (1984) has shown how the curriculum developers in mathematics in America, who were often academics, ignored the learning needs of students.

However, as Fitzgerald (1983) shows, the selection of basic skills is not a simple matter. For example, it is questionable whether it should be necessary to use logarithms when calculators are available, and their use called for, in the same syllabus. It is surprising that whereas in the National Science Board's report competencies in computing are called for there is no mention of this in the Manpower Services Commission's list. Little is known about the response of the less able to computing but it may be that it is the kind of device which will motivate such students (Heywood, 1974a). Computers are already being used with some success in remedial reading and arithmetic. In all countries and especially in America, there is a drive to install microprocessors in primary schools. Both reports call for skills which will help develop spatial ability, although the Manpower Services Commission emphasizes drawing skills in addition to basic geometrical skills. But if past experience is anything to go by many such abilities could remain unused because of lack of training and curriculum development in education.

Clearly, as things stand, there is need for a substantially different curriculum for the less able. Much of what is being tackled in post-16 schemes in the areas of communication, decision-making and planning is to make a wider range of subjects available in schools (Davies, 1982; FEU, 1979). Schemes of this kind may be derived from the analysis of jobs and considerable developments in the application of task analysis to education and training schemes have been made during the last 20 years (Singer and Ramsden, 1969). Studies of technologists and technicians at work (Youngman *et al*, 1978) have led to the simple yet obvious view, also expressed by Mant (1979), that every man or woman is a manager; for every individual exercises direction and control over himself or herself, his or her job, and sometimes over other people.

If we examine the kind of skills we use when we design something from scratch, we find that they are the same kind of skills which historians or scientists use when they solve problems. What differs primarily is the context within which a problem has to be solved. The context of history is very different from that of science, but at the fundamental level the designer, historian and scientist are faced with the evaluation of solutions, the recognition of assumptions, the need to generate hypotheses and skill in making judgements. This point is illustrated in Figure 5.2 (see p 88). These skills embrace those involved in critical thinking, as for example:

(a) A model of how a scientist solves problems. (From J Heywood and H Montagu-Pollock (1976) *Science for Art Students: A Case Study in Curriculum Development* Guildford, Society for Research into Higher Education

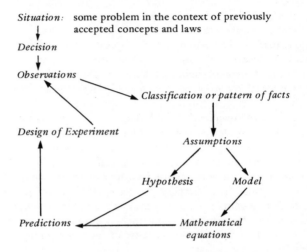

After a number of cycles there may emerge new *concepts*, *laws*, or *practical applications* of this knowledge.

(b) *A model of the design process*

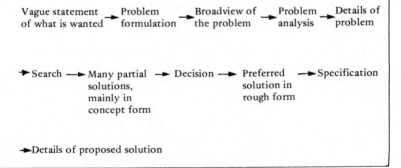

Figure 5.2 *A model of how a scientist solves problems compared with a model of the design process*

The ability to

☐ recognize the existence of a problem;
☐ select information relevant to the problem;
☐ recognize assumptions bearing on the problem;
☐ make relevant hypotheses;
☐ draw valid conclusions from the data obtained;
☐ judge the validity of the data/process leading to the conclusion;
☐ evaluate a conclusion in terms of the initial plan, etc.

Such skills, as the syllabus in Figure 5.1 (see p 84) shows, are required by historians in the interpretation of data. It has been argued that if students are to learn these skills some form of process-approach to learning is required. This might be through discovery learning or by the more formal activity of a substantial project. Projects may be undertaken in any subject, but this is not to advocate their general use in all subjects for they may be of more value in some subjects than others. It is held that projects in science and technology help to develop skills in the areas of design, planning, specification and evaluation. Discovery learning has been found to be of great value in retraining adults (Belbin and Belbin, 1972).

A learning skills approach to the analysis of work leads to the conclusion that the subjects of the curriculum may assist the development of life skills and are also important in drawing out an individual's capacity, skills and values (McPeck, 1981). Thus there needs to be content in the curriculum which relates to life, work and interests (Fitzgerald, 1983). Exactly how this might be done is another problem. In this respect it is relevant to take note of recent developments in life skills learning which is largely non-dimensional and independent of subject-centred content.

Life skills learning

In 1970 G Holroyde (quoted by Heywood, 1974a) listed 14 skill areas common to most adult situations which were in the main picked up haphazardly. These were in the areas of perception, unstructured problem-solving and judgement, communication, understanding, sympathy and tolerance, personal management, the management of other people, working co-operatively in groups, handling frustration, personal responsibility, taking risks, emotions (emotional resilience) and physical dexterity and endurance.

Since then, several attempts have been made to provide for the formal development of these skills. It will be seen that the student teachers believe that their subjects can contribute to such development, as for example in economics where it is possible to use business games both in the conduct of business and decision-making. Several exercises have been developed for decision-making in schools (Hopson and Scally, 1981) and a course was developed in decision-making at Reading (Juniper, 1976). Such strategies pervade the cognitive and affective domains.

The Further Education Curriculum Review and Development Unit in Britain has described seven models for social and life skills development, four of which they claim are product-oriented and three process-oriented (FEU, 1978, 1979, 1980, 1981).

The product-oriented models relate to the development of basic skills in which a pupil is deficient: the development of specific competencies for which the criteria are well defined as in specific tasks at work; the provision of information that is a necessary requisite of development and the development of values and attitudes derived from the world of work, adult life and society (socialization). The process models relate to experiential learning, reflective learning and counselling. In the first the aims are derived from *a priori* principles and situational analyses of such things as community action and team work. In the reflective model the student is helped to 'pattern' experience or data in alternative ways, to make and check generalizations and to develop conceptual frameworks, skills which are essential to problem-formulation and problem-solving. The counselling model emphasizes individual or group reflection on experiences in the affective domain; this aims to help control behaviour and to understand the feelings and behaviour of others.

It seems to the author that history teachers, who could claim that their programme met the aims suggested in Figure 5.1 (see p 84), would in fact be meeting the aims of the three process models, and such aims could be written for any subject in the curriculum. These are the aims of liberal education. Thus it is of considerable interest to establish why the traditional subjects do not achieve these goals. Is it more a question of method than relevant content?

The City and Guilds of London Institute (C and G, 1984) have designed a course for vocational preparation. This course (number 365) includes career planning involving work experience in three different kinds of activity-related studies which enable an individual to look at the organization of a specific firm and so learn to identify both management structure and union organization. Sections are also included on understanding society, economic and environmental understanding.

It is difficult to believe that such a course which embraces the commonly understood aims of liberal education should be for those who have achieved little in the school system. In attempting to overcome deficiencies, educationalists often create a 'vogue' which for a while dominates education thinking.

At the present time this applies to experiential learning which has for many years been a norm in management education (Roskin, 1976). Surprisingly few teachers seem to be aware of this fact, yet there is now much interest in experiential learning, particularly among teachers of religious education (O'Brolchain, 1983). Following in the footsteps of the second volume of *The Taxonomy of Educational Objectives* (Krathwohl, 1965), Steinaker and Bell (1969) have developed a taxonomy for experiential education. The main categories in this taxonomy are:

Exposure   seeing, hearing, reacting and recognizing
Participation   observing, discussing, listening, ordering

Identification	classifying, explaining, experimenting, writing and drawing
Internalization	generalizing, comparing, contrasting and transferring
Dissemination	communicating, debating, presenting, motivating and influencing

Careers specialists have been particularly interested in the development of life skills and have been involved in a number of experiments which have used computers as interactive devices in career selection. Such programmes developed with IBM were also intended to develop skills in decision-making. Since then they have done much work in the development of life skills teaching, a lot of which involves pupils and students working in groups. Nowhere have group processes of learning been more explored than in British higher education (Abercrombie, 1970; Abercrombie and Terry, 1978) and Abercrombie's (1960) *Anatomy of Judgement* has been a powerful influence in this direction. But the major impetus has come from isolated subjects or counselling. It is work which requires teachers to adapt their roles to become facilitators of learning rather than experts who pass on knowledge (Hopson and Scally, 1981).

That teacher training is beginning to take into account group methods is indicated by the student teacher respondents. In one of the courses in Trinity College Dublin, 140 graduate trainees are taught together in a combination of buzz group and syndicate techniques. This undoubtedly encourages students to try such methods in the classroom. Many other similar experiments have been reported (Collier, 1983).

But what of the curriculum generally? One of the most promising developments in recent years has been the introduction of a transition year in second-level education in Ireland (Egan and O'Reilly, 1977). The general pattern of the curriculum in Ireland is that pupils transfer from primary to secondary school at the age of 12, undertake a three-year programme for the Intermediate Certificate and a further two-year programme for the Leaving Certificate which is set at honours and pass levels and is also used for university entry. The school leaving age is 15 and a lot of pupils stay on at school, although many of them are unlikely to be successful and leave before completing the Leaving Certificate. Richard Burke, when Minister for Education, introduced a special fourth-year course which became known as the transition year. It was a school-based curriculum development. The course was evaluated in Newpark Comprehensive School (Harris, 1981) where it is provided for all students, many of whom do not take the Intermediate Certificate examination. It emphasizes preparation for work, for living in the community, for use of leisure time and includes courses in such areas as media education, consumer education, home-making and film appreciation. Its overall aim is the personal growth and development of the pupils who are engaged in it. Pupils seem to hold a positive view of the effectiveness and usefulness of the course.

A break of the kind offered by the transition year solves many of the structural problems within education which occur when the world of employment tries to remedy, with deficiency models, things which should have been accomplished within second-level courses. Moreover, it highlights the fact that students of all abilities have much to gain from such studies. Otherwise the most able can go through the education system and not come into contact with life skill development as it embraces interpersonal relationships on the one hand and decision-making and critical judgement on the other. Such courses can embrace both community and work activities. There should not be any need for separate Youth Training Schemes which in any event are no solution to unemployment (Rees and Atkinson, 1982).

This is not to argue that there is no need for courses of this kind in higher education. That they can be successful is illustrated by the work at Alverno College in the United States (Doherty *et al* 1978; Read, 1980) where a systems approach has been used to the development of its general education programme. The College considers that there are eight characteristics which equip a student for life.

1. Effective communications ability
2. Analytical capability
3. Problem-solving ability
4. Valuing in a decision-making context
5. Effective social interaction
6. Effectiveness in individual/environmental relationships
7. Responsible involvement in the contemporary world
8. Aesthetic responsiveness

In its student prospectus the first four levels of competence required of every student in the pursuit of these goals are outlined. For example:

	Level 1	Level 2	Level 3	Level 4
3. Problem-solving ability	Discerns problems	Formulates problems	Resolves problems	Integrates approaches
4. Valuing in a decision-making context	Identifies own values	Discerns expressed values	Infers implied values	Applies valuing process

The college adopts a heuristic approach to teaching, which involves the teacher in both summative and formative evaluation, criterion and norm referenced tests. Its work on valuing is of special interest (Alverno College, 1983). As with all brief illustrations this description does the course and its associated materials less than justice. I have argued that as the structure of employment changes so programmes like this will become increasingly necessary (Heywood, 1981b).

Even though it is possible for teachers to argue that their subjects meet the aims of education for work and life in terms of knowledge, skills and values, the evidence of pupil performance and subsequent behaviour at work suggests that they do not. It seems that an alternative curriculum is required for very many students. For example, the European Economic Community is sponsoring the development of an alternative Leaving Certificate based on St Patrick's School, Shannon. The provisional areas for development are:

1. Literacy, Numeracy, Computer Awareness
2. Social/Cultural Studies, Art/Design, Music, Films
3. Craft/Design/Technology/Applied Science
4. Horticulture/Agriculture/Food Technology/Catering
5. Business Studies/Information Technology, Language Studies
6. Mini-Company (or Social/Community Work)
7. Recreational/Practical
8. Religion/Moral development

During the first half-year of this two-year programme there are plans for students to participate in a Community-based learning project or a mini-business development, schemes of this kind having already been successfully undertaken by the St Patrick's School.

It becomes clear that the academic curriculum does not achieve the general aims of education such as those described in the organizing section of the chapter (see pp 77 - 79). By and large schools do not help children to develop life skills but rely on individual teachers and their understanding of what can be achieved within their subjects. A conflict between the academic and economic ideologies, leaving the able relatively untouched while seemingly providing more stratification among the less able, seems apparent. In these circumstances life skills are but a form of compensating education (Rees and Atkinson, 1982). The success of the Youth Opportunities Scheme in Britain which incorporated such training in many of its schemes seems to have been limited by the economic climate in which it was undertaken (Main and Raffe, 1983). In any event, if all students are to benefit from such programmes it seems that in any system of education there must be a radical restructuring of the curriculum immediately before and after the school leaving age. This is as important, if not more important, for individuals as the transition from primary to second-level education.

References

Abercrombie, M L J (1960) *The Anatomy of Judgement* Penguin: Harmondsworth
Abercrombie, M L J (1970) *Aims and Techniques of Group Teaching* Society for Research into Higher Education: Guildford
Abercrombie, M L J and Terry, P (1978) *Talking to Learn* Society for Research into Higher Education: Guildford
Alverno College (1983) *Liberal Learning at Alverno College* Alverno College Prospectus: Milwaukee: USA
Belbin, R and Belbin R M (1972) *Problems in Adult Retraining* Heinemann: London
City and Guilds of London Institute: C and G (1984) *Vocational Preparation (General): Profile and Report Form* (Course 365) London
CMND 9703 (1956) *Technical Education* Her Majesty's Stationery Office: London

CMND 1254 (1961) *Better Opportunities in Technical Education* Her Majesty's Stationery Office: London

CMND 2154 (1963) *Higher Education* Her Majesty's Stationery Office: London

Cockcroft, W H (1982) *Mathematics Counts* Her Majesty's Stationery Office: London

Collier, K G (1982) Ideological influence in higher education *Studies in Higher Education* 7 (1) pp 13-19

Collier, K G (1983) (ed) *The Management of Peer Group Learning: Syndicate for Research into Higher Education:* Guildford

Council of Europe (1972) *Curriculum Reform in Post-Secondary Education. List of Problems* Council of Europe: Strasbourg

Davies, B (1982) What most young people really want in a job *The Guardian* 9, 10 August

Doherty, A, Mentkowski, M M and Conrad, K (1978) Toward a theory of undergraduate experiential learning *in* Keeton, M T and Tate, P J (eds) *Learning by Experience, What, Why, How?* Jossey Bass: San Francisco

Egan, O and O'Reilly, J (1977) *The Transition Year Project* The Educational Research Centre, St Patrick's College: Dublin

Embling, J (1974) *A Fresh Look at Higher Education* Elsevier: Amsterdam

Further Education Curriculum Review and Development Unit (FEU) Department of Education and Science: London (1978) *Experience Reflection Learning Suggestions for Organizers of Schemes of Unified Vocational Preparation*

FEU (1979) *A Better Start in Working Life: Vocational Preparation for Employed Young People in Britain* DES: London

FEU (1980) *Developing Social and Life Skills: Strategies for Tutors* DES: London

FEU (1981) *Vocational Preparation* DES: London

Fitzgerald, R (1983) Part I Mathematics in employment '16-18' project: its findings and implications *Mathematics in School* 12 (1) pp 14-18; Part II *Mathematics in School* 12 (2) pp 6-10

Fitzgibbons, R E (1981) *Educational Decisions: An Introduction to the Philosophy of Education* Harcourt Brace Jovanovich: New York

Government Publications: Dublin (1965) *Investment in Education;* (1980) *White Paper on Educational Development;* (1984) *Rules and Regulations for Secondary Schools* (annual)

Halsey, A H (1972) *Educational Priority. EPA Problems and Policies* Her Majesty's Stationery Office: London

Harris, J (1981) The evaluation of school-based curriculum development, PhD thesis, The Library of the University of Dublin: Dublin

Heywood, J (1974a) *Assessment in History (Twelve to Fifteen)* First report of the Public Examinations Evaluation Project, The School of Education, The University of Dublin: Dublin

Heywood, J (1974b) Remedial pupils, computer-assisted learning and guidance, Appendix G2 of the *Final Report of the Committee on the Form and Function of the Intermediate Certificate Examination* Government Publications: Dublin

Heywood, J (1981a) Manpower requirements *in Arts (Humanities). Their Place in Higher Education* University of Dublin: Dublin

Heywood, J (1981b) Curricula, teaching and assessment *in* Oxtoby, R (ed) *Higher Education at the Crossroads* Society for Research into Higher Education Guildford

Heywood, J, McGuinness, S and Murphy, D E (1981) *Final Report of the Public Examinations Evaluation Project to the Minister for Education* School of Education, University of Dublin: Dublin

Hopson, B and Scally, M (1981) *Lifeskills Teaching* McGraw Hill: London

Juniper, D F (1976) *Decision-Making in Schools and Colleges* Pergamon: Oxford

Krathwohl, D (ed) (1965) The affective domain (Vol 2) *The Taxonomy of Educational Objectives* Longmans Green: London

Main, B and Raffe, D (1983) The transition from school to work in 1980/81: a dynamic account *British Educational Research Journal* 9, p 57

Mant, A (1979) *The Rise and Fall of the British Manager* Pan: London

Matthews, D (1977) *The Relevance of the School Learning Experience to Performance in Industry* Engineering Industry Training Board

McGuinness, S (1984) PhD thesis, School of Education, University of Dublin: Dublin

McPeck, J E (1981) *Critical Thinking and Education* Oxford University Press: Toronto

Manpower Services Commission: MSC (1980) *Basic Skills Reference Manual* Report DTP 20, London

National Science Board: NSB (1983) *Educating Americans for the 21st Century* National Science Board Commission on Pre-College Education in Maths, Science and Technology: Washington

O'Brolchain, C (1983) An evaluation of an experiential approach to religious education in Kenya, NLitt thesis, The Library, The University of Dublin: Dublin

O'Connor, S (1968) Post primary education: now and in the future *Studies* 57, p 233

Organization for Economic and Cultural Development (1974) *Problems for Higher Education* OECD: Paris

Read, J (1980) Alverno's Collegewide approach to the developing of valuing *New Directions in Education* 31, pp 71-9

Rees, T L and Atkinson, P (1982) *Youth Employment and State Intervention* Routledge and Kegan Paul: London

Roskin, R (1976) *Learning by Experience* MCB monograph: Bradford

Singer, J and Ramsden, J (1969) *The Practical Approach to Skills Analysis* McGraw Hill: London

Steinaker, N and Bell, M R (1969) *An Experiential Taxonomy* Academic Press: New York

Youngman, M B, Oxtoby, R, Monk, J D and Heywood, J (1978) *Analysing Jobs* Gower Press: Aldershot

Chapter 6

Examinations, Society and the Curriculum

Summary

Examinations perform many functions and among the most important is selection for jobs and/or higher education. The educational admission requirements of the professions and the entrance requirements of universities and colleges exert an undue pressure on the secondary curriculum. This is to be seen even in countries like the United States where the level of access is high through the emphasis that students put on good scores in the scholastic aptitude test. In Britain there are signs that the traditional highly specialized study of a single subject for three years in a university is being reconsidered.

In all countries there are also signs of curriculum change in second-level education and much thought is being given to the nature of assessment and examinations. There is much interest in competency tests and associated profile reporting. The chapter concludes with a student illustrated section on the concept of a common curriculum, for at the moment in England, unlike France, it is possible for students and schools to choose from a very wide range of subjects. Those thought to be lacking in 'ability' are likely to take fewer subjects and find their access to both jobs and higher education limited. It is argued that, apart from literacy and numeracy, subject listings depend very much on the cultural heritage in which a curriculum came to be. It is also argued that a simple listing of subjects is inadequate to the task of defining a common core curriculum and that a fundamental rationale is required.

Examinations and the meritocracy

While it is increasingly recognized that individuals will need to be adaptable, and that for this reason some form of continuing or recurrent education is a necessity, the structure of our education systems is such that most individuals finish their formal education between the ages of 15 and 17, and do not subsequently participate in any formal study. In this respect they are hindered by the fact that much further and continuing education is related to the provision of studies for qualifications. The number of people who participate in education for its own sake in adult classes of one kind or another is small.

It is in the context of utilitarian, as opposed to liberal study, that examinations have come to play such an important part for they are essential to the meritocratic society. Their positioning in the structure of that society is related to the positions at which an individual can safely leave the formal education ladder for the career that he or she seeks. A major consequence of the meritocracy is that examinations have to perform several functions and by and large the 'conditioning' of learning is the least of these.

Prime among these functions is the role of examinations as agents of selection. In this respect they measure potential to do a job or pursue a course of study rather than attainment, although the content of the course is often said to have relevance to that job or study. Selection is often made between primary and post-primary institutions of education; it is also made between post-primary (second-level) institutions and the institutions of higher education such as universities and polytechnics. All this creates a downward pressure on the examination system: universities create demands for certain subject areas and certain kinds of subjects which reverberate throughout the secondary school curriculum. The curriculum as defined by the subjects taught in schools becomes dominated by the demands of university faculties, and subjects which could have some importance in the general education of individuals may well be dropped because they are not part of the university requirement. Universities receive the support of the articulate group in society and schools are forced to adapt to the needs of this particular group. Moreover, schools which do not usually cater for this group find that their curriculum 'drifts' toward that which is acceptable to the articulate middle class. But the meritocracy can only function if examinations operate as a syphon that is increasingly selective, and in this sense the all-important examination is the one which is related to the school leaving age. It is an examination (or assessment) which forces the system, pupils and parents to make decisions about the value, for a particular child, of remaining within the educational system. If the examination which the child takes at, say, 16 is academically oriented because it is designed to feed a senior secondary cycle course geared to university entry, then it may not be a satisfactory indicator of performance in terms of the school leaving requirements. At the same time it may also have created a curriculum in the schools which is not suited to the many who, for one reason or another, will be unable to pass that exam.

For this reason there is considerable interest in criterion-referenced measurements which would produce a profile of the child in terms of attitudes, knowledge acquired, and skills developed for courses of vocational preparation of the kind mentioned in the previous chapter. In social terms such measures serve to maintain the elite. However, we have yet to establish the psychological impact of these courses on attitudes and learning, for a person's disposition to his or her place in an examination or society is as important as the place he or she is ascribed. Examinations, as Eggleston (1977) points out, play a major role in the hidden curriculum, for they help children learn what they can and cannot do.

Unfortunately, examination systems are slow to change. They do not

97

respond readily to the changing demands of society which often seem to be hidden from society itself. In this respect children for one reason or another are tending to stay in school for longer periods. The school leaving age has been increased in many countries. In England, related to changes in the school leaving age, there are two examinations, one of which was designed for 15-year-olds leaving school (the Certificate of Secondary Education) and one for 16-year-olds intent on further education of some kind (the Ordinary level of the General Certificate of Education). Since 1971 when the school leaving age was increased to 16, there has been a demand for a common examination, 'the 16 Plus', and the abolition of the CSE and O level. But even so it is very difficult if not technically impossible to examine the total population so that a gaussian (bell-shaped) distribution will be produced. In England it is customary to talk about the 60 per cent who are examinable and the 40 per cent who are not and so examinations are designed for the 60 per cent. This is the major reason for the interest in profile reporting, for it may provide a suitable means of assessing the 40 per cent. It is conceivable that the present two-tier system, if it is offered in all schools, may provide more incentives in 'learning terms' than a single system. Since a CSE grade I pass is equivalent to an O level pass of the General Certificate of Education children may prefer such a pass to a very poor performance in the General Certificate. There is unfortunately no cut-and-dried answer to this problem.

There is however another aspect of the problem. Marshall (1939) (see Chapter 3) makes it clear that the use of qualifications as a means of entry to the professions, semi-professions and trades combined with the lengthening of the school leaving age transfers competitiveness from the world of work to the world of education. Once one is in a track it is difficult to change to another track because the points are few and far between. By the age of 21 most individuals are firmly fixed in tracks; a few are on the fast lines, most are on the slow. Necessarily such structures operate against a general acceptance of the idea of recurrent education, and they assume that an individual's development is predictable and age-related. No concession is made to slow learning, readiness as a general function of learning any subject, or a human being's natural state which is learning, for all action results in learning.

In this respect it is worthwhile putting the question whether in England the predominantly part-time system of higher education which prevailed in the 1950s was, despite the high wastage (Heywood, 1971), more flexible and more open to continuation.

The structure of full-time formal education is reinforced not only by examinations which are essentially age-related but by the system of grants; in Britain it is not easy to get a grant if you return to the system having left it at an earlier stage. So competition starts in school and not merely in the later years of schooling but in those that are early and formative. For example, a recent Scottish study in so-called unstreamed comprehensive schools showed that by the end of the second year (14+)

the pupils were in effect streamed into examination and non-examination groups (Ryrie, 1981), and in some schools the English CSE was introduced to cope with some of the non-examinable pupils in the Scottish single system of examining. Such decisions are based on teacher perceptions of the 'ability' of pupils which legitimate the decisions which they make. In those circumstances:

> 'most students, it appears, simply came to realize sooner or later what the most appropriate thing for them to do would be in the light of their performance.'
> (Ryrie, 1981)

It is no wonder that Scottish investigators like Weir (1980) should call for totally different structures and institutions to provide education at all ages. This experience, on the surface at least, would seem to provide a substantial argument for the retention of CSE in the English system even though it provides yet another hurdle at a relatively early age. Arising from two Committee reports (Scottish Education Department, 1983) new examination structures are being introduced in Scotland.

However, none of these ideas get away from the fact that meritocracies create elites, and the example of the French system over the last 20 years serves to illustrate the point (Halls, 1976). In that system, on transfer to secondary education at the age of 11, and on the recommendations of the primary school teachers, pupils enter into one of three tracks in the same school although parents' wishes are taken into account. Modern I is for the most able children, Modern II for less gifted children who are nevertheless capable of academic study, and Transitional III for the 25 per cent of the pupils who had for one reason or another fallen behind in primary school. Sorting between the tracks takes place after a two-year interval. At 15 the decision is made as to which track the pupil will follow in upper secondary education. Some of these tracks are for technical education which comes under the umbrella of secondary education.

The effect of these structures is that 35 per cent enter a *Lycée* which may be either classical, modern or technical. Studies at the *Lycée* are followed by higher education. The next 40 per cent (Modern II) go to a college of technical education and enter employment at around 18 while the remaining 25 per cent may receive some pre-vocational training before entering employment.

Halls (1976) writes:

> 'According to a pioneer in the reforms, Roger Gal, the orientation process should "try to grasp how there may be developed to the utmost the forces latent in every unfinished personality and seek out in what direction each human being will achieve fulfilment". Thus conceived orientation resembles a turntable which may be adjusted to the direction appropriate for the pupil and send him off on the right track. It contrasts with the selection process, which may be compared to a filter through which all may not pass. But parents fear that orientation gives too much power to the teachers, despite the safeguard that the conventional examination offered as an alternative undoubtedly provides. Consciously or unconsciously, it is argued that teachers may misjudge children.'

This is the kind of power which many teachers in England and Ireland seek when they recommend the abolition of examinations and the adoption of school-based assessment. However, it is not without relevance that 60 per cent of the whole age group in France take a diploma at 15 which does not affect their subsequent allocation in upper secondary education. Moreover, the pass rate is 80 per cent which is analagous with the Intermediate Certificate in Ireland. But it does serve as a terminal examination for those who will leave at 16, and is required for intermediate grades in public administration even though it is not required as a qualification for higher education. Pupils take tests in French, mathematics and a modern language. There is an option in physical education. In this sense there would be a case for the retention of the CSE and the abolition of both O level and 16+. But this would require direction at 16+ and the English might well prefer to have this done by competitive external examinations, for as Boyson argues, 'External marking means that teacher and pupil are allies, not enemies.' (Boyson, 1975).

At the upper level of secondary education in France there are short and long courses. For those on long courses the Baccalaureate examination is the climax of their studies. Similar criticisms to those made of A level are made of the Baccalaureate (eg some subjects are more difficult than others).

The upper sections of the *Lycée* represent the dominant area of study of the pupil but in the final two years of the three-year course, the three options broaden out into five sections. It is interesting to note that philosophy is a compulsory subject although its content varies according to the section in which the pupil studies. The syllabus and level of the six compulsory subjects are weighted so that depending on the section taken some subjects are studied to a greater depth than others. In some respects it resembles the old Higher School Certificate in England (prior to 1951) which had both main and subsidiary subjects. But breadth is achieved at the expense of a longer university course and a much higher drop-out rate from university at the end of the first year.

In France in 1974 it was argued that the tracking system had failed, and in consequence the Minister for Education proposed that it should be replaced with mixed ability groupings, 'setting in certain subjects, or semi-mixed ability grouping or mixed ability grouping in all subjects' (which approximates to the Swedish solution for this age group). One approach already in use in France was to select for the transitional track and choose Modern I and Modern II by alphabetical order. Sadly, even if teachers undertake mixed ability teaching, the aforementioned Scottish study suggests that the net effect will not be largely different because the notion of ability will remain the same.

The French system is very different from that in Britain and it is a system which in the past has not allowed any choice. But its dilemma is no different from that of the British for as White writes:

'Fundamentally, the dilemma of the academic secondary curriculum at this stage arises from attempting to illustrate and exemplify as many different

facts of knowledge as possible, whilst at the same time preparing pupils for
the next stage of education or for employment.' (White, 1971)

Different societies make different responses to this problem. For example
in England, while there has been much experimentation with a 16+ examination, a Certificate of Extended Education has been introduced for those
who stay on until they are 17 or so. It is like the CSE in reverse and
produces the equivalent of an O level but with syllabuses which are
supposedly oriented to the needs of that particular group. This brings us
again to the universities and their influence not only on examinations
but through examinations on the curriculum.

The universities, school examinations and the curriculum

In the British Isles the universities use school examinations of both
Advanced and Ordinary level as their means of selection. In Ireland and
Scotland leaving certificate examinations are used. The candidates take
five or more subjects in all three systems and a minimum competency is
ensured. This is in marked contrast to some American universities which
have to provide remedial courses in English and mathematics (Menacher,
1975).

Nevertheless, in the University of Dublin and Scottish universities
honours degree students take four years as do undergraduates in the
United States. But this is in contrast to the English system where the
majority of courses in the sciences and the humanities are of three years'
duration. This is made possible by the fact that at 16 most university
entrants will, having taken eight or nine Ordinary level subjects of the
General Certificate of Education, participate in a two-year course of
specialist study in three, perhaps four subjects to Advanced level. This
means that by the end of the course they have covered much of the first-
year work which would be done in many courses in universities in Ireland
or Scotland. Unlike the United States, students pursue a specialist study
in a subject (eg history) and not a general liberal arts course (that is,
apart from engineering) in which credits can be collected in a variety of
subjects. Thus at the end of a degree course in the British Isles a student
is highly specialized.

Wilby (1982) has suggested that the job of university entrance could
well be done as it is in America — by sophisticated intelligence tests for
which no cramming is required. (I say university although Wilby uses the
term profession.) The fact of the matter is that many professions use
university or Council for National Academic Awards degrees as exempting
qualifications and take the entry requirements for their own qualifications
to be those required by the universities. So the issue is whether or not a
scholastic aptitude test with a school record should replace A level as a
means of selection. A massive experiment was conducted by the Committee
of Vice-Chancellors in the 1960s to answer this question. The results
led to the conclusion that the A level was as good a predictor as the
experimental test of academic aptitude (Heywood, 1971). From a cost

point of view, the A level makes the British system very efficient.

The comparison which Wilby makes with the Scholastic Aptitude Test is not necessarily a good one. There is a widespread belief in American schools that more work on mathematics will lead to higher scores in the mathematics section of the test. This causes them to study maths at the expense of courses which would be better for their interests and aptitudes (Eisner, 1979).

However, the issue which Wilby raises about the relevance of qualifications is of considerable importance. There is no doubt that the professions and the semi-professions have used educational qualifications as a means of gaining prestige (see Chapter 3) but it is by no means clear that what is learnt is relevant to professional practice. The point is made clearly by Clements and Roberts in respect of engineering technicians when they argue that the mathematical requirements of the Business and Technician Education Council certificates are far in excess of those required for industry. At the same time, technicians do supervisory and managerial work for which they receive little training (Clements and Roberts, 1980).

Wilby's more important point is that the education with which a professional is provided should enable him or her:

'to keep up to date with developments in his profession after he is qualified. The real absurdity of the qualifications spiral — and of the professions argument about the "knowledge explosion" — is that it involves an ever-increasing concentration of resources on initial full-time education in the teens and twenties. Yet in a fast changing society, it is in their thirties and forties that most professional people require extra education.' (Wilby, 1982)

This is a point with which Mant (1979) would doubtless agree.

The contention would seem to be that personal growth in a profession should be a function of both continuing practice and education. The present author has heard the 'heresy' offered by a former chairman of the British Engineering Professors' Conference that the A level in engineering science of the Joint Matriculation Board would be more than suitable (with one or two modifications) as a basic qualification in science for engineers in industry. (He had worked some 30 years in the electrical industry.) Neither are the A levels in maths particularly suited to those needs, yet maths and physics are essential requirements for science and technology studies at university which are carried on and developed in the A level academic tradition. It is possible to argue that the most appropriate curriculum for a BEd degree in design and technology would produce individuals equally capable of working in industry as in teaching. The necessity of having an honours arts degree to teach, say, history at second level might also be questioned. Teaching is a profession which is beginning to recognize the need for the regular provision of in-service training.

The other important criticism of the English system is that it causes children to specialize too early. In Scotland the leaving certificate is necessarily at a lower standard because of the larger number of subjects which are taken. In Ireland there are two levels, pass and honours. But since it is possible to argue that a good grade at the Ordinary level of the General Certificate of Education is equivalent to a pass leaving certificate subject, and since most pupils entering university in England take seven or more O levels, it is difficult to sustain the argument that the English system is more specialized than the others. Indeed some children might benefit in the other systems if they had to take fewer subjects. Nevertheless, the fact that faculty entrance regulations in England require students to take particular subjects (eg science for a science degree, humanities for an arts degree) means that pupils are biased early in their careers. It also means that certain subjects acquire more status, to the exclusion of others. In England, in contrast to Ireland, pupils may choose the subjects they wish to take at Ordinary level since they are not related as in a university matriculation examination where the number taken and level achieved determines whether the certificate is awarded or not. Although minimum entry qualifications require three Ordinary and two Advanced levels the faculties may limit choice. In practice, university entrants tend to take a much wider range of subjects at Ordinary level. But choices have to be made as early as 14 years of age and these will be dictated by children's perception of the career they wish to pursue. It is this early disposition towards specialization that so many find objectionable, for an inappropriate choice of subjects can be very harmful but they forget that children entering higher education are taking seven or eight subjects. Overall the influence of the universities on second-level examinations is such that it minimizes any debate about the nature and purposes of post-primary education. They would certainly not meet the criteria of liberal education as set out by such authorities as Newman in his educational writings (Newman, 1947). While the same is true of the Irish second-level curriculum, all entrants to university take the eight subjects at the intermediate certificate which, in contrast to the British system, offers a restricted range of subjects. Student teachers in Ireland consider this to be a core curriculum, and, as will be shown later, 'believe' their subjects to meet the goals of liberal education. So, like the French system, there is very little choice. At least this simplifies the problem for parents and pupils.

Apart from the influence on choice, every pupil is placed in an examination system which is geared to the entry requirements of higher education. Those who opt for any other scheme which a school may offer also opt for a lower status track. If they remain in the high status track they may have to follow a curriculum which is not suited to their needs. A leaving certificate becomes a matriculation. In Ireland there has been much discussion about the possibility of adding a third year to the senior cycle of second-level education. This additional year would take place after the leaving certificate and would aim at a matriculation for university entrance (Mulcahy, 1981). It is argued that this would minimize the influence of the universities on the content of the second-level curriculum but it is difficult to believe this will be the case unless universities change their curriculum to the kind of liberal arts curriculum offered by many colleges in the United States.

These issues raise questions about the structure of higher education which have only recently bothered critics in Britain. Carter (1983) now considers that the Robbins Committee Report which heralded the expansion of higher education was misconceived, and that this was due to the fact that its recommendations were based on the conventional wisdom of the universities at the time. A recent report from the Leverhulme Foundation (Leverhulme, 1983) calls for two-year rather than three-year degree studies.

In spite of the conservatism of educationalists, changes do take place as, for example, the response to the Munn and Dunning reports in Scotland (Scottish Education Department, 1980), and ideas abound. One response to the problem of choice in England is the concept of the common curriculum and it is with that idea that the next section is concerned.

The common curriculum debate

Introduction

It is appropriate now to introduce some student teacher ideas about the curriculum although the organizing question only partially directs our thinking since it relates to the less able. If, however, it is remembered that 40 per cent of pupils in Britain fail to have their performance assessed, then the question below has a great deal of relevance, as do the student responses even if they do not come to grips with the fundamental philosophy of the common curriculum. This is partially due to the fact that in Ireland it has been traditional for all pupils to take the wide range of subjects necessary to gain an Intermediate Certificate (see example 3. on p 105). Unfortunately, the situation in England with its much greater range of examination subjects, and much greater range of choice, makes that system more difficult to understand. This section begins with an organizing question about the curriculum and is followed by extracts from student examination responses.

Organizing question

'The principle that schooling should be provided which meets the needs of individual pupils conflicts with the concept of a "common curriculum". Discuss this statement with reference to the needs of the children you teach.'

Organizing responses

EXAMPLE 1: RELATING TO MATHEMATICS

'I firmly believe that in the case of my own subject, mathematics, the idea of all students studying the same course is incompatible with the goal of enabling all students to realize their potential. One is, of course, hesitant about aiming ideas that may be interpreted as inegalitarian or elitist but I believe that false adherence to fashionable ideologies is not a good thing — after all that is the antithesis of critical thinking.

I firmly believe that mathematics is an elitist subject in the sense that only a small minority will ever be able to appreciate its structure, power and enormous aesthetic appeal. This is hardly surprising as it represents the pinnacle of human intellectual achievement.'

'The ideal solution then would be three curricula. I feel that the third group should be given a strictly functional curriculum. Scopes reject this as being "joyless" but abstraction when you are incapable of coping with it is "joyless" and also debilitating. After all Bondi has said that the average person only needs a grasp of statistics and their application.'

EXAMPLE 2: THE STUDY OF ENGLISH BUT IN RELATION TO FACTORS INFLUENCING LEARNING OTHER THAN THE CURRICULUM. (THIS IS ALSO A GOOD EXAMPLE OF THE HIDDEN CURRICULUM.)
'There is also the important factor of peer-group pressure. There is a strong ethos, for example, amongst the boys in my classes, that being interested and working at English (and presumably other subjects) is "uncool". Therefore those who are enthusiastic and keen feel pressurized not to become engaged in class activity as much as they would like. There is a strong anti-imaginative writing bias, for instance, which makes it difficult for those who like to express their deeply felt ideas to do so without being attacked as a "sissy" or generally disapproved of. So I would not say that the curricula itself is wholly responsible for the individual's problems, for any group of 25 to 30 exerts its own pressures in the accepted mode of behaviour and kind of interest which is not suited to each individual's needs.'

EXAMPLE 3: RELATING TO A CERTIFICATE-TYPE EXAMINATION AS IS SET IN IRELAND
Emmet I were lucky. The overall common curriculum, the second-level common curriculum and needs of the children overlapped. But Emmet II were not so lucky. Emmet II are just above remedial and so they are expected to sit the group cert. Half of these children will fail the certificate while the other half will probably pass. This class is the debate between the needs of the pupils and the common curriculum in microcosm. I tried to balance the needs of the pupils with the needs of the "second-level common curriculum" but it just did not work. The needs of the children were stronger — they needed to know how to look up a bus timetable not how to look up a table of logarithms.
    In the end then what we call the common curricula and what it has come to be are two very distinct things. With the exam system to a large extent common, I don't think we can ever say we are catering for the real needs of a large section of our pupils.'

EXAMPLE 4: RELATING TO ART AND ITS VALUE IN CREATING SUCCESS
'Of course some of them will be more dexterous than others. I chose media because it did not require precision for the less able, eg pastel is a very "broad finish" medium with quick and effective results. We also used brightly coloured papers. Several other media give a professional and "finished" result with a minimum of skill, though to use them well to exploit their possibilities is obviously an art. However, "success breeds success" and gradually pupils became more interested and tried harder. Before I knew it I had dispelled the idea that "art is an innate capacity", everybody was capable of producing something of a certain level of quality. I was very happy with this because just as everybody can write, and few will be great authors, so also everybody can paint but few will be artists. Again I had not intended this felicitous result; had I been aware of the hidden curriculum I might have striven after it, but occasionally even our faults work for us.'

EXAMPLE 5: RELATING TO ECONOMICS
'On the purely economic side, people are realizing that economic knowledge

is becoming increasingly important if they are to operate efficiently within present day society. Every day they pick up a newspaper, they are reading figures and statistics on the economy given by efficient interested parties . . . Therefore people are formulating opinions as figures and statements that can be conciliatory or contradictory but that they know little about. Formulating opinions as strong as these can make or bring down a government.

It is therefore essential that the future electorate at least will have a basic knowledge in economic affairs . . .'

EXAMPLE 6: RELATING TO MODERN LANGUAGES
'I see modern languages as having a fundamental connection with language in general, language as the common denominator in the curriculum, the key to all subjects and areas of knowledge. I see my subject as a "source of knowledge, a moulder of values, a developer of skills and a way of thinking" . . . I do believe that modern language should be at the core of the curriculum, and hold its place alongside the English language as a developer of the essential skills necessary for learning.'

EXAMPLE 7: ALSO RELATING TO MODERN LANGUAGES
'The aim of developing an awareness and an appreciation of a foreign culture and people is more closely related to the higher cognitive domain, but it also moves into the affective domain where pupils will be expected to receive and respond to another culture, begin to form values and make judgements on it, and organize and characterize the information they receive. This area of foreign language teaching has vast implications for a pupil's whole approach to foreign peoples and cultures, and if approached correctly should help to make the pupil more open-minded and receptive of ideas and customs other than his own. This is essential in life, and unfortunately objectivity in assessing new or strange ideas is too often lacking.'

EXAMPLE 8: RELATING TO SCIENCE
'By introducing pupils to a wide selection of areas from scientific to artistic in a common core curriculum one is providing a person with a wide range of schemata in the brain. This, coupled with an introduction to the skills of problem-solving, is the basis of a liberal education. By providing pupils with integrated courses one is enabling them to develop a wider view. Thus in science, I believe one should stress the concepts, etc, but also the aesthetic, moral, social, mathematical, etc, sides of science. I attempted this year to get the pupils to be creative within the science class. I had realized that most of my homework, etc, were neat, convergent problems so I decided to give the class an essay on "A day in the life of a carbon dioxide molecule". The pupils after the initial shock settled down and enjoyed the work. We also in class had discussions on "Should a scientist work on atomic theory when it could lead to weapons?" It was after trying these things that I realized that many of our subjects were viewed as autonomous and that the method of teaching contributed to this. I think this has the effect of restraining individuality and that a common curriculum which does not view subjects as having strict barriers offers a greater potential for individual development.

Thus I believe that a curriculum which does not have a common core has a danger in that some pupils will miss out on aspects of their education which are essential to their development as individuals. A common curriculum which treats subjects as strict disciplines without stressing interconnections is also I believe undesirable for individual development.

EXAMPLE 9: A COMMON CURRICULUM FOR THE NON-ACADEMIC
'The needs of the pupils I teach are social rather than academic and I feel

more activities and experience could be beneficial. They are being frustrated by failure and a lack of interest in the academic race for results and so tend to join the "delinquent" sub-culture of the school (Hargreaves). I feel such pupils should be exposed to a liberal education that is relevant to their lives today and will be relevant and beneficial in later life. A common curriculum that would include English, maths, local history and geography, cookery, commerce, sewing, basic science, music, art, physical education and sports and such items politics, how to vote, what is a democracy? how do trade unions operate? This would include education for work and leisure as Maritain suggests. We live in a world of vast change, and so pupils must be taught to cope with this, to be adaptable and creative. Leisure is on the increase and so the arts are important. There are areas that all pupils will benefit by, while the range of learning and interest can be created by the teacher. Flexibility in a common curriculum I would also suggest, where a pupil can choose the area he would like to devote time to outside of class, eg choice of project between a few subjects.'

Commentary

There has been a long discussion about the common curriculum in Britain and reference has already been made to Lawton's suggestions for a common culture curriculum (see Chapter 2) (Lawton, 1975). At the present time there is in theory a wide range of subjects which can be chosen for examination which, in practice, is limited by the entry require-ments for jobs. But should such choice be allowed? If we happen to believe with Hirst (1974) that there are a number of fundamental forms of knowledge then we will believe that training in these elements will be the main objective of the curriculum *sine qua non*. White (1971) writes of the 'high culture' to which secondary pupils should be initiated, the com-ponents of which cannot be understood unless the pupils are actively engaged in their study. Everyone should study these subjects until 'they understand why its devotees are satisfied with it'. In principle he seems to be at one with the authors of the French system. His answer to the problem of mixed ability is simply that it is up to the teachers to find ways that are satisfying to the pupils. Yet, even within the French system, there is a third track in the lower secondary school and remedial education is provided both in order to keep within the track and to change between the tracks for it is recognized that pupils differ very widely in aptitude and motivation. Wringe, who is very much a supporter of the forms of knowledge approach, argues that:

'we must recognize that pupils are very differently equipped (for all sorts of reasons to do with their ability (example 1), motivation (example 2), pressure on motivation (example 3) and so on) to make progress within the forms of knowledge. This means that the greatest flexibility is needed in planning approaches which meet pupils on their own terms and truly start from where they are. But this flexibility should always be seen for what it is — namely an attempt to make some initiation into the forms of knowledge a real possibility for all pupils.' (Wringe, 1976)

Of course, as we have seen, it is possible to derive educational needs from an analysis of what individuals require to live, work and vote. After all, the content of knowledge derives from what we do. That what we are able to do creates identifiable and restricted forms of knowledge goes without saying. The crucial factor, it may be argued, is not these patterns but the mental mechanisms of knowledge handling and problem-solving. Looked at in this way a quite different common curriculum might arise as, for example, in the area of mathematics which was also discussed in the last chapter.

For example it would be necessary to make a distinction between a mathematical ability heavily dependent on spatial ability and the numerical ability associated with aptitude tests (MacFarlane Smith, 1964). To get 'inside the subject' might be taken to mean that kind of numerical ability which will enable a person to read quality newspapers (Heywood, 1976) (see examples 1. and 9. on pages 104 and 106).

It is evident that very little 'attempt' to screen the aims of the curriculum in depth has been made and much of what is written about the curriculum is culture bound (see Chapters 9 and 10 and Furst, 1958). The examples suggest that, by the age of 16, the amount which can actually be common to the whole ability range may be rather small. It may also be argued that the Irish experience points to the value of offering three grade levels within a school leaving certificate (eg basic and pass and honours academic) (Heywood, McGuinness and Murphy, 1981). While this seems to support the retention of the CSE in Britain it unfortunately, as we have seen, provokes the issue of status as defined by examination levels.

But it also shows the difficulty of a fixed time curriculum with a fixed school leaving age which cannot take into account the differential learning rate of pupils. In a system where there is much choice, motivation and interest play an important role in learning and may lead to poor performance in some subjects, and possibly more significantly, to not wanting to learn other subjects, a fact which can in some instances be blamed on poor teaching. One has to want to learn a subject to get into it for, as Bruner (1966) says, one learns to be a mathematician by doing what a mathematician does, a view which is held by Mascall (1957) about theology and the theologian. If by reason of ability or some other factor we are put off a subject we will in general not learn it.

If Whitehead's theory (Whitehead, 1933) is accepted, individuals require a stage of romance before they will embark on the detailed study of a subject. This romance can occur at any age and any stage of education. For example, because of the many factors involved in choice and selection it was felt necessary to make liberal studies compulsory for diploma in technology students who, it was thought, would otherwise receive a limited education. However, these students did not like this and rebelled against liberal studies which they felt interfered with their engineering studies (Davies, 1965). When a few years later it was seen that graduates were not required for research they began to see the value of the other studies, particularly in management, as the Nuffield Foundation General Engineering Education project showed. (This is not to say that those students or their predecessors did not do things which would be regarded as 'broadening' in their private lives — they did (Carter, 1983; Heywood, 1969).

All this relates to the present structure of the curriculum and the location of particular subjects and examinations at specified age levels. As the precise relationship between jobs and qualifications disappears the aims of education must require something more than a dependence on either an academic or an economic ideology (Collier, 1982). They must derive from a view of the person as agent in the activity of life (MacMurray, 1957) and for this reason curriculum structures should be seen within the concept of lifelong education. The curriculum has to be seen as a continuum and curriculum theory cannot simply be applied to primary and secondary education without reference to further and higher education, even though it is necessary to argue that pupils should be given a range of insights before they officially leave school.

Bennitt (1982) argued that each subject should offer a series of graded examinations, as is already the case in music. These would start early and may result in some 12-year-old children taking classes with 16-year-olds and vice versa.

An alternative concept of the common curriculum was offered by the present author within the Irish context in 1977. It was argued that:

> 'the notion of the multiple-objective curriculum stems from the view that each subject has something particular to offer as a source of knowledge, a developer of skills, a way of thinking, and a moulder of values. The failure of curriculum development has been its piecemeal approach to the explosion of knowledge. It is only within the context of a multiple-objective curriculum framework that the value of a subject, be it of the traditional or integrated kind, can be perceived. Figure 6.1 is an attempt to illustrate this theory. It shows a part

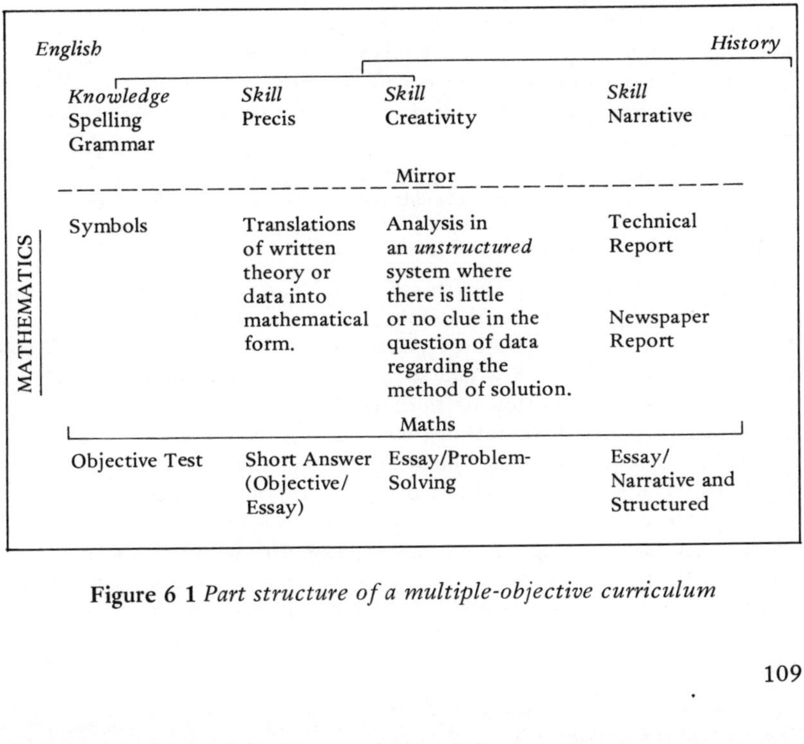
English
History
Knowledge
Spelling
Grammar
Skill
Precis
Skill
Creativity
Skill
Narrative
Mirror
MATHEMATICS
Symbols
Translations of written theory or data into mathematical form.
Analysis in an unstructured system where there is little or no clue in the question of data regarding the method of solution.
Technical Report
Newspaper Report
Maths
Objective Test
Short Answer (Objective/ Essay)
Essay/Problem-Solving
Essay/ Narrative and Structured

Figure 6 1 *Part structure of a multiple-objective curriculum* structure of a multiple-objective curriculum. The subjects considered are English, history and mathematics. The skills particular to English and history (in this example) are outlined in the top half of the diagram. There is some overlap which, in this case, is considered to be desirable. The objectives are stated in terms of the language of the subject.

The same skills are mirrored by mathematics. This time, however, the skills, except for those under narrative, are presented in the terminology of the behavioural method using Wilson's (1970) terminology.

English may aid the development of skills in creative writing. The same view is mirrored in mathematics if skill in the analysis of an unstructured system is developed. (This would correspond to Avital and Shettleworth's level of analysis and synthesis.) Similarly, skill in the writing of narrative using history is mirrored by skill in technical or newspaper report writing. While this may not be regarded as a skill to be developed by mathematics, it might be regarded as an essential feature of the curriculum in which the teachers of English and mathematics collaborate. A multiple-objective curriculum also takes into account the type of learning experience, such as the project, so that the time allowed for each activity is adequate. Timetabling becomes an art which is dependent on the school's theory of education. Development of a curriculum such as this cannot be accomplished without clearly defined objectives.'
(Heywood, 1978)

It may be argued that Hirst's forms of knowledge can be structured in this way. It seems evident that whatever model is used, the debate about the aims of education is of crucial importance and is often treated superficially, particularly at the level of policy-making. White (1981) has made this criticism of a recent paper on the school curriculum issued by the Minister for Education in England and Wales (HMSO, 1981). Apart from the view that its aims are muddled he finds the paper difficult to interpret and concludes that it is illiberal.

A liberal curriculum would lead to an education which would help pupils understand their common humanity and the society in which they live. By illiberal White means a curriculum which is dominated by subjects that occupy key positions — in this case English, mathematics, science and modern languages.

'a diet of basic skills, plus science, a modern language, religious education, physical education and vocational guidance is not going to help the older secondary pupil to understand herself (or himself), her own life and its possibilities and the complex social world in which he lives.' (White, 1981)

None of the authors of this critique would say that the paper met the spirit of example 9., however simplistic it seems. Where, for example, is the discussion about the role of politics in the curriculum or the significance of aesthetics which would seem to be important in a world where people increasingly have time on their hands?

It is striking that those authors who claim, as White does, that a liberal curriculum is required, do not mention the fact that philosophy is taught in French schools and is a subject in the international Baccalaureate. This in turn points to the fact that much of what happens in a country arises from its cultural heritage. For example, Ogborn and Black (White *et al*, 1981) note that British teachers have never been interested in integrated studies; they teach physics or chemistry or biology. In Ireland however this is the norm, for there is only one examination in science at the 15+ level and it is interdisciplinary; teachers who graduate as specialists expect to have to teach the other science subjects. The student example below indicates this willingness. ISCIP, to which the student refers, is an integrated science project for the less able developed by the Dublin Vocational Education Committee's Curriculum Development Unit.

'In my own teaching situation, teaching science to first-years in a vocational school, I am given a very set body of knowledge to be covered, and the methods to be adopted are prescribed in a textbook, lesson by lesson. To simply follow the course from lesson to lesson according to the textbook (which is very good in itself), asking the questions set in it and using the inquiry and methods set out in it, would be a received perspective. The course itself, ISCIP, also involves an element of project work in third year, and to that extent the entire course is a restructured one; however at first-year level it is received. Having covered the first term a week in advance, I then undertook a basic study of the solar system, which I would think would hold a fascination for children of all ages. I started off by considering the position of the earth in relation to the sun, and then went on to consider the other planets, the seasons, day and night, etc, in a very informal atmosphere, and bringing in previously acquired concepts such as gravity, metric units, mass, volume and change of state. The method I used, having no set time to cover any specified material, was dialectical in that it depended on the interaction between me and the pupils and what would be the next step for the next day given the learning outcome of the previous, given my view of the children's interests and my knowledge of the relatedness of the material.'

An even better illustration is the contrast in attitudes of teachers in the British Isles to science and technology to those relating to the junior secondary curriculum in France. Writing in White (1981), Ogborn and Black argue for compulsory science thus:

'to make a limited course in science compulsory for all from 14 to 16, as the further study of science for those not pursuing it in another part of the curriculum, and as a complementary for those who are. This would mean reducing the content of the science subjects (a good thing in itself) to create space for such complementary science. It would have to be a study, not in a science or sciences but about science. A part could usefully be technical, about how to install central heating, control a diet, deal with chemicals in the home, stock and maintain a pond, and so on. This part could usefully be learnt from one aspect of science that ordinary people will pay good money for — magazines which tell one facts, both mundane and astounding. Another part could valuably be a study of problems and decisions relating to science, the problems of control of information, of supplying power, of siting and controlling factories.' (White *et al*, 1981)

The philosophy of this approach is well expressed by one of the students who wrote in an examination answer:

'Pupils need to be honest in the observations and exercise as little bias as possible in their perceiving if they can hope to be objective in their solving of problems of answer situations that present themselves to them. Science as a subject can contribute greatly in such developments as it requires keen and honest observations and if we are to make reasonable hypotheses then we have to eliminate bias in our viewing of the relevant situations. This leads to the need of the pupil to be able to hypothesize reasonably and subsequently make reasonable deductions which lead to action. This is the very method of the scientist and so encouraging the children to take part in such activities helps them answer the associated needs (Bruner). Such "actions" may be in the form of devising an experiment to test the hypotheses, the results of which behave as further information/output/observations.'

So in Britain there are developments toward a compulsory common core science curriculum and the Scottish idea is of special interest since it embraces a competency approach (SEB, 1983). By contrast, in France, science has only a small role in the junior cycle of second-level education. Only biological sciences are taught in the first four years of second-level schooling. Since 1970, however, technology has been introduced in lower secondary schools. The subject has been defined as 'the critical study of objects and simple mechanisms conceived by men for the satisfaction of their needs'. Teachers have been warned against teaching it as a branch of the physical sciences or mathematics. The object is to develop the scientific curiosity of the pupil, to enable him or her to apply reasoning to scientific and technical mechanisms and to bring education closer to real life. It is argued that technology is a way of organizing science for use, which is a mental operation requiring as much intelligence as the understanding of science itself. As such it is a part of the general culture for the present age (Halls, 1976).

The criticisms of the British document on the common curriculum (HMSO, 1981) show that a simple approach, which is almost a straightforward listing of subjects, is no criterion for the design of the curriculum. It is a view that is supported by the study of the educational systems in other countries. Such a curriculum requires a rationale that is at once more critical, a point made by Lawton when he says that the document ought to have examined: 'whether all pupils should be required to come to grips with history and, if so, what kind of history, and why' (White, 1981). Anyone who has worked in Ireland or who has any understanding of the complex relationships which exist between Ireland and England will probably give even more significance to Lawton's comment than he intended. The student example which follows illustrates just how important this issue is.

'During my teaching practice I taught history to fifth-year boys in a vocational school in a working class suburb. They were classed as "post-remedial", ie low ability. They did poorly in all the academic subjects but were reported to do well in woodwork, mechanical drawing and computer science. They obviously had never come to grips with abstract ideas or theorizing, and this was a grave disadvantage in the study of history. Bruner believed that anything could be taught to anybody at any time in an intellectually honest form. I would be more inclined to agree with Gagne that you can teach anything to anybody providing they have the prerequisites. In this case the majority of the boys didn't have the prerequisites — several could read only with difficulty, and their writing was poor. What these boys need is practice at the very basic skills of communication, at organizing their ideas and at developing a critical attitude to some extent at least. I found it very difficult to cater for these basic needs within the confines of the common history curriculum. But to some extent it was possible. Everything had to begin at a concrete level — concept teaching became possible only if we moved through Bruner's enactive — iconic — symbolic stages. For example, we dealt with democracy through a class election, then role-play on decision-making, then discussions of institutions of democracy, then examples of what democracy was not, etc. In doing this the boys gradually came to develop a confidence and their abilities to grasp historical information and their progress improved. I did find that the history curriculum was quite useful in helping the children to come to terms with their own environment – the topics of violence, unemployment, etc, and other concepts they need to understand if they are to make sense of what happens. Violence in particular was an issue which was raised again and again, both in relation to political violence (the IRA, etc) and in relation to personal violence. For many of them the fact was that violence was seen to work, but discussion did help to bring out the other possibilities.'

The reference to violence in this illustration draws attention to the need to develop critical skills in the handling of the media or of coping with the knowledge explosion and moral development with some integrated framework. Clearly the concept of a common curriculum is not an easy one to handle. It is with problems of integration and interdisciplinarity and their role in coping with the 'knowledge explosion' that the next chapter is concerned.

References

Bennitt, C (1982) Down with the competitive spirit *The Guardian* 17 August

Boyson, R (1975) *The Crisis in Education* Woburn Press: London

Bruner, J (1966) *Toward a Theory of Instruction* Norton: New York

Carter, C F (1983) The Robbins Report Twenty Years On *Times Higher Educational Supplement* October

Clements, I and Roberts, I (1980) Industrial needs and course unit structure. What the practitioners say *in* Heywood, J (ed) *The New Technician Education* The Society for Research into Higher Education: Guildford

Collier, K G (1982) Ideological influences in higher education *Studies in Higher Education* 7 (1) pp 13-20

Davies, L (1965) *Liberal Studies and Higher Technology* University of Wales Press: Cardiff

Eggleston, S J (1977) *The Sociology of the School Curriculum* Routledge and Kegan Paul: London

Eisner, E W (1979) *The Educational Imagination: On the Design and Evaluation of School Programmes* Macmillan: New York

Furst, E J (1958) *Constructing Evaluation Instruments* David Mackay: New York

Halls, W D (1976) *Education, Culture and Politics in Modern France* Pergamon: Oxford

Heywood, J (1969) An evaluation of certain post-war developments in higher technological education, thesis, The University Library of Lancaster: Lancaster

Heywood, J (1971) A report on wastage *Universities Quarterly* 25 (2) pp 199-237

Heywood, J (1976) *Assessment in Mathematics* Second report of the public examinations evaluation project, School of Education, University of Dublin: Dublin

Heywood, J (1977) *Examining in Second-Level Education* Association of Secondary Teachers, Ireland

Heywood, J, McGuinness, S and Murphy, D E (1981) *Final Report of the Public Examinations Evaluation Project to the Minister for Education* School of Education, University of Dublin: Dublin

Hirst, P (1974) *Knowledge and the Curriculum* Routledge and Kegal Paul: London

Her Majesty's Stationery Office (1981) *The School Curriculum* HMSO: London

Lawton, D (1975) *Class, Culture and the Curriculum* Routledge and Kegan Paul: London

Leverhulme Report (1983) *Excellence in Diversity: Towards a New Strategy for Higher Education* Society for Research into Higher Education: Guildford

MacFarlane Smith, I (1964) *Spatial Ability* University of London Press: London
MacMurray, J (1957) *Persons in Relations* Faber and Faber: London
Mant, A (1969) *The Experienced Manager: A National Resource* British Institute of Management: London
Marshall, T H (1939) The recent history of professionalism in relation to social structure and social policy *in* Marshall, T H (1966) *Sociology at the Crossroads and Other Essays* Heinemann: London
Mascall, E L (1957) *Christian Theology and Natural Science* Longman: London
Menacher, J (1975) *From School of College Articulation and Transfer* American Council on Education: Washington, DC
Mulcahy, D G (1981) *Curriculum and Policy in Irish Post-Primary Education* Institute of Public Administration: Dublin
Newman, J H (1947) *The Idea of a University* Longmans Green: London
Oakeshott, M (1962) *Rationalism in Politics and Other Essays* Methuen: London
Ryrie, A C (1981) *Routes and Results. A Study of the Later Years of Schooling* Hodder and Stoughton: Sevenoaks
Scottish Education Department (1980) *The Munn and Dunning Reports: The Government's Development Programme* Her Majesty's Stationery Office: London
Scottish Examination Board (1983) *Joint Working Party Report on Science at Foundation and General Levels* Scottish Examination Board: Dalkeith
Weir, A D (1980) A context for technician education *in* Heywood, J (ed) *The New Technician Education* Society for Research into Higher Education: Guildford
White, J P (1971) *The Curriculum: Context, Design and Development* Oliver and Boyd: London
White, J P (1981) *No Minister. A Critique of the DES Paper The School Curriculum* London University Institute of Education: London
Whitehead, A N (1933) *The Aims of Education* Benn: London
Wilby, P (1982) Exam results: the real absurdity *The Sunday Times* 15 August
Wringe, D S (1976) The curriculum *in* Lloyd, D I (ed) *Philosophy and the Teacher* Routledge and Kegan Paul: London

Chapter 7
Synthesis

Introduction

While student teachers see the role of their subject within the totality of the curriculum it is not sufficient to be able to rely on traditional subjects to cope with the changing demands of life brought about by the knowledge explosion. Additionally successful problem-solving often depends on a synthesis of knowledge from more than one subject area. Together, the response to the knowledge explosion and the need to develop the skill of synthesis demand that there should be some studies in the curriculum which are both integrated and interdisciplinary.

Given Whitehead's (1932) theory of rhythm in learning, integrated studies belong especially to the stages of romance and generalization, although some precision is both possible and necessary. There needs to be continuing attention to the romance in the second-level cycle and this may be provided through the inclusion of new areas of study. Various experiments in integrated studies at both second and third level are described. Key concepts are shown to be of considerable value in the design of integrated courses and are illustrated by a middle schools project in history, geography and social studies. The American programme in Man: A Course of Study (Bruner, 1961) is discussed but the main focus in this section is on the British humanities project. Following Adams (1976) the present author concludes that the programme's major value may be in teacher training because of the challenge that it offers the traditional role of the teacher.

In the last section an argument for integrated studies in design and technology embracing studies in technology and society on the one hand and organizational and business studies on the other is presented.

Student responses to examination questions about the role of their own subjects in the curriculum are used to show that, while there is an understanding of their liberal role, more than what is at present on offer is required. Throughout the chapter recognition is made of the fact that the status ascribed to subjects prevents new and valuable developments — a fact which seems to be as true of the curriculum in the United States (Eisner, 1982; Riesman and Jencks, 1962) as it is in Britain.

Education in and through a subject

Organizing question

'We might thus think in terms of a distinction between education in and

education through a subject' (*Teacher Training in the Secondary School*, Department of Education and Science, an HMI Report, 1981).
What is meant by this statement and what implications does it have for the subject you teach?

Some responses to the organizing question

1. MUSIC AND THE ENRICHMENT OF LEISURE THROUGH CRITICAL THOUGHT
    'There is so much to learn *in* the subject of music, and yet so much to learn *through* music. One of the most obvious benefits of musical knowledge and appreciation is that it enriches the leisure time of a person very much. This is especially important today in a world which is offering a greater concept of leisure time. It is essential, therefore, to train children in school to develop interests during leisure. The music teacher stands in a strategic position in relation to this. Often a student is learning about the various concepts and principles of music; he also has to develop the skill of critical thinking. This is aided by the encouragement of critical listening to music. The student is encouraged to listen for the form of a song or a piece to try and recognize the style of the composer through his use of harmony, melody, counterpoint, orchestra, etc. If a student has been trained to develop such skills in listening, his appreciation of music is greatly deepened and so his leisure time is greatly enriched. The student has also gained the aesthetic experience of music. He appreciates its beauty to a much deeper level. This further develops a person's ability to be independent, not only physically but mentally. His greater physical independence is due to the fact that he may not need company as often as possible, since there is great fullness and comfort in music. This benefits his independence of mind also, because he is experiencing a healthy isolation through his listening.'

2. HISTORY, SCIENCE AND MORALS
    '. . . science teaching can easily be related to history. For example, when dealing with nuclear power the question of nuclear weapons is bound to come up and reference can be made to Oppenheimer's contribution to the ending of the Second World War. In fact a discussion could be held not merely about the morality questions involved in dealing with nuclear weapons but also about nuclear power itself. For example, shortly after that accident in Long Mile Island in the US about a year or two ago, the number of miscarriages around the area increased significantly. Such matters might well be discussed with children.'

3. HISTORY, THE MEDIA AND AUTONOMOUS LEARNING
    'School does not prepare pupils for life. It does not educate them to cope with the influence of the media. I think that a subject like history can develop these skills within a pupil so that he/she will be able to cope with "unseen" situations in later life . . . For example, television has become a source of history. Many historical programmes are now viewed by thousands of young people every week. The claim that the camera cannot lie is a fallacy. Pupils should be educated in this. These historical programmes provide a good opportunity to educate the pupils in this. An example which comes to mind is that of Kee's history of Ireland. How objective was that? One could discuss the use of music and symbolism which Kee used to get his point across. Another example is the history of the papacy as illustrated by the Borgias. How accurate was that? From the use of these illustrations one could use history to train children to be more critical of what they see on television. The same is true for newspapers and the question of bias. History textbooks provide excellent examples of how the evidence of two people can differ so radically. One could get two pupils in class to write an account of an incident. The two stories would be completely

different. This would help them to see the uncertainty of history and of the
life which they are facing. No question has a definite answer; no situation
can be interpreted solely in one way. It is this transferability which is important.
Bruner argued that it forms the basis of motivation and autonomous learning.'

4. MATHEMATICS AND THE DEVELOPMENT OF JUDGEMENT
'. . . every subject can help a pupil perceive things as they are, ie develop skills
in objectivity. Mathematics can help the pupils in that they must perceive what
it is they are being asked to do (ie what does the question require of them).
 All subjects aid the development of language. Mathematics does this in that
it encourages clear, concise, precise expression. Mathematics can also contribute
to many other areas. For instance, it contributes to the aesthetic sense in that
it develops a sense of *order*, seeking patterns in numbers, etc. A sense of
symmetry of form can also be developed. Contributions to creativity are made
in that the pupil formulates a problem and must arrive at a solution (self-
initiated).'

5. MATHEMATICS AND OTHER SUBJECTS
'How can I as a teacher of mathematics help a student be aware that not all
knowledge is of a rational nature? I can do it by introducing the notion of
creativity in mathematics — by showing that man does not always function in
a logical manner. Poetry may be seen as man's expression of his sickness
and union with an aspect of reality. He does not plan a poem, usually, but
rather allows his thoughts to take the shape of the poem. Koestler postulates
that invention is one of three forms of creativity. Mathematics is suitable
breeding ground for invention of formulae and so forth. One can emphasize
the origin of many widely accepted formulae and often show how they came
in a sudden flash of insight.'

6. ENGLISH AND FRENCH: COLLABORATING WITH OTHER TEACHERS
'Knowledge of the vernacular language influences performance in most other
subjects on the curriculum. In this way, I consider myself to have been teaching
a general education *through* my subject this year.
 The first time I encountered this was when the French teacher spoke to me
about co-operating with her in teaching a first-year class. She explained to me
that she was having great difficulty teaching her class adjectives and adverbs
in French. She felt that this was because they did not understand these concepts
in English. We decided to work together on grammar. I would teach adjectives
to my class and the next day in French class she would teach adjectives in
French. This worked very well for both of us in grammar teaching as the pupils
received reinforcement of their learning in the French class.'

7. LEARNER-CENTRED LANGUAGE TEACHING AND
   COLLABORATION IN CHEMISTRY
'When I walk into my classroom I do not essentially perceive myself as a French
or Spanish teacher but rather as a facilitator of learning whose primary aim is
to do all that is possible to enable the learners to acquire the knowledge, skills,
values and strategies for them to achieve their highest potential. . . The social
interaction in the language classroom — role-making, role-playing, group work,
project work, games, activities, etc, all help the child to understand that school
is not divorced from society; it is an integral part of society and enables the
child to learn how to develop interpersonal relationships.
 . . . in finding opportunities for meaningful communication I have directed
pupils' attention to their own lives at school. When one day we (second year
students) were discussing recent "flops" in cooking — the cakes which did not
rise in the domestic economy class! — I realized that our explanation of the
rising power of yeast was essential. I consulted the chemistry teacher and

checked out the validity of a science experiment using yeast, sugar — a bottle and a balloon — which shows how a chemical reaction takes place and carbon dioxide is given off. This, in turn, inflates the balloon over the bottle. I then devised a set of work cards with simple instructions in French and illustrations of the various steps in the experiment. Ten minutes one day was spent explaining the reaction between yeast and sugar in French and then I distributed a set of introductory cards to five groups with instructions concerning what was to be gathered for the experiment. There was an air of anticipation and excitement — the children did not know exactly what we were going to do (arousal, expectancy functions) as the cards illustrating the step by step procedures were not distributed until the following day in the science lab. They all arrived complete with balloons, bottles of sugar, spoons, etc and I provided the yeast which in the introductory lesson I had passed around for them to handle, feel, smell, etc.'

Discussion

In their criticism of teacher training the British Inspectorate argued that secondary teachers were too subject-oriented and did not see the place of their subject within the wider perspective of the curriculum. The organizing question at the beginning of this chapter was set to see how our trainees reacted to this view and the examples which followed would suggest that these trainees, at least, had a wider perspective of their subjects which they were able to illustrate in practice. It is evident that they regard developments in the affective domain to be as important as those in the cognitive, and that often the two are seen to go hand in hand. This is not to say that such views should be accepted without questioning, especially as to whether such enrichment really takes place. Perhaps, too, these respondents had a particular view of what the examiner wanted but it has to be said that they are representative of the spontaneous responses given during discussions on this topic. It would seem that subject-orientation is something that develops after initial training.

However there is another question which is raised by these extracts. 'Is it sufficient to rely on broadminded subject specialists for the achievement of the aims of education when these are expressed in terms of the cultural goals of society, the "knowledge explosion", and the ways in which problems are solved?' In the sections which follow it is argued that this is not sufficient and a theory of integration (integrated disciplinarity) is suggested, followed by descriptions of some attempts to develop integrated studies at both second and third level.

Synthesis: the integrating ability

Synthesis is that ability which draws from many subject specialisms and pieces them together in the unique pattern dictated by each and every problem.

In higher education the subjects of teacher education and management are integrating subjects. Unlike history, geography and mathematics they bring together a range of disciplines in the solution of practical issues which occur in the classroom or on the shop floor. In planning a lesson a teacher is at once a subject specialist, strategist, philosopher, sociologist and psychologist. In implementing the lesson he or she is subject specialist and psychologist and, if involved in disciplinary problems, he or she requires both moral and social dimensions to his or her way of thinking. This is true in any walk of life, be it the family and the housewife, interpersonal relationships in the street or on the shop floor. More often than not, however, we have very little information on which to base our decisions and so we 'play it by ear'. In this way, intuition and experience come to be highly valued, and often they lead to wrong decisions if the new experience is not treated as a learning situation (Hesseling, 1966; Heywood, 1982). Thus in the British Isles most people value practice and are terrified of the academic. This attitude has created a dualism which has afflicted thinking about educational method and curriculum, and nowhere is this better illustrated than by developments in engineering education in the universities (see Chapter 3).

Engineering education, the world of work and the need for synthesis

In 1963 when the Robbins Report (CMND 2154) was published the Committee drew attention to a well-known study by Hutchings (1963) of six-formers in Britain. It showed that students entering engineering departments at universities had poorer qualifications than those entering physics departments. This created a furore in engineering departments, for over the years engineering departments had turned themselves into engineering science departments and could in many respects be called applied physics departments. So much so was this that industrialists complained that their courses were suitable only for research and development and that far more graduates of the 'wrong type' were being produced than was necessary (Bosworth, 1963). A survey by Lee (1969) supported these contentions by showing that many engineering graduates felt that laboratory work was good because it was the only time in their courses they experienced an identity with engineering.

In 1962 Furneaux reported that examinations in mechanical engineering, with the exception of engineering drawing, all measured the same kind of limited ability. One interpretation of his results was that, because the examination questions tested the application of mathematics to problems in applied science, they were all testing in terms of *The Taxonomy of Educational Objectives* (Bloom, 1964), a restricted skill of analysis which would produce a single solution (Heywood, 1968). Furneaux suggested that there was a need both to clarify and examine for specific objectives. Following on from this, D T Kelly and the present author designed an examination for the Advanced level of the General Certificate of Education in engineering science which was intended to develop the key skills required for the application of science in design (Heywood and Kelly, 1973).

In order to obtain approval from schools for this examination it had to be accepted by the universities as equivalent to physics, and so had to have much in common with physics. However there were several significant differences as, for example, a major 50-hour design project for assessment in schools. But the present author was never able to persuade the Examination Board that there was a need for a syllabus component in design although a note on design was eventually included in the *Notes for Guidance* (JMB, 1972).

As a subject which 'failed' (as measured by the numbers taking the course) it is of considerable importance in the study of educational innovation in Britain. Its significance in this context was that it gave rise to a new style examination which attempted to test specific objectives in its sub-tests, and that in the coursework students would be expected to make a considerable synthesis of information through investigations and design-and-make activities. The examiners also argued that the teaching approach could influence attitudes toward engineering and listed desirable attitudes to be fostered in the course in the syllabus. The acceptance of such views represented a quite remarkable change in the thinking of the Examination Board.

It is not without significance that the low status subjects in universities and schools are often those which draw together a range of information from a variety of subjects in the solution of problems, as for example design and technology and home economics. The traditional approach is in-depth study for single or joint subject honours which is primarily analytical and critical.

This point is laboured because it would seem that the primary objective of an integrated studies programme is to develop the skill of synthesis or, if you prefer, skill in the solving of problems to which there is no perfect answer and for which a variety of data is required. The present author believes that the development of the skill of synthesis is more important than programmes designed simply to cope with the explosion of knowledge. An interdisciplinary programme which simply causes the students to study two subjects is not necessarily interdisciplinary unless specific steps are taken to ensure that it is. This point may be illustrated by the Man, Industry and Society programme which was designed by the present author in 1971 for A level in response to a perceived need to complement the engineering science syllabus mentioned above. The aims of this programme were:

1. To assist school leavers to adapt more quickly to the environment of industry by giving them some familiarity with industrial principles and practices and with some of the specialist terms employed in industry.
2. To assist young people to communicate fruitfully by providing some understanding of the roles, objectives and problems of people in industry.
3. To give an appreciation of the principles underlying the behaviour of individuals and groups in corporate situations and to use these principles in the study of current industrial problems.

4. To illustrate the constraints imposed on individuals and companies by legal, social and economic considerations and to examine some of the current issues facing industry and society in relation to these studies.

5. To develop creative and critical thinking and to enhance confidence in the use of the knowledge and skills gained throughout the course by emphasis on the development of skills in the transfer of learning.

6. To appreciate the dynamics of social and technical development and their interaction (by history).

It was anticipated that a variety of learning strategies would be required if these goals were to be achieved. The syllabus headings were (a) Man the Inventor and Innovator, which included notions of creativity (psychology), the design process (engineering) and organization structures for effective innovation (organizational behaviour); (b) Man, Society and Technological Change, which included the industrial revolution (history), its characteristics (behavioural sociology), social structure and institutions (sociology) and interactions between technology and man, resources and the price of labour (economics); (c) Man and his Economic and Social Environment, including studies of the concept of wealth, the trade cycle and technology and society; (d) Man and the Third World; (e) Living with Management, with two major sub-titles, (i) Man and (ii) Organizations, and (f) Techniques and Practice in the Handling of Projects.

The interdisciplinary nature of the study is self-evident although its effectiveness would depend on the skill with which the examinations were designed to draw out the syntheses. Unfortunately it did not find favour because schools required it to satisfy university entrance requirements before they would embark on such a course.

Integrated and interdisciplinary studies have been developed at all levels of education (Newell and Green, 1982). Some of these developments as they relate to particular aspects of the curriculum (eg the role of the teacher, theories of motivation and the curriculum and school design) are discussed below. The examples have been chosen to illustrate certain features of the curriculum and are not described in full.

The first two examples come from the University of Liverpool. Although they began in the early 1970s there was no collusion between the two teachers, even though the participants were known to each other. One was undertaken in the Department of Industrial Studies in the Faculty of Engineering Science and the other in the School of Education. This gives some idea of the difficulty of implementing innovation in the university context when there are no formal mechanisms within the university for bringing the innovators together. It also indicates indirectly the reluctance of university departments to seek help from their own education departments who by and large are accorded low status, yet as will be shown on p 127, the educational project was based on a similar idea to the School of Education Project and had in the present author's opinion a better conceptual framework.

Industrial studies at Liverpool

Mention has already been made of the fact that industrialists were highly critical of the products of universities and in particular their attitudes toward industry. In the second half of the 1960s the Faculty of Engineering Science introduced a programme of orientation lectures on various aspects of industry. By 1969 the Faculty had created a Department of Industrial Studies for this purpose. Its major function was to provide a service course on the engineer in society for the Department of Mechanical Engineering. This was a requirement for membership of the Institution of Mechanical Engineers. This course was 72 sessions in duration. The Departments of Building, Science and Electrical Engineering also took modules from the course. Between 1970 and 1973 courses were developed for joint honours with science courses and at the general degree level as a third course in the third year of the programme. Although the Department helped a three-year honours degree programme in engineering science and management, it was not given responsibility for the course although a third of the work was to be in management.

When the present author joined the Department the main teaching load was carried by Dr N Carpenter with very limited help from other departments (eg Law). Although the engineer in society course is but a single unit within a very extensive three-year programme, the Institution of Mechanical Engineers and Council of Engineering Institutions' syllabus was very broad. It demanded study in the areas of the history of technology, industrial relations, personal management, economics, financial and production control. To accommodate the course Carpenter had designed a series of modules, some of three sessions' duration, some six and others 12. The course was examined by continuous assessment and examination (Carpenter, 1975). The present author's task was to develop the courses in the areas of economics, history, industrial relations, personal management and organization theory, all of which had to be achieved within 32 sessions. The courses have been described in detail elsewhere (Carpenter and Heywood, 1973; Heywood, 1974). By the second year Carpenter and the present author were planning the course objectives. One group of objectives is shown in Figure 7.1 (see p 123).

An integrated course cannot approach the problem from the viewpoints of the individual subjects from which it is desired to take the concepts for integration; nor can it approach them from the traditional subject viewpoint. One cannot precede a course on organizational theory with full courses in sociology and psychology. Nevertheless, without certain basic concepts from these disciplines the treatment of organizations must be descriptive and based on current practice. The problem was to see if it was possible to develop certain concepts out of a discussion of practical problems for in this way students may be encouraged to develop the problem-finding skills which Livingstone (1971) in his critique of the Harvard courses thought industry needed. Some concepts were selected and formed one of the core themes for all subsequent courses. The choice was eventually determined by the ease with which concepts

Basic areas in which knowledge is to be acquired	Understanding and skills to be developed	Attitudes which it is desirable the student should develop
Factors contributing to the social and economic behaviour of individuals or organizations. Attitudes to economic growth and technological and social change. Problems of innovation and achievement and the motivation of individuals and groups. Applications to current problems such as advanced and underdeveloped countries, pollution, population growth and resource conservation.	Ability to relate individual and corporate acts to their global consequences. Understanding of real facts in situations which are currently highly charged with emotion.	Appreciation of the value and limitations of historical studies in explaining current situations. Appreciation of the interactive nature of our economic and social situations and problems; of the need for analysis and synthesis in situations where controlled experiments are impracticable.

Figure 7.1 *Extract from a statement of objectives for a course in industrial studies for students of engineering and science*

such as role and stereotype could be derived from practical issues as a means of understanding these issues.

The first lecture programme failed on four counts. First, some of the concepts discussed were presented in too abstract a form. Second, in order to achieve integration the general themes of the lectures became obscure. Third, because of an awareness of the well-known limitations of the lecture (McKeachie, 1962; McLeish, 1968) the printed notes were arranged in such a way that students would have to complete the essential principles. This was to avoid excessive notetaking and provide reinforcement, but in the event it led to disintegration and the method was abandoned half way through. Detailed sets of notes were then printed which were complementary to the required reading. The associated lectures were discourses dealing with complementary themes to the reading. In retrospect it was evident that no clear links existed between the first course (which was basically about organizations) and either the examination or the required reading. The course was teacher-centred and the students were not involved in case studies. The cases were illustrations within the notes which were referred to in the lectures.

The examination at the end of the first course was disappointing for it showed that some students did not read widely and that others had difficulty with the reading. Many of the answers, particularly in the area of industrial relations, were opinions unsupported by evidence and the standard could be put at O level of the General Certificate of Education.

To try to remedy these defects a number of changes were made in the second course. First, prior notice questions were used. The students were told that the questions in the June examination would be taken from a list of questions issued at the beginning of the course. These questions were in the traditional form of a statement from a book followed by some action phrase like 'discuss'. The questions were selected from three books carefully chosen for their brevity and skill in synthesizing and analysing a range of factual and sometimes uncertain information. The questions were also selected in such a way that the student would have to read all of the material in order to answer them. This approach was found to be effective and many respectable answers were presented.

Second, each student was required to present a substantial seminar. Traditionally students in science and engineering attend lectures and laboratories; thus the idea of an oral presentation of a piece of critical thinking for discussion by their peers was an unfamiliar activity for most of them. The object of the exercise was to get them to read yet another book, in order to critically review the text and to back up, by logical argument, their reasons for agreeing or disagreeing with the views on industrial relations presented by the authors. In this way it was hoped they would learn to be more objective in their approach to matters of common opinion, gain some understanding of the method of sociological analysis, rid themselves of prejudices and evaluate their own efforts in comparison with their peers.

Fortunately, most of the small groups had sufficient diversity of opinion to make for satisfactory debate and it was evident that the students enjoyed the exercise. They did far more work than was expected and each student was provided with a copy of his or her work. The seminars were constructed around the texts which were associated with the prior notice examination and then used to exploit the basic themes and enlarge on them through particular attention to the illustrative material. Among the themes were (i) the idea of organizations as open and closed systems; (ii) the idea of a firm as a social technical system; (iii) an awareness that each new situation had to be considered on its own merits; (iv) the idea that the view we have of humanity has a profound influence on our behaviour toward others; (v) to give students an insight into types of study quite different from their own and to increase the level of understanding between scientists and non-scientists; and (vi) to help students to adapt themselves to the industrial environment with minimum stress and to be effective in this environment as quickly as possible.

For example, in relation to the fifth theme, although there was no historical section as such within the prepared notes, the first chapter outlined the history of the trade union movement, and the section on innovation was introduced through a brief note on the recent history of technology. This section aimed on the one hand to lead the student to a judgement about the characteristics which go together to determine the productive potential of a technology and to look at cause and effect in the development of technology on the other. In order to avoid a simplistic view, the behavioural sociology of Homans (1969), who specifically discusses causation in relation to the industrial revolution and entrepreneurship, was introduced. Through using history as a lead to the understanding of present-day problems (but still under the heading of innovation), issues such as the extent to which industry initiates industrial trends, rather than solves the problems created by the general movement of industry, provided a framework for a discussion of the interrelations between science and technology, and the role of government in innovation and its implications for management.

In the third year a joint honours course was introduced. Substantially more time was available and experiential learning procedures were introduced. One of these, at the time, was relatively novel, for instead of approaching the problem of 'interviewing' by filmstrips, lectures or classroom demonstrations, the students were split into four groups and asked to (i) read the available literature on interviewing and (ii) make a documentary on interviewing. Four excellent 20-minute video-tape films emerged from this exercise. Although the students thought the exercise was well worthwhile they suggested a reorganization and restructuring of the strategy. The examination question on interviewing was, however, poorly done but this was probably due to the fact that the students did not consider the topic in seminar after they had done their project.

Educational implications: theoretical and practical

The introduction to the course textbook which the students used is probably unique for that period in that, written for engineering and science students, it contained a description of an educational theory in its preface. This was Whitehead's rhythmic theory of mental growth which suggested that all learning begins with a stage of romance which is followed by stages of precision and generalization (Whitehead, 1932). The purpose of the course, it was said, was primarily to provide a stage of romance with some precision, for the solution of human problems necessarily involved an integrated approach, and in the initial learning these responded to the need for romance. The examination questions and coursework assessment procedures responded to the need for precision, for they required wider reading and a greater depth of understanding. The experiential learning activities belonged more to the stage of romance. All learning begins with romance for it is interest which drives us forward and it is the inability to cope with the circumstances we find that drives us away from learning. Whitehead (1932) wrote of this stage that the subject matter is novel and 'holds within itself unexplored connections with possibilities half disclosed by glimpses and half concealed by a wealth of material'. In this stage knowledge is not dominated by systematic procedure. Such a system as there must be should be treated piecemeal, *ad hoc*.

We continually enter into cycles of romance and sometimes we pursue them through to generalization. In this theory the subject discipline belongs to the stage of precision. The stages of romance and generalization clearly benefit from an integrated approach to knowledge even when it is on a narrow scale as is evident from Whitehead's treatment of education in mathematics (Whitehead, 1932). The student examination responses indicate that there needs to be continuing attention to them in the second-level cycle and this may be provided through the inclusion of new areas of study.

Students who take 'subjects' for the first time at school or university will find them difficult if they are not first introduced to the romance of the subject. This is part of the problem in the transitions from primary to post-primary school and school to university. For example, in some universities it is possible to read philosophy as an interest subject in a first-year course. If it is approached as an ordinary honours course with methods appropriate to the stage of precision, the course will in all probability conflict with the perception which philosophy has for students who are interested in the solution of practical problems. In consequence they are likely to be disappointed with the course and withdraw. These rhythmic cycles are a matter of everyday experience and it is the speed with which the stages are passed in learning new material which differentiates the adult from the child as well as the adult's ability to be selective.

But is there a reason why such a curriculum should not be followed in schools and so better prepare pupils for life? Life and work are processes which require the continuous integration of widely disparate packages of knowledge for which an understanding of the humanities and the social sciences is essential. Yet there are other, and probably better, ways of achieving integration than through the use of rather general themes as, for example, in the use of 'key concepts'. However, before describing a middle school programme which utilizes key concepts there are two other aspects of this development which merit discussion.

First, the type of activities which can best achieve aims in subjects where the affective domain is as important as the cognitive often require more time than is allowed for by a university or school timetable. Educationalists have as yet to examine the implications of their learning theories for school timetables.

Second, it has been argued that school examinations only test the cognitive and for this reason should be abolished (Masters, 1982; Ryrie, 1981), but there are equally valid arguments against this view. It is true that examinations are concerned with a whole range of cognitive skills, but they must inevitably be value-oriented. That is to say the judgements which are made will more often than not be value judgements and such judgements depend on the totality of the human disposition. Examination and assessment procedures in an integrated study of this kind should force students to think about their disposition in relation to the major assumptions made about human beings, industry and society. Nowhere is this better illustrated than in the training of general practitioners.

'Surgical operations involving the replacement of human organs tend to place the surgeons and close relatives of the patient in the role of vultures waiting until an injured or seriously ill person can reasonably be declared dead. The distinction between homicide and post-mortem dismemberment of a corpse becomes very narrow and dubious. The educated person must confront these value conflicts and relate various patterns of behaviour and their effects to his own values. Failure to relate the cognitive and affective is simply an unwillingness to take a stand on what constitutes good education . . .'
(Dressel, 1971)

Much more has to be done to relate the two domains but that is no reason to deny the positive effect that a well-designed examination can have on learning. The problem with public examinations, as shown in the last chapter, is that the subjects which they examine acquire status and make it difficult for the examining system to respond to changes made necessary by the knowledge explosion, and in particular by our improved under-standing of human behaviour. In the future much greater attention will have to be paid to ways of integrating knowledge prior to studies in precision, and in this respect the 'key concept approach' has much to offer.

Key concepts

The best known programme to use key concepts in the British Isles was the Liverpool middle schools programme in geography, history and social studies for the age range 8 to 13, which was sponsored by the Schools Council. It had as its objective the production of materials for these subjects, whether taught separately or in combination. The principal emphasis was to show how, with some examples and handbooks as a guide, teachers could be helped to develop procedures and materials appropriate to their own situations. A substantive illustration of its application to second-level geography by G Plunkett is to be found in *Pitfalls and Planning in Student Teaching* (Heywood, 1982).

The Liverpool team feel that a course cannot be imposed on teachers, for the commitment of the teacher cannot be guaranteed when everything is done for him or her. They were well aware of what had happened in the Nuffield Curriculum projects about which Waring had written:

'Again by 1966 there was considerable evidence to show that normative re-education on course or in seminars is not necessarily sufficient to sustain change once teachers return to their normal setting, and that mere possession of knowledge does not guarantee its use.' (Waring, 1979)

Likewise the model used for the Irish 15+ studies began with the principle that teachers should be trained to design and develop their own examinations (Heywood, 1977). Murphy in his evaluation of part of that project showed that, apart from the social pressures preventing change in schools, those teachers who were committed to the new approach experienced great difficulty in internalizing the concepts put to them in a way which would not only make them their own but cause them to develop them further (Murphy, 1976).

The Liverpool team borrowed and modified the idea of the 'key concept' from the work of Taba in the United States. Key concepts are procedural devices to help teachers in the selection and organization of course content.

An American study of 16 college courses has shown that in 11 of these courses the concepts were used in a linear hierarchy and that the most important key concept was the most inclusive one used. In all but one of the courses the key concept had the preordinate role (Donald, 1982). For example, in Figure 7.2 (see p 129) the whole of the physics course shown is seen to be built around the concept of 'wave shapes'. In contrast to courses in the humanities (eg English) where the concepts often followed a linear formation, the branches in the physics tree went from the more important to the less important concepts. Donald (1982) states that these differing formats suggest different learning patterns. For example, the key concepts in science are more tightly structured than those in English, while those in the social sciences are loosely structured with certain key concepts acting as pivots or organizers. This seems to be the sense in which the Liverpool middle schools project use their key concepts which are shown in Figure 7.3 (see p 130), and it is evident from these examples that that is the way they would have to be used in the design of integrated courses. Derricott and Richards (1980) of the Liverpool team discuss the relationship between key concepts and the disciplines of knowledge:

> 'A theme planned in the way that this project advocates should not lose sight of the distinct nature of the contributory disciplines. There are, however, difficulties. Key concepts that are high-level abstractions which over-arch several subjects can have an epistemological status that they do not possess. They may even impose upon children an idiosyncratic structuring of ideas about society, in place of traditional and tried disciplines that they have superseded.'

The Liverpool middle schools project is of interest for two other reasons. First, the course team stated six fundamental abilities (objectives) which they hoped would be developed during the course, but they also gave equal weight to social and physical skills. These are set out in Figure 7.4 (see p 130). Apart from giving a direction to the activity, this schema provides a relatively simple method of profile assessment in the school, given that it is scaled in a more sophisticated way than a series of numbers. Teachers everywhere need to know what a good or bad performance is. Descriptive scales have been developed by several examining authorities which illustrate this need. Assessment, whether we like it or not, involves discrimination and those who want to take into account the assessment of factors other than the 'cognitive' have to recognize this as well as the fact that such assessments can be very unreliable. Moreover, once one enters into this field, allowances have to be made for both school and family background. This 8 to 13-year-old project also throws light on this problem for the Liverpool project team felt that the pupils would perform in such a way that discriminations could be made in the area of interests (Figure 7.5, p 131) and attitudes and values (Figure 7.6, p 131).

Reproduced by kind permission of Janet G Donald and the Editor of the
Journal of Higher Education from Knowledge structures: methods for
exploring course content *Journal of Higher Education* 54 (1) pp 31-41

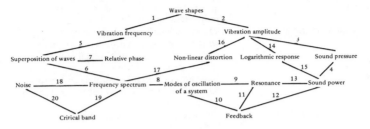

(a) Tree structure of key concepts in a physics course

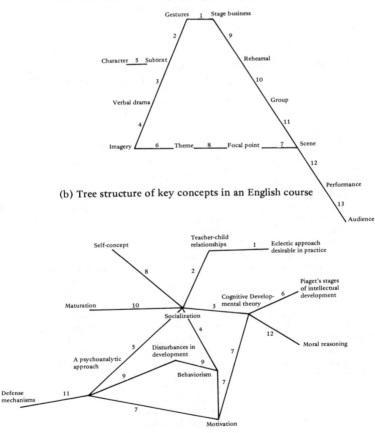

(b) Tree structure of key concepts in an English course

(c) Tree structure of key concepts in a developmental social psychology course

Figure 7.2 *Key concept structures in physics, English
and developmental psychology*

1. Communication	—	The significant movement of individuals, groups or resources or the significant transmission of information.
2. Power	—	The purposive exercise of power over individuals and society's resources.
3. Values and Beliefs	—	The conscious or unconscious systems by which individuals and societies organize their response to natural social and supernatural disorders.
4. Conflict/Consensus	—	The ways in which individuals and groups adjust their behaviour to natural and social circumstances.
5. Similarity/Difference	—	Classification of phenomena according to relevant criteria.
6. Continuity/Change	—	Distinction of phenomena along this essentially historical dimension.
7. Causes and Consequences	—	The notion that change in a state of affairs can be attributed to the phenomena preceding.

Figure 7.3 *Suggestions for key concepts in history, geography and social sciences for 8- to 13-year-olds* (Blyth *et al*, 1973)

Skills

Intellectual	*Social*	*Physical*
1. The ability to find information from a variety of sources. in a variety of ways.	1. The ability to participate within small groups.	1. The ability to manipulate equipment.
2. The ability to communicate findings through an appropriate medium.	2. An awareness of significant groups within the community and the wider society.	2. The ability to manipulate equipment to find and communicate information.
3. The ability to interpret pictures, charts, graphs, maps, etc.	3. A developing understanding of how individuals relate to such groups.	3. The ability to explore the expressive powers of the human body to communicate ideas and feelings.
4. The ability to evaluate information.	4. A willingness to consider participating constructively in the activities associated with these groups.	4. The ability to plan and execute expressive activities to communicate ideas and feelings.
5. The ability to organize information through concepts and generalizations.	5. The ability to exercise empathy (ie the capacity to imagine accurately what it might be like to be someone else).	
6. The ability to formulate and test hypotheses and generalizations.		

Figure 7.4 *Skills to be developed in history, geography and social science for 8- to 13-year-olds* (Schools Council Project) (Blyth *et al*, 1973)

Interests which it might be possible to discriminate between:

A Child:

1. Who shows a passive interest in people and physical features of the environment.
2. Who considers, willingly, questions asked by teachers about the environment.
3. Who asks, willingly, questions about the historical, geographical and social science features of the environment.
4. Who collects, spontaneously, materials from the environment for observation.
5. Who has a strong desire to find out things for himself or herself about the environment.
6. Who is enthusiastic about a particular set of interests related to the environment.
7. Who recognizes that others identify him or her with a discrete but evolving set of environmental interests.

Figure 7.5 *Schools Council history, geography, social science project age 8 to 13* (Blyth *et al*, 1973)

Attitudes and values which it might be possible to discriminate between:

A Child:

1. Who acquiesces in response to attempts to develop a study of the environment.
2. Who responds willingly to a study of the environment.
3. Who shows awareness of the variety of ways of studying the environment and of testing ideas and hypotheses.
4. Who shows awareness of the variety of ways of communicating the findings of his or her enquiries.
5. Who is wary of over-commitment to one framework of explanation and is alert to possible distortion of facts and omission of evidence.
6. Who is willing to identify with particular attitudes and values about the environment and relates these to other people.
7. Who has a characteristic set of attitudes and values but remains open to change.

Figure 7.6 *Schools Council history, geography, social science project age 8 to 13* (Blyth *et al*, 1973)

Second, the project was associated with a particular development in British schools called middle schools which were intended for pupils in the age range 8 to 13. It seems that by and large they emerged as a function of the reorganization of secondary education and, following their creation, it seems that those responsible for them had to justify them in educational terms. This they did in terms of the child-centred ideology and the cognitive developmental theory of Piaget (Blyth and Derricott, 1977; Derricott and Richards, 1980).

The 8 to 13 study at Liverpool was an attempt to work out a curriculum for the middle years of schooling related to a system of organization which, if it is to be a: 'new and progressive force, must develop further curriculum methods and attitudes which exist at present in junior schools. It must move forward into what is now regarded as secondary school work, but it must not move so far away that it loses the best of primary education as we know it now' (Plowden, 1967).

The Liverpool team took a broad developmental view and designed a framework intended to lead the child from pre-disciplinary to disciplinary activities and through three levels of concept development. Level I concepts are specific, closed, easy to define, narrow in scope and can be experienced through the senses or through carefully evoked experiences using language, movement and drama. Level II concepts are not so readily experienced and more difficult to evoke, while Level III concepts are the 'key concepts', broad in scope and open to differing interpretations and meaning. For example, they give a teacher an illustration of the key concept of communication for differing ages as follows:

8+ Transport in local setting. Local road patterns. Local transport services.

9+ National network of motorways. Railways. Airports. Why is the pattern as it is?

10+ Barriers to communication and how these are overcome. Crossing rivers, estuaries.

11+ Communication through the media. Newspapers, radio, TV.

12+ Advertising. Can we believe all we are told?

The team's experience challenges the view that children cannot accept the uncertainty of there being no unique answer to a particular problem either cognitively or emotionally until mid-adolescence. They also note that children gain in confidence through the increasing capacity of being able to ask as well as answer questions.

People and society

Not content with his studies in the psychology of learning, Bruner also developed Man: A Course of Study which has had an influence on developments on both sides of the Atlantic. Its place in 'The Humanities Jungle' is well described by Adams (1976).

'The content of the course is man: his nature as a species, the forces that shaped his humanity: three questions recur throughout:

What is human about human beings?
How did they get that way?
How can they be made more so?

We seek exercises and materials through which our pupils can learn wherein man is distinctive in his adaptation to the world and wherein there is a discernable continuity between him and his animal forbears.' (Bruner, 1966)

So Bruner is led to compare humans with their ancestors and other animals in a five-dimensional framework, that is as toolmakers, language creators, engineering social organization, with a prolonged childhood, and the urge to explain the world.

The course developed by Bruner which is provided with materials, film, games, books, etc, is designed to meet the requirements of his own theory of instruction which at the time underlined the importance of process as opposed to product in learning (Bruner, 1961) but it is not based on totally free enquiry or child-centred education. Materials for its use in Britain have been developed by the Centre for Applied Research in Education at the University of East Anglia but they are only sold to teachers who have been thoroughly trained in their use.

Jones (1972) makes the point that there are many ways of achieving the aforementioned goals, and Adams (1976), in a substantial analysis of this project, argues first that the model of human beings used in the production of materials is very much the American middle class white; second, that the male and female roles are stereotypes of traditional thinking: 'Mother does the shopping and drinks coffee with the neighbours' (Adams, 1976); and third that there is a cultural bias in the materials.

Adams also suggests that the study neglects the affective domain although this argument has been refuted by Dow (1970) who directed the development of the programme in the United States. The selection of materials and the methods of teaching, especially questioning, do involve the affective domain and this is a view which is supported by Bruner. But Adams suggests that the materials (myths and poetry associated with a section on an eskimo family in this case) are used but not *felt* or *understood* by the pupils. It is the issue of notional versus real assent and it is clear that involvement in the affective domain through the cognitive is difficult and has to be planned. It has also to be recognized that much of what happens affectively is neither measurable nor open to observation by teachers.

The effect of the materials on children may not be that which the educators want to obtain. Adams says that several films involving the killing of animals made him squeamish. There is much harshness and violence even in the marketed version of the course which causes him to ask:

'Is there any gain in giving young children pictures in which they see animals skinned alive in this way, or are we simply adding to a general coarsening of the sensibilities that studies of this kind can all too easily induce?'

It is surprising that, in a course which has been the subject of so much research, evaluations to test the influence of the materials on children's sensitivities have not been made. Questions about the effect of courses are as important as questions about the effects of the media even though the answers are difficult to come by.

Adams goes on to suggest that there was a marked change in Bruner's thinking between 1961 (Adams, 1976) and the publication of *Relevance in Education* in 1972 (Bruner, 1972). There was a shift away from the importance he attached to the 'process' of learning toward the significance to those things that have relevance to a particular child's learning. Adams illustrates this point by two quotations from Bruner which are presented here from his discussion:

1. 'Let me say a word about a point of view quite different from ours. It holds that one should begin teaching social studies by presenting the familiar world of home, the street, and the neighbourhood. It is a thoroughly commendable ideal; its only fault is its failure to recognize how difficult it is for human beings to see generality in what has become familiar. The friendly postman is indeed the vicar of federal powers, but to lead the child to a recognition of such powers requires many detours into the realm of what constitutes power, federal or other, and how, for example, constituted power and wilfully organized force differ.' (Bruner, 1966)

2. 'Could it be that in our stratified and fragmented society, our students simply do not know about local grocers and their styles, local doctors and theirs, local political activists and theirs? And don't forget the styles of local bookies, aspiring actresses, or illegitimate mothers. No, I really believe that our young have become so isolated that they do not know the roles available in society and the variety of styles in which they are played. I would urge that we find some way of connecting the diversity of the society to the phenomenon of school, to keep the latter becoming so isolated and the former so suspicious.' (Bruner, 1972)

Adams comments that the pursuit of 'generality' to the neglect of the 'friendly postman' underlies the lack of understanding of other 'life styles' and the consequent progressive alienation of the schools from society that Bruner deplored in 1971.

In terms of the previous discussion on the relationship between theory and practice, there is clearly a shift from the Platonic to the position of MacMurray (1954) who argues that our theories derive from the need to solve the practical and whose emphasis is on the self as agent in the process of discovery.

Adams is led to argue that the course is better suited for teacher training.

'Most teachers, at whatever level of education, could learn much about the process of education by working through the study. The teachers too, being generally at a later stage of intellectual development than their 11- or 12-year-old pupils, may be able to transfer from the enactive process of learning to an ability to formulate more abstract conclusions from their experiences.' (Adams, 1976)

One approach to the study of the humanities in Britain

Organizing examples from student responses to an examination question

1. ON DEVELOPING INDEPENDENCE
'If we look at the need of the pupil to gain independence, the curriculum doesn't really go anyway toward helping this need. As an adolescent grows he needs to be given more and more responsibility so as to achieve independence. The curriculum doesn't allow this. With the examination system being so competitive students and teachers are forced to get through the course first so that the pupil can do well in the examination and there is very little responsibility put on the students' shoulders. Instead it is firstly on the teacher to get the pupil through the exam.'

2. IN RESPONSE TO QUESTION ON THE INFLUENCE OF TECHNOLOGY IN THE CLASSROOM
'Despite all that has been written about the ability of the computer to act as a tireless, personal tutor, it is necessary for the child to be motivated to learn first of all, and secondly, someone has to write a program for the computer. Apart from this the exclusive use of computers in teaching smacks too much of an exclusively behavioural objective approach to teaching. As Stenhouse remarks in his book on *Curriculum Development and Research* teaching is much more than a matter of proceeding expeditiously in the direction of one's self-imposed objectives. It should be a more opportunistic affair, with the teacher exploiting all chance occurrences in the classroom to aid the learning process. The computer on the other hand is limited in its response by the fixed number of variables the program has allowed for.'

3. ON VALUES AND INDOCTRINATION
'Today our values and ideologies are selected in all subjects of the curriculum. It is important that education incorporates current social values because it is only then that the student will fit into the society. This is not to say however that we indoctrinate the young with these values but rather that we present them for analysis. It is not therefore to become a platform for the individual teacher to indoctrinate his or her own personal values either since this would be in conflict with the democratic ideal and may also be in conflict with the values of parents.'

These three illustrations serve to introduce a quite different approach to the humanities developed by Stenhouse (1970) for the lower half of the ability range. The first draws attention to his goal of turning pupils into students, the second indicates the spirit of his approach to teaching, while the third is yet another reminder of the central problem of 'values' in any humanities curriculum.

The humanities project

A pluralist society, with its various philosophical and theological dispositions, will produce a corresponding variety of approaches to the humanities. For people with a religious disposition the aim of understanding their fellow human beings will be developed within the context of religious education and much work has been done in this area (Hull, 1982). To some extent the influences on any humanities project must be cultural and inspection of examinations in Christian Responsibility serve to illustrate this view. In England religious education is the only compulsory subject in the curriculum whereas in Ireland religious education is not compulsory for it has no need to be. There is as yet no school examination in religious education although a leaving certificate is intended. In a pluralist post-Christian society there is a need to protect the rights of minorities. In a Christian society this problem should not arise although small minorities in Ireland would dispute this proposition.

In pluralist societies anything that is done in this area is likely to be controversial and so it has been with the humanities curriculum project sponsored by the Schools Council (Stenhouse, 1968). This was undoubtedly one of the most successful curriculum projects undertaken in Britain (Munro, 1977). The project is associated with Stenhouse, who directed it and subsequently wrote a book on curriculum development. Its remit was clearly interdisciplinary:

'To offer to schools such stimulus, support and materials as may be appropriate
to the mounting, as an element in general education, of enquiry-based courses,
which cross the subject boundaries between English, history, geography,
religious studies and social studies. The project is expected to concentrate
upon such support as will in particular meet the needs of adolescent pupils
of average and below average academic ability.' (Quoted by Adams, 1976)

This principle applies as much to technology as it does to the humanities
which must be borne in mind when attempts are made to cope with the
explosion of knowledge through integration. It is illustrated by the
approach of the Institute for the Sociology and Politics of Work in
Germany which aims to establish a single theory for work at the conceptual level and to bring together as much sociological, economic
and psychological information as possible at the data level (OECD,
1972; 1974).

Since the purpose of the humanities course was to devise materials
for consideration by the pupils in areas of understanding where there
can be real differences of opinion, it is not surprising to find that the
course hinged on small group discussion with the teacher.

Stenhouse (1970) asked the teachers who were involved in the project
to act as chairmen of these discussions but to remain neutral. 'The
teacher as chairman of the discussion should have responsibility for
quality and standards in learning.' (Stenhouse, 1970). This concept of
neutral chairmanship was provocative in the teaching world as it
demanded a change in the role of the teacher and provoked the comment
that teachers cannot be neutral. Stenhouse and his evaluator Elliott
(1971) argued that neutral chairmanship is a 'procedural role' and in
any case pupils know that teachers are not impartial. They also know
that teachers are not experts on every subject under the sun. Discussion
methods have been used over the years in higher education where there
have been many different attempts at syndicate learning (Collier, 1983).
They have as their purpose the development of critical thinking which is
the essential skill that university students in the humanities have to
acquire.

Stenhouse argued that the purpose of the course was to turn the
pupils into students and thus teach them how to learn. He was not
unaware that the successful implementation of the course in a school
could have profound consequences for the organization of the school,
since the students would be able to articulate their own views about its
management.

Notwithstanding the problem of neutrality, it is clear that the
selection of materials which are to contribute to the discussions is also
value-laden. It is the opinion of Adams (1976) that the materials have a
left-wing, middle class bias being progressively liberal humanist in their
position. For this reason some teachers of a different persuasion might
find it impossible to use the materials and Adams argues that teachers
can only use materials they respect.

'This is of course to restore the teacher to more of his traditional role as
initiator than Stenhouse would allow for but, although his position is one that

I can both understand and sympathize with, it does not seem to me one that in the end I am able to accept. This does not mean necessarily a return to an authoritarian position: it could, and in my view should, imply a more democratic pattern of work with the teacher and pupils together engaged as partners in a dialogue in which they are both participating members.'
(Adams, 1976)

Adams goes on to argue that the long-term value of the project is likely to be the contribution it has made to our understanding of classroom discussion and techniques for its conduct. As with so many other projects, the need for in-service related training is made abundantly clear. In a society in which organized religion has only a small role the search for school approaches to humanities, which are concerned with the problems of living, is bound to continue. Stenhouse is likely to remain influential in this field.

The subject jungle

Despite the views of the students at the beginning of this chapter, it is clear that achievement of those aims of education which will fit a person for life and work can only occur in a haphazard way by education in and through the traditional subjects. The experiments in the humanities reported in this chapter show new ways of developing curricula and greater understanding of the significant features in learning. Even so they only deal with the aesthetic side of the curriculum or with science and technology.

The demands for new subjects are great. The much misunderstood demand (by those who make it) to make education relevant to work is opposed by those who, like Barker (1982), argue that the basic subjects should come first, and that economics (for example) should not be included in an already overcrowded curriculum. He argues against Warnock's view that moral education is the key for it will give employers what they want (Warnock, 1982).

In contrast to France and Ireland the English curriculum allows schools very considerable freedom. The Boards which examine the Certificate of Secondary Education allow schools to submit and examine their own syllabuses (mode III). There is some mode III work in the General Certificate of Education where eight matriculation boards offer schools this possibility. The range of subjects offered in the traditional mode is wide. There are as many as six different approaches to mathematics as compared with the single unified approach in Ireland.

Contrast the brief discussion about science in English schools with technology in French schools in the last chapter. Given the British Government's view that education should prepare pupils for work it should surely be trying to change the curriculum so that technology has higher status. Yet technology is a low status subject usually associated with woodwork and metalwork. During the last 10 years there has been a substantial endeavour to change these subjects and now the area of most rapid growth is design. Despite this growth it is unlikely to gain status if the case of engineering science is anything to go by. Nevertheless, very much larger numbers of students will take design as a subject, but like mathematics there is a proliferation of subjects in this area, as Figure 7.7 (p 139) shows. (Add to the list electronics and control technology to give some idea of the range.) Some of the special features associated with these papers are also listed. Thus there are developments in materials and processes which replace the traditional divide between woodwork and metalwork. Some syllabuses require design-and-make projects: others do not. Two syllabuses emphasize skills in the development of design such as those described in Chapter 5. Others relate design (or technology) to society and call for a basic understanding of economics and the way technology and society interact. Several of the syllabuses recognize the importance of technology. One or two relate their studies to business.

These courses have been developed without cognisance of what it is people do at work. For example, had the course designers looked at what engineers do (Youngman *et al*, 1978) they would have found a range of skills are required, and that such courses do not need to place heavy emphasis on mathematics (Clements and Roberts, 1980). There would also need to be considerable emphasis on practical work involving design-and-make activities. Integration would require that business skills relating to decision-making and organization be incorporated which, except for content, are not different from the skills of learning (Holt, 1977; Juniper, 1976). They would require the provision of business games, case studies and role-playing, through which life skills would be developed, for such skills cannot be developed without content (McPeck, 1981).

The purpose of these last few paragraphs has been to illustrate the potential value of an integrated approach to the study of design and technology in schools as an alternative to the traditional science-based curriculum. Focused on design, the integrated approach requires the development of a wide range of skills for solving technical and inter-personal problems. No attempt has been made to work out a programme or to examine the ways in which the structure can respond to the needs of the different ability groups. It also seems clear that such an approach (which may be made highly responsive to individual needs) in the sixth form might provide a two-year course of substance which, while related to work experience, would nevertheless be in the education rather than the labour system.

The provision of such courses would require substantial changes in our attitudes to science as well as in the training of teachers. For example, such training would provide intending teachers of design and technology with the possibility of an alternative career in business, given the findings of Clements and Roberts (1980) on what is actually done at work! More generally, support for an integrated approach in this area is to be found in the document *Understanding Design and Technology* which came from the consultative committee of the Assessment in Performance Unit (Department of education and Science, 1982). The Committee argues that abilities in this area relate to design, planning, implementation and

Traditional	Geometrical (Technical) Drawing Metalwork Woodwork Workshop Technology	These are developments with definitions of aims and objectives leading to improved examination.
Recent developments (craft-based)	Design	A level AEB – emphasis on development of design skills. But no requirement for activities and projects in the use of tools and machines to make things. Requires study in the influence of economics, environment and culture on design. Includes awareness of electronic circuits and their uses. Science syllabus includes control systems, force and work.
	Design and Technology	A level/O level London exam papers encourage skills in hypothesis forming, generation and evaluation of alternative solutions and decision-making. O level calls for study of materials; A level calls for study of production techniques.
Recent developments (science-based)	Technology	O level Cambridge: positive and negative aspects of the interaction between technology and society. Detailed study of three of structure pneumatics, mechanisms, electronics. Materials or polymer-technology.
	Elements of Engineering Design	A level Cambridge: syllabus is of interest because of particular aspects of applied science which are selected: especially mechanics. O level courses include a course on materials and method.
	Engineering Science	A level JMB includes written paper on project planning and design: 50-hour design-and-make project. Notes for guidance give aims in the affective domain.

Figure 7.7 *Trends in technological subjects in Britain indicating some characteristics of the examination syllabuses*

evaluation, that knowledge is required in the technological concepts of control, energy and materials, and that technology is never free of value judgements which occur in the technical, economic and aesthetic domains. Integrated studies pose all sorts of problems for the curriculum. While they provide romance and respond to the need to develop the ability of synthesis, there is also a requirement for depth study in the disciplines if pupils are to learn to handle problems. However, the education system is almost wholly devoted to this stage of grammar (precision), and this prevents the development of the 'whole' person, because it is a stage which only acquires meaning in the context of work and life.

References

Adams, A (1976) *The Humanities Jungle* Ward Lock: London

Barker, B (1982) Why our belief in self help can be a hindrance *Times Educational Supplement* 27 August

Bloom, B (1964) (ed) *The Taxonomy of Educational Objectives* Vol 1 Longmans Green: London

Blyth, W A L and Derricott, R (1977) *The Social Significance of Middle Schools* Batsford: London

Blyth, W A L, Derricott, R and Cooper, K (1973) *History, Geography and Social Science: An Interim Statement* School of Education, University of Liverpool: Liverpool

Bosworth, G S (1963) Towards creative activity in engineering *Universities Quarterly* 17, p 286

Bruner, J S (1961) *The Process of Education* Oxford University Press: Oxford

Bruner, J S (1966) *Towards a Theory of Instruction* Oxford University Press: Oxford

Bruner, J S (1972) *The Relevance of Education* Penguin: Harmondsworth

Carpenter, N (1975) Continuous assessment and student motivation in management studies *International Journal of Electrical Engineering Education* 12, p 5

Carpenter, N S and Heywood, J (1973) Undergraduate preparation for industry: a design for learning *Proceedings of the Design Activity International Conference* The Design Research Society: London

Clements, I and Roberts, I (1980) Industrial needs and course unit content *in* Heywood, J (ed) *The New Technician Education* Society for Research into Higher Education: Guildford

CMND 2145 (1963) *Higher Edcation* (Report of the Robbins Committee) Her Majesty's Stationery Office: London

Collier, K G (1983) *The Management of Peer Group Learning: Syndicate Methods in Higher Education* Society for Research into Higher Education: Guildford

Derricott, R and Richards, C (1980) The middle school curriculum, some uncharted territory *in* Hargreaves, A and Tickle, L (eds) *Middle Schools Origins, Ideology and Practice* Harper Row: London

Dressel, P (1971) Values, cognitive and affective *Journal of Higher Education* 42, p 400

Donald, J G (1982) Knowledge structures: methods for exploring course content *Journal of Higher Education* 54, p 31

Dow, P (1970) Teachers book No 6, The Netsilik eskimos at the inland camps *Man: A Course of Study* Education Development Centre: Cambridge, Massachusetts

Eisner, E W (1982) *Cognition and the Curriculum: A Basis for Deciding What to Teach* Longmans: New York

Elliott, J (1971) The concept of the neutral teacher *Cambridge Journal of Education* Easter issue

Furneaux, W D (1962) The psychologist and the university *Universities Quarterly* 17, p 33

Hesseling, P (1966) *A Strategy for Evaluation Research* Van Gorcum: Aassen

Heywood, J (1968) Technical education *in* Butcher, H J (ed) *Educational Research in Britain* University of London Press: London

Heywood, J (1974) American and British influences on the development of a transdisciplinary course on the engineer and society *Proceedings of the ERM division annual conference American Society for Engineering Education* 12

Heywood, J (1982) *Pitfalls and Planning in Student Education* Kogan Page: London

Heywood, J and Kelly, D T (1973) The evaluation of coursework in engineering science in England and Wales *Proceedings of the Third Frontiers in Education Conference* Institute of Electrical and Electronic Engineers: London

Holt, K (1977) *Product Innovation* Newness-Butterworth: London

Homans, G C (1969) The sociological relevance of behaviourism *in* Burgess, R L and Bushell, D (eds) *Behavioural Sociology — The Experimental Analysis of the Social Process* Columbia: New York

Hull, J (1982) (ed) *New Directions in Religious Education* The Falmer Press: Lewes

Hutchings, D G (1963) *Technology and the Sixth Form Boy* Oxford University Department of Education: Oxford

Joint Matriculation Board (1972) *Notes for the Guidance of Schools: Engineering Science at the Advanced Level* JMB: Manchester

Jones, R M (1972) *Fantasy and Feeling in Education* Penguin: Harmondsworth

Juniper, D F (1976) *Decision Making in Schools and Colleges* Pergamon: Oxford

Lee, L S (1969) Towards a classification of the objectives of undergraduate practical work in mechanical engineering, MLitt thesis, University of Lancaster: Lancaster

Livingstone, J S (1971) The myth of the well-educated manager *Harvard Business Review* Jan/Feb

MacMurray, J (1954) *The Self as Agent* Faber and Faber: London

Masters, K (1982) The real world of school *Catholic Pictorial* 8 August

McKeachie, W J (1962) Procedures and techniques of teaching: a survey of experimental studies *in* Sanford, N (ed) *The American College* Wiley: New York

McLeish, J (1968) *The Lecture Method* Cambridge Institute of Education: Cambridge

McPeck, J E (1981) *Critical Thinking and Education* Oxford University Press: Toronto

Munro, R G (1977) *Innovation: Success or Failure* Hodder and Stoughton: London

Murphy, D E (1976) MEd thesis, School of Education, University of Dublin: Dublin

Newell, W H and Green, W J (1982) Defining and teaching interdisciplinary studies *Improving College and University Teaching* 30, p 23

Organization for Economic and Cultural Development (1974) *Interdisciplinarity: Problems of Teaching and Research in Universities* OECD: Paris

Organization for Economic and Cultural Development (1975) *Future Structures of Post Secondary Education* (Two volumes) OECD: Paris

Plowden, Lady (1967) *Children and their Primary Schools* (Two volumes) Her Majesty's Stationery Office: London

Riesman, D and Jencks, C (1962) The viability of the American college *in* Sanford, N (ed) *The American College* Wiley: New York

Ryrie, A C (1981) *Routes and Results: A Study of the Late Years of Schooling* Hodder and Stoughton: London

Stenhouse, L (1968) Humanities curriculum project *Journal of Curriculum Studies* November

Stenhouse, L (1970) *The Humanities Curriculum Project: An Introduction* Heinemann: London

Waring, M (1979) *Social Pressures and Curriculum Innovation. A Study of the Nuffield Foundation Science Teaching Project* Methuen: London

Warnock, M (1982) *Times Educational Supplement* 27 August

Whitehead, A N (1932) *The Aims of Education and Other Essays* Benn: London

Youngman, M B, Oxtoby, R, Monk, J D and Heywood, J (1978) *Analysing Jobs* Gower Press: Farnborough

Chapter 8
Evaluation and Accountability

Introduction

Nowhere in teacher education is it more difficult in the absence of experience to deal with such topics as curriculum, school evaluation and professional and public accountability. Although student teachers soon formulate views about accountability as the examples from their responses to examination questions in the middle sections of this chapter show, some of the organizing responses, and especially those at the beginning, have been taken from work for masters' degrees.

Evaluation and accountability have in principle the same ends in view. They are concerned with the extent to which pre-specified outcomes have been attained and the factors which have influenced or impeded their attainment. Historically, evaluation came on the scene first, and was concerned with curriculum projects. Evaluations were conducted both internally and externally and many questions were raised about the purposes of evaluation (eg for whom and for what?) and in consequence the role of evaluators. There remains much confusion about the role of evaluation. There was a considerable debate about methodology and the traditional scientific model based on testing came in for heavy criticism. A new model, given the name illuminative evaluation, based on anthropological procedures, emerged. In this chapter it is argued that the problem is not measurement as such but when and what to measure. An investigator has to be aware of the range of available techniques. Evaluation is an activity which allows for changes in tactics as the evaluation progresses: it can only ever be 'partial'.

Accountability as an activity finds itself with much the same problems but since it is concerned with the performance of teachers in the classroom and schools, it is a much more emotional issue as the student examples on p 153 show. The idea that accountability can be measured simply by testing the performance of pupils is rejected. Performance of both teachers and pupils, like curriculum innovation, is greatly influenced by management attitudes and organizational structure. The argument that since teachers are professionals they should be responsible for what goes on in the classroom is rejected on the grounds that they are inadequately trained for the task, have a restricted notion of professionalism and that, in any event, society has an input to make on curriculum decisions. Nevertheless, teachers need to develop skills in self-evaluation which can only come with reflection on experience. In-service staff development is therefore essential because initial training can only provide a framework of ideas.

Defining accountability

'My interpretation of this term is that professional accountability refers to the concern and interest shown by teachers (both as a professional body and as individual teachers) for all aspects of their work from curriculum design and evaluation, through effectiveness of teaching methods to measurement of behavioural outcomes in students. The term would embrace Hoyle's notion of extended professionalism which stresses aspects of a teacher's work other than those confined to the classroom. Concern and interest in the professional aspect of their work would need to be monitored by both internal and external checks to ensure that standards in the above mentioned areas were being maintained.'

Predicting teacher attitudes to accountability

'With respect to professional accountability I expect to discover as a result of a survey of teachers' attitudes that:

☐ teachers are sceptical about being evaluated on the basis of pupil accountability;
☐ they have a restricted professional perspective;
☐ they are discontented with the present system of control and evaluation;
☐ they do not feel competent to execute evaluation of self, curriculum and pupils with any degree of skill, due to lack of training.

As a result of these findings, a system of accountability along the lines of the self-evaluation schemes adopted by many English Local Education Authorities would not be appropriate unless there was greater investment in teacher education, greater opportunities for teachers to develop competence related to curriculum development and evaluation, and greater opportunities for professional recognition.'

Evaluation and evaluators

The projects described in the previous chapter were undertaken in a large number of schools and in Britain substantial funds were found for their development by the Schools Council and the Nuffield Foundation in particular. Both in America and Britain there was concern about the effectiveness of projects in terms of dissemination, student learning and teacher participation and, in consequence, evaluators were assigned to project teams. Sometimes, as in the case of the environmental studies project financed by the European Economic Commission in the Dublin Vocational Educational Education Committee Curriculum Development Unit, an external evaluator was assigned (Callan, 1982). In other cases, as for example the Liverpool middle schools project and the humanities project, the evaluators worked with the projects (Cooper, 1973). In the science for arts project at Lancaster the evaluator was invited to participate in the project by the lecturer concerned (Heywood and Montagu-Pollock, 1976).

Evaluators have to decide what is to be evaluated and this is determined in no small measure by their employer. Most of them prefer to use the

143

term 'client' instead of employer for often the funding agency has no direct expectation of them so the determination of who one's client is becomes an important issue. For example, in the case of the Dublin project, was the evaluator's client the EEC who financed him, the Irish Department of Education, the project unit whose work he evaluated, or the teachers for whom the project was intended? All these groups would have different expectations of him. (Sometimes evaluators are called 'stakeholders'.) Equally important decisions have to be made by evaluators about their roles. For example, should they adopt an action-oriented approach and try to influence the direction the project takes, or should they stand back and simply present their observations for discussion by all concerned? Essentially these are the issues in project accountability and evaluators may have fewer problems if they are seen in this light.

Clearly an external evaluator is in a much more difficult position than an internal one, for it is easy for a project group to argue that an external evaluator was unsympathetic to them and did not really understand their mode of operation. Equally, an internal evaluator can be isolated by the project group. The situation may be complicated if both sides have to report to a steering committee which is not sure of its own powers. (The present author has witnessed all these situations.) But these problems also raise the issue of the responsibility of the project team not only to the evaluator but to the sponsoring agencies which may include the financial sponsor and a university, and the extent to which they should respond to the recommendation of an evaluator. Each of these issues has to be resolved and it is evident from the reported case studies that all sides need clear remits in terms of the role of the evaluator and purposes of evaluation. No wonder that early in the history of evaluation the purposes, problems and techniques associated with it became a major study, and that by the end of the 1960s the American Educational Research Association had produced a series of monographs on evaluation (Scriven, 1967).

A major contribution to the debate about method, which was very influential in Britain, was by Parlett and Hamilton (1972) who argued that the anthropological model of investigation was more appropriate to educational situations than the traditional input-output measures based on the scientific model of verification. The next section is a paraphrase of that particular debate about method. Following Munro (1977) it is concluded that the problem is not measurement but when and what to measure. There still remains, as we shall see, much confusion about the purposes of evaluation.

Evaluation as illumination

In Britain by 1972 a controversy had arisen over the appropriate methods for evaluation. Parlett and Hamilton (1972) argued that the traditional input-output model used in testing was inadequate for the task because:

(a) Such programmes allowed for little or no change during the period of study.
(b) Large samples must be used in order to achieve randomization or the experiment must be strictly controlled. The former is expensive in time and resources. The latter involves the manipulation of personnel which may be unethical.
(c) Large-scale sampling smoothes out local perturbations which may be important.
(d) It often ignores the questions posed by various interest groups.
(e) Quantitative methods restrict the design of the study and may neglect other important data which is disregarded as being 'subjective', 'anecdotal' or 'impressionistic'.

Scriven (1967) helps us to understand this attack on the traditional mode of research which uses tests when he draws our attention to the areas which an educational innovation is likely to influence. At one level it is likely to affect pupil performance and expectations. A test will tell us about the former but not the latter. At another level it is likely to influence teacher performance and expectations, which tests can tell us little about except by inference. Finally, at yet another level, the expectations of other people can be changed as, for example, parents when they hear the results of their children's performance in examinations. But there are likely to be equally important effects on administrators and taxpayers.

Since traditional evaluation methods were associated with intelligence testing, it is not surprising that Parlett and Hamilton's critique found a favourable response among many educationalists. They proposed an alternative model which they called 'illuminative evaluation', in which the educational researcher recognizes that:

'he is being addressed by the products of human experience — an experience which he understands in a different way than any mere organic process is understood. Hence, rather than simply impose his own methodological scheme on the data, he must be prepared for the data to tell him something new, and to tell him in a challenging manner which may even break asunder the methodological classifications and categories designed to accommodate and process data.' (Hogan, 1980)

Thus Hogan is led to argue that the researcher must be sensitive to the historical influences on not only the evaluated but the evaluator and for this the most appropriate model is the 'hermeneutically trained mind' (Gadamer, 1975) of the person involved in biblical studies.

Munro, who has evaluated some evaluations of Schools Council Projects, analysed the differences between traditional and illuminative evaluation and distinguished between primary (pupils), secondary (teachers) and tertiary (head teachers, etc) effects (1977). At the primary level the experimental method specifies and measures pupil performance whereas the illuminative approach does neither, although it may measure generalized educational attainments. Similarly it will not obtain pupil expectations in interview or observation but evaluate them from questionnaire responses. At the secondary level illuminative evaluation notes teacher performance as it occurs, whereas the experimental method will define desired teacher performances and assess the extent to which they are attained. The same contrast applies to the evaluation of teacher expectations. At the third level the experimental approach is not concerned with the outcomes except on examiners and members of selection committees, whereas the illuminative method is very much concerned with these aspects more especially as they influence head teachers and education officials.

But what is evaluation? The present author has always taken it to mean the determination of whether one achieves what one sets out to achieve. It involves the evaluator in the use of techniques appropriate to the solution of the problem posed by the aims of a project involving the evaluator in an illuminative strategy in which traditional techniques (tests) and strategies (input-output) may or may not be used.

Elley (1972) (quoted by Munro) argues 'that it is the collection, analysis and reporting of information about the effects of an educational innovation, with a view to making judgements about it'. Since, according to the Organization for Economic and Cultural Development (also quoted by Munro), innovation is a deliberate attempt to improve educational practice it is also purposive and therefore the evaluation of an innovation must also embrace an evaluation of its purposes.

Because it soon became clear from the studies of the major projects that information diffusion was a major problem (Munro, 1977), project units had to be clear about who their clients were and present their information in formats suitable for their clients and this might need three or four different presentations. Any definition of evaluation has to embrace the client for as Nevo writes:

> 'Educational evaluation is the process of delineating, obtaining and providing useful information to various audiences, regarding the merit of goals, designs, implementations and outcomes of educational activities, to serve formative and summative roles.' (Nevo, 1979)

To measure or not to measure?

In the course in science for arts students which the present author was invited to evaluate, the methodology included participant observation, independent discussions with students in groups and as individuals, attitude tests and input-output studies of knowledge (Heywood and Montagu-Pollock, 1976). These approaches combine process and product philosophies which the present author also takes to be the approach used in the *Evaluation of Science Teaching Methods Project* discussed by Munro (1977). That investigation argued that there was a danger that the illuminative method could be too subjective and, in a world where there is an almost anti-scientific measurement bias, the illuminative philosophy can provide an escape route for those who do not wish to be faced with unpleasant facts about the outcomes of their work. J F Eggleston and his colleagues argued that grave errors can arise when research findings and interpretations are based on personal selection and a few isolated events and for support they cited Popper's 'degree of corroboration' test in which:

> 'every hypothesis which the model generates should use not only the maximum amount of available data but should also attempt to build up a chain of interdependence. The final acceptance of the hypothesis should be conditional upon a number of predicted directional changes in the intervening chain of events. The longer the chain the more severe the test.' (Quoted by Munro, 1977)

Before and after measurements can be used to corroborate observational data.

Psychologists involved in mental testing have always insisted that a wide range of tests are necessary if a reliable picture of performance and potential is to be obtained. There is no better illustration of both process and product approaches to be found than in Freeman and Byrne's (1976) attempts to evaluate the training of general practitioners. (It is essential to read the second edition of their study.)

Munro (1977), having looked at several British projects, concludes that the problem is not measurement as such but when to measure a decision which is taken as a function of the evaluation process. He argues for a balanced approach. It seems to me, however, that in contrasting the two paradigms, Parlett and Hamilton's (1972) axiom that the problem should create the method and not the opposite will only hold if an investigator is aware of the range of methods and techniques and of what they have to offer. It is the paradigm of the engineering design process which allows for changes in tactics as the evaluation progresses. Finally, evaluations can only ever be partial, a point which is examined in more detail elsewhere (Heywood, 1977).

Many of these points may be illustrated by contrasting the small group studies of teaching arts to science students (Heywood and Montagu-Pollock, 1976) with the Irish 15+ examination investigation (Heywood, McGuinness and Murphy, 1981). In the former no control group was possible. It was a typical teaching situation with one class of about 20 students per year. Because the class was small it was possible to collect a huge amount of data for comparison with the class in the following year, and as it was also agreed that the evaluator should be a participant observer, it was possible to make changes as the course went along. Any change would necessarily destroy some, but not all, components of an input-output analysis. For example, if information about levels of interest was available at the beginning of the course then the effects of the changes could be seen in the post-course analysis if other variables could be excluded. Because there was continuing participation in the class other forms of corroborative evidence could be obtained. Taking all the evidence together the course for the following year could be modified to see if the aims were better achieved or could be modified, or the course could be changed to meet modified aims.

All this occurred during the three-year study and at the end it was possible to look at the whole activity in terms of some well-accepted

147

principles of learning. It was also possible to compare this approach to one by Epstein (1970) used at Brandeis and Oxford Universities based on Bruner's theory of instruction and in particular discovery learning in which non-scientists learnt through the study of published research papers.

My evaluation and report on the Science for Arts Students programme (Heywood and Montagu-Pollock, 1976) was criticized for not describing the institution's attitude to the innovation, the authors having only been concerned to see if the course objectives were achieved. Many evaluators would argue that institutional views of the innovation were important which serves to illustrate the breadth of role given to evaluation in some models. Insofar as the institution was concerned, the authors had already discussed this problem in a report to the Leverhulme Foundation (Dew-Hughes *et al*, 1966).

Contrast this with the Public Examinations Evaluation Project of the Irish Committee on the Form and Function of the Intermediate Certificate — a 15+ examination. The research unit received a precise remit (Heywood, McGuinness and Murphy, 1981) to try to design examinations which would test higher order skills than those currently tested by that examination. The Committee, greatly influenced by *The Taxonomy of Educational Objectives* (Bloom, 1964), felt that the examination as it was tested knowledge of recall although it had had no time to test that assumption. Thus only two judgements were open to the Committee's research unit:

Statistically:
1. Did the experimental examinations test the objectives they were designed to test?

Opinion:
2. Did teachers believe the examinations tested the objectives they were designed to test?
3. Which style of examination did the teachers prefer?
and so on . . .

The project was further limited by an inability either to change teaching methods in the classroom or to influence the syllabus, even though it was anticipated that the data would have to be compared with the results obtained by the pupils in the public examination. To a large extent this is the position in which the examining boards and teachers find themselves in England when they evaluate examinations.

Statistically the problem is fraught with difficulties as the final report shows (Heywood, McGuinness and Murphy, 1981). Nevertheless, the assumptions made by the Committee that:

1. teachers were interested in change;
2. change could not be brought about without a national programme of in-service training;

enabled the research unit to work with teachers in an in-service programme which had as its goal the design of experimental examinations by the teachers in the programme. This meant that some degree of illumination was possible, since the teachers would be able to look at the 'apparent' effects of the experimental examinations on themselves and their pupils. Thus the important finding was not so much that the examinations probably tested a different range of skills but that teachers preferred the new style examinations.

As a research worker the statistical results always disappointed the present author, but who were his clients? Certainly not himself as a research worker. The team's clients were the teachers, the Committee and society. Even though the Committee financed the research it could not claim to be the sole client since a reaction by the teachers against this work would have led the Committee or the Minister to ignore it in their consideration of the examination system. We were particularly concerned with society since there was no doubt from the response to the recommendations of the Committee's own report and the findings of an American investigator of the Irish system (Madaus *et al*, 1979) that the public was content with what it had. There is no doubt that in making their recommendations the authors of the subsequent research report were greatly influenced by this assumption which was supported by other studies of the problem of change in industry (Burns and Stalker, 1961) and education (Hoyle, 1969). There was nothing value-free about these judgements and the authors were conscious of this fact.

From the educational point of view the inferences about the relationship between examinations, teaching and learning were probably the most important and, some would argue, especially as they apply to mathematics. Others might say that the fact that the teachers' trade union published a textbook (without prejudice) was the most significant result (Heywood, 1977b). Thus, although aims determine procedures, the relative importance of the outcomes will depend on the perception of the different groups and individuals involved in the project.

Purpose and practice in evaluation

By inference the preceding paragraphs indicate some of the problems which faced evaluators, in Britain especially. It is not surprising that Munro (1977), from his study of recent evaluations, argues that there is so much confusion about the purpose of evaluation and that often the findings of the evaluators do not relate to the 'real world' of the school and classroom.

'Curriculum evaluation remains a young, over self-conscious development in educational affairs. By questioning the value of aspects of schooling, it has entered a field in which it is not always sure of its responsibilities. Because of this, evaluators have readily pretended to value-free positions in an attempt to escape the consequences of their own judgements. Yet whether they wish it or not, they are involved in commentaries which reveal what they believe to be "good" and "bad" practices in education. Analysis of much of their work reveals a fierce belief, for example, in the importance of such human capacities as respect for evidence, rational analysis and tolerance of divergence. In the future, we must hope that evaluators will be more honest in distinguishing between the value process which reflects their own social background and upbringing and the more clinical data-collecting process. To produce "good" evidence about effects depends on the careful application of techniques which can be checked by others. To make a "good" judgement is to take a stand within a value system to which only *some* like-minded people will subscribe. Thus, by revealing the bases for their judgements, evaluators can present themselves as humanly credible — a condition their audiences are entitled to expect of them.' (Munro, 1977)

A teacher has to be accountable to others just as they are accountable to him or her insofar as their organization of his or her work, development and resources contributes to the effectiveness of his or her teaching.

As McMahon (1976) has shown in a replication of the Burns and Stalker (1961) industrial studies in Dublin, schools which are 'organically' organized so that communication is both lateral and vertical and communication decision-making more communal, are more likely to innovate in the curriculum than mechanistically organized schools that operate like bureaucracies with orders coming vertically from the top. McMahon also showed that the key figure in innovation in both types of school was the principal.

Insofar as teachers are concerned, the evaluation of their programmes should help them to improve their work and in so doing it may help their personal growth. But personal development is also a function of the organization as is the effectiveness of teaching. In industry such development is called staff development. It is a concept that is relatively new in education but already there is much discussion about its potential. The debate about accountability did not begin with any 'reciprocity theorem' of accountability, rather with criticism of the educational system insofar as it was not perceived to be doing the job it was required to do for society. It is with this debate that the next sections are concerned.

Organizing questions

1. No system of accountability will work if teachers have security of tenure. Discuss with special reference to the school system in which you work.

2. A teacher is only accountable to himself in respect of his actions in the classroom. Discuss with reference to the school system in which you work.

Organizing responses from student answers to these questions

EXAMPLE 1. THE FUNDAMENTAL QUESTIONS

'In approaching the problem, let us be mindful of some pertinent questions: why should teachers account for their teaching, teaching methods and curriculum content? To whom should teachers be accountable? Is is to their peers? Inspectors? Parents? The community? Society? Or all of these?

How can teachers, or other interested parties, evaluate their work? Is a teacher only accountable to himself in respect of his activities in the classroom? If we accept that other agents have a role to play, what is it?

Finally, can a workable system of accountability be found if teachers continue to enjoy security of tenure?'

EXAMPLE 2. ACCOUNTABILITY TO PARENTS AND PUBLIC

'In a more specific review of public accountability we must not forget the position of parents and their role as primary educators of their children as laid down in the constitution of this country.

Cox and Boyson rightly point out parents and tax payers demand a say in education and will indeed refuse to send their children to schools whose values they reject or whose teaching efficiency is suspect. They do advise that the aims and purposes of education must be made more responsive to the general public — the parent — than is now the case.

One feels that we must respond to the public desire for more information and involve parents and their elected representatives in policy and decision-making and, at the same time, increase the profession's capacity to evaluate its work.

The school can readily make itself accountable to the public, and parents in particular by:

(a) Providing the names, qualifications and relevant occupational experience of the staff and their institutional responsibilities and those of the Board of Management members, Department Inspectors, and local back-up services in regular contact with the school.

(b) It can provide information about appointment procedures of staff; about how to lodge a complaint and the school approach in dealing with them; about the school's aims and objectives in academic and non-academic fields.

(c) The school can provide information on the decision-making process in relation to distribution of responsibilities, internal forms of accountability and on how practices are reviewed.

(d) It can provide information on school rules for pupils and staff, school policy on academic attainment, extracurricular activities, curriculum content and planning; pupil assessment, pastoral care and advise on post-primary education and the selection of schools.

(e) The school can also provide much information on its provision for remedial teaching and the professional qualifications of the staff responsible.

Further steps might involve the school compiling and publishing accounts of its instructional strategies in different knowledge areas, its choice of textbooks and teaching aids and the criteria used in their selection, its views on learning needs of pupils and the staff members' approach to these problems. It is understood here that any document published by the school providing information along these lines also includes the school's balance sheets in a statement of accounts.'

EXAMPLE 3. ACCOUNTABILITY TO PRINCIPALS

'Elliott suggests that there is no point in creating an evaluatory mechanism which succeeds only in apportioning blame to the teacher. The aim of any evaluatory system must be to modify teaching processes for the better. This would apply to both formal and informal evaluation. Because much of the nature of the evaluation that is ongoing in the school is of an informal nature it often is left undone, eg principals are not encouraged by teachers to enter their classroom and monitor their teacher effectiveness. This situation appears to be contradictory. Teachers, contractually, are accountable to the principal teacher but yet will not entertain any evaluation upon them by the principal. This clearly demonstrates the fact that the accountability issue is an emotive one. Teachers are very defensive about being held accountable. They would claim that teacher evaluation should never occur unless the methods used have proven validity and reliability. They are concerned about the possible misuse of results of an evaluation procedure. If effective accountability systems are to be introduced, intelligent use must be made of the evaluation results. This use must include a constructive feedback procedure for a teacher's benefit, to help him refine his teaching skills. Teacher involvement in the evaluatory process is essential. There is likely to be much to gain for teachers, pupils, parents and other groups in society if teachers were to incorporate into their roles a critical examination of their goals and their effectiveness in achieving them. The theory behind the method for self-evaluation is based on J Elliott's writings on the Ford Teaching Project 1976. By "self-monitoring" the teacher becomes more aware of the consequences of his actions, the extent to which he can be held responsible for them, by reflecting on his practice. He must overcome subjective obstacles to give accurate accounts of his actions. First person reports are not always infallible. People can describe their intentions and situations so inaccurately despite being in an ideal position to do so accurately. Elliott states that outside help should not be ignored, objective observations can give much insight. He also suggests the use of tape-recorders and video equipment. The main thrust of the self-monitoring concept is that a teacher should never be self-satisfied. There is always room for personal and professional development. There are a number of disadvantages to this approach. These would include the fact that self-evaluation too easily degenerates into self-justification. It also increases the teacher's workload. It has been suggested that the process lacks objectivity and therefore credibility and that it could lead to excessive "looking over your shoulder". G Elliott expands this notion of self-evaluation and describes a model of evaluation. It comprises:

1. Self-evaluation
2. Formal evaluation
3. Informal evaluation
4. Internal evaluation
5. External evaluation

The purpose of the framework is to keep the school and its members under review. This would involve staff and pupils and would include the school's curriculum, organization, management and performance. Elliott stresses that this framework is still in its infancy and it will have to be further refined and developed if it is to be used satisfactorily. The advantages of this model according to Elliott are:

(a) individual teachers feel less threatened by it;
(b) it can be applied to any part of a school;
(c) it encourages schools to act independently;
(d) it is a formative process involving staff development;
(e) it is likely to provide a greater volume of information than any other evaluation process.'

EXAMPLE 4. CONCERNING PROFESSIONAL STANDING AND ACCOUNTABILITY

'Does the fact that there is security of tenure prohibit any further developments in the present system? There is the danger that security of tenure can lead to complacency. There is also the risk that only the negative aspects of accountability will be considered by teachers. On the other hand teachers are continually striving to increase their professional standing. In other professions eg medicine and law a system of accountability does operate. If a person is reported for malpractice a registration council will investigate the case. If it can be proved that malpractice has occurred then the practitioner could be struck off the professional register. This has the effect of standardizing practice and of raising the overall professional standard. This same procedure could be applied to the teaching profession. If teachers could be persuaded to see the advantages as well as the disadvantages of a similar procedure for them perhaps they would not feel so threatened by the accountability movement. Teachers should not see this movement as an attempt to undermine their position but rather as an attempt to raise the general standard. Built into this movement should be a mechanism whereby a teacher would have to attend in-service training at given intervals. This would help him to keep abreast of innovation. The process of accountability would also apply to principals. Generally speaking, principals are appointed for an indefinite period. Perhaps contracts for a fixed period would be more appropriate as they would lead to more innovation and job mobility. Obviously teachers have a right to security of tenure but when this right blocks or prohibits discussion and possible implementation of an evaluatory process then this right must be questioned.'

EXAMPLE 5. TEACHER ATTITUDES TO EVALUATION AND THE ROLE OF THE HEADTEACHER
'Not all teachers appreciate the role of the headteacher as an evaluator, but then not all teachers have the same attitude towards evaluation. Those who see in their evaluation the possibility of desirable rewards tend to have a favourable attitude towards the process. Ironically, these are often teachers who are already strong in self-evaluation and who see themselves as competent professionals. Many teachers, however, dislike and resist evaluation. Some argue against evaluation on ethical grounds, ie that no one has a right to evaluate another person. Paradoxically, these same teachers evaluate their pupils regularly. Furthermore, the criteria for evaluation may be incompatible with the instructional objectives and values supported by an individual teacher. For example, one teacher may be firmly committed to long-range development of pupils' problem-solving skills, yet she may be evaluated on the basis of pupil performance of rote memory tasks. Another teacher may be actively engaged in cultivating pupil independence and initiative, yet evaluation may be in terms of how quiet and orderly are his classes. Professor Eric Hoyle in a paper to the Education Section Association at its Swansea meeting (1971), while giving "guarded" support for planned innovation has confessed to "misgivings" about the accompanying threat to the satisfaction that teachers derive from their freedom within the boundary of their classroom, to develop their own skills in personal relationships with pupils and in understanding of children's learning processes. It seems from this argument that some teachers want to be involved in collective planning in order to develop and use their organizational skills, whereas others like to follow their own bent within the relatively private domain of a classroom. Thus, the Head's framework of accountability must take cognizance of the teacher's initiative from which new ideas will flow rendering a professional service to society.'

Control and accountability

The accountability issue seems to have been brought to public notice in Britain through parliamentary reaction to the so-called student revolt. The fact that taxpayers' money was given to the University Grants Committee (which did not account for its expenditure to anyone) was highlighted. Should, for example, its funds and work be open to inspection by the Auditor General?

Colleges in the public sector of higher education were subject to local authorities who in turn received the majority of their findings from the Exchequer via the Department of Education and Science. Both the colleges and the local authorities were subject to considerable controls and, as events in the late 1970s and early 1980s showed, the Department could close colleges at will. In contrast, the only control which the Exchequer had over the universities was the amount of money made available to the University Grants Committee.

Control mechanisms available to the English Department of Education and Science are complex. At a simple level it can reduce the allocation to a local authority with a *dictée* as to how expenditure should be utilized. At a more complex level it can encourage or discourage the implementation of courses through the Inspectorate who are members of statutory regional advisory councils charged with the overall supervision of the provision of higher and further education in the public sector. More subtle mechanisms of control exist through the Council for National Academic Awards and other similar agencies who vet course submissions once they have been approved in the advisory councils (Church, 1983; Jones, 1982; Gaskell, 1982). In 1981, after much debate, a National Board was established to control developments and develop a national policy. Even so there is very little accountability directly to Parliament. At the tertiary level, as in Australia, Ireland and Norway, two systems also operate side by side.

In the higher sector in Britain there are a number of course controls which have operated successfully to reduce expenditure, but their value may be questioned. Consider two examples relating to the Department's proposals for 1982 which relate to education in two areas of high unemployment.

First, although Sunderland Polytechnic, which is located in an area of high unemployment, was not hit too badly by the spending cuts, its School of Education was told to reduce its physics and mathematics training programmes, yet in both subjects there are acute shortages of teachers.

Second, widely reported in the local and national newspapers in 1982 was the fact that the City of Liverpool College of Higher Education was told to stop its teacher training, including its provision for teaching the mentally handicapped. Not only was the mentally handicapped programme the only one in the North of Engand, but the teacher training programme was excellent. The effect of these cuts was to reduce the student numbers to around 800, all studying for degrees validated by the University of Lancaster. It soon became apparent that the purpose of the exercise was to merge the remnants of the college with the polytechnic as a means of raising the polytechnic's academic standing and this has now happened. The effect of the redundancies was to reduce substantially the income available to Knowsley (the area in which the college was located), a borough with one of the highest unemployment levels in England. It also meant a loss of income to Liverpool of over one million pounds per annum. The only conclusion which can be drawn from this is that the Department intended to close the college independently of the needs of Merseyside and a Minister in another Department of State was given responsibility for them.

The American observer Martin Trow (1974) has long advocated the need for systems as opposed to pragmatic planning in education. These two cases cited above would appear to vindicate his view, as in neither case was there accountability to the wider society which education is supposed to serve.

Similarly, in the university sector the University Grants Committee was instructed in 1981 to make severe cuts (as much as 40 per cent) with recommendations as to which subjects should be cut. There was no doubt that the Committee was both pragmatic and biased in favour of the older universities, the technological universities in areas of high un-employment being hit the hardest.

Probably the most important issue relating to accountability arose in August 1982 when, in a letter to the Open University, the Department of Education and Science (which directly funds this institution) asked the University to comment on an apparent left-wing bias in the teaching of some of its courses in education and sociology. It said it had received complaints from students.

Even *The Times*, not generally sympathetic toward the universities, wrote in an editorial:

'The Open University, which has to be specially alert about the possibility because a part of its instruction takes place not in closed classrooms but on open airwaves, has its own procedure for the assessment of its courses. On this occasion it appears that the Department of Education is taking a hand itself by forwarding the allegations of bias and asking for an explanation. The Open University is established by royal charter which consists of the same elements as the charters of other universities. Unlike them it is not funded by the University Grants Committee but directly by the Department. But that financial tie does not alter the position by which academic matters, including the content of particular courses, are the responsibility of the University itself and of nobody else. It is not answerable to DES officials for what it teaches. It may choose to answer those officials' questions, or not. If it does, prudence suggests that it should not allow its questioners to forget that they are entering an area in which they possess no authority.' (*The Times*, 1982)

These examples raise the question of how universities should relate to society. In Britain they have been able to hide behind a variety of myths about liberal education acceptable to both Government and the public, yet the evidence is that they are exceptionally conservative in their response to changing patterns of knowledge. In the United States teachers and courses are subject to evaluation (Flood Page, 1974), but in Britain endeavours to provide minimal university teacher training programmes were among the first of the cutbacks despite the fact that much university teaching is notoriously bad. It seems that the cutbacks did not cause reformation but rather retrenchment to traditional subjects and values.

In the public sector the Inner London Education Authority (ILEA) is embarking on a college review which begins with a checklist of these headings: the role of the college (in relation to local authority policy); organizational structures (committee structures, communication processes); finance (budgetary control); staff (staff development policy); accommodation (room loading/utilization); plant and equipment (purchasing procedures); consumables (stock control); publication (prospectus); self-assessment for teaching staff; considering learning materials; teaching methods; and student response. This work was developed by the ILEA from their work on school reviews which will be mentioned later.

More generally at the level of school organization in England there was a move to make schools more accountable to the public and parents. The Taylor Report suggested that the governing bodies of schools should be reorganized to achieve this end (Taylor, 1977). Contrast this with Ireland where similar proposals for the management of primary schools have been seen more in terms of a relinquishing of control by the Catholic hierarchy than as a tightening of control by the public (Hogan, 1978). It is questionable whether any real sharing of management has developed because the patron can still appoint the chairman and representatives.

Accountability, therefore, has as many facets as evaluation, and the same questions which are asked about evaluation have to be asked about accountability, as comparison of the reports by Munro (1977) and O'Rafferty (1984) makes clear. Just as Elliott (1980) has demonstrated that no one form of evaluation can satisfy all the purposes which it is supposed to meet, so the same is true of accountability. Sizer (1981) has noted that indicators such as staff-student ratios and costs per full-time student are only partial performance indicators, many of which are process measures of performances and not measures which indicate whether an institution is achieving its goals or not. A system which makes a teacher accountable may not improve his or her teaching, and a system of tight control may inhibit innovation. Although the response to accountability in different societies is very much a response to the historical development and organization of the system of education, there are significant issues which are common to all countries. Some of these issues will be considered below and for this it is necessary to return to the concept of the received curriculum (see Chapter 2).

The received curriculum and government control

Apart from the organization of schools as a means of social engineering, the vehicle for meeting the needs of society is the curriculum. The question of 'who controls the curriculum' is thus central to the management and control of an educational system. At the apex of the system of education is the government of the day which spends huge sums on school education. Since these monies are obtained from taxes, the first level of accountability in education is of the government toward the society from whom it collects taxes. However, education is not an issue which excites the electorate, although in England planning and method have tended to become ideological and good ideas from either side of the political divide can be dropped by a particular administration simply because of an ideology that may or may not be without foundation. For example, if project methods are linked with progressive education and progressive education is linked with the left, right-wing educationalists may oppose project methods even though their value has been proven.

There has therefore to be some means of maintaining an independent debate about curriculum and method. This, many would argue, should be the *raison d'être* of university departments of education but governments sometimes believe that such departments are biased against their ideology. This seemed to be the case with the 1979-84 Conservative Government. It was greatly influenced by the Black Papers which were highly critical of many organizational, curriculum and teaching developments which took place in the 1950s and 1960s (Cox and Dyson, 1971). In both political parties many people were concerned with standards. Moreover, the regular assessment of standards at particular intervals in a child's life became the *cri de coeur* of this group, and after a speech by a Labour prime minister, a unit (called the Assessment in Performance Unit) of the Inspectorate was set up to measure standards at several given ages. Although there was no public debate about the meaning of standards it was clear that the measurement of 'something' in the areas of English, maths and science was intended to make the system more accountable. The danger of a system of this kind as was argued above is that it can so easily place a straitjacket around educational development. It is difficult to know whether the work of the Assessment in Performance Unit is still taken seriously, although some of its reports have provided valuable information (APU). In any event the choice of what should be assessed is a decision of major importance.

A ministerial document on the 'Common Curriculum' (see Chapter 6) represented another attempt at control in that it required headteachers to report on the curriculum in their schools within two years in order to show its approximation to the proposals.

None of this goes as far as the centralization in the Irish system. In Ireland the Inspectorate controls the secondary examining system and wrote the curriculum which is common to all national (primary) schools. Many teachers in England fear that the present trend in Britain is toward a much greater central control of the curriculum.

One argument in favour of central direction, as in France and Ireland, is that it is easier to breed change. Teachers tend to be 'conservative' and bound by their subjects. They tend to resist change unless it is absolutely necessary. In Ireland the Inspectorate says that their new primary curriculum (Government Publications, 1970) was not as radical as it might have been because they did not trust the professional competence of the teachers at that time. In contrast, the syllabuses of the second-level examinations have remained remarkably constant although the present Government has created a board for the curriculum and examinations with the intention of change.

The Inspectorate, local authorities and accountability

In contrast to Britain there is no local authority network to control State education in Ireland. The national (primary) schools are run by the Department of Education as are most of the comprehensive schools. The secondary schools are run by religious bodies and the vocational schools are run by vocational education committees, funded by the State. They

157

are the nearest organizational equivalent to a local education authority. There are separate inspectors for the secondary and vocational sectors. Much of the work of the Inspectorate at the secondary level is devoted to examining and this role has been the subject of much debate among teachers. In contrast, the Inspectorate in Britain has changed its role in the past decade but the substantial inspections with which it was associated are once again being reported. At the same time it conducts other enquiries among schools. Its report on comprehensive education (HMSO, 1979) which sparked off the debate about the curriculum caused much controversy and in 1982 it issued a list of local authorities who, in its view, were making inadequate educational provision which was equally controversial. It has also made known its views on teacher training. Nevertheless, it cannot be said that the Inspectorate's role in policy-making and accountability is absolutely clear.

Some local authorities also have their own inspectorates. In Britain it is the local authorities who nominate the boards of management (governors) of schools and run the system of publicly financed education. These authorities have been especially concerned with accountability. By 1981, Elliott had identified 69 local authorities which were in the process of drawing up self-evaluation. Among the most publicized was the ILEA's scheme for schools published in 1977 under the title *Keeping the School Under Review*. Birchenough (1982) records that among the lessons learnt was the value of reviewing the work of an institution at one particular point, even though some staff would necessarily be involved in continuing self-evaluation. He also noted that 'the whole institution needs to be stressed'. It was easy to look at departments and undervalue the importance of general school and college policies, and it was also easy to produce descriptive, rather than evaluative, material.

Birchenough argues for the use of external agents with a knowledge of the school — in this case the local authority inspectorate — in self-evaluation since this will produce more effective action. He also argues that evaluative materials will only emerge if aims and objectives are clearly stated at the beginning.

If the evaluation of the educational process leads to only one set of aims and objectives then such objectives might be defined by the authority. However, in simpler organizations (eg the running of a steel plant), it has been found in the evaluation of in-company training schemes associated with staff development that their failure arises from the fact that the personnel on them do not have common goals and often have difficulty in perceiving the company's objectives. In one experiment conducted by the present author, it took four days of modified T-group work for a group of managers to perceive that they all had common training needs. One result of this study was the suggestion that courses should begin with an evaluation of aims and objectives by the staff concerned which would allow for positive modification of the proposed course (Heywood, 1972). There is every reason to believe that a more positive evaluation of the work of an institution would arise if staff were involved in the determination of aims and objectives, and this view is supported by Robinson (1982) as a result of the experience of self-review in New Zealand. School staff cannot develop an internal commitment to review unless they develop a clear sense of the specific problems that will be addressed. Robinson adds that some models are only appropriate in settings where there is an openness between staff at all levels as well as a willingness to experiment and take risks. Where this is not the case the review should be conducted with the aid of an outsider. Survey feedback, argues Hopkins (1982), is much to be recommended.

Most recently the Schools Council has established a project (GRIDS) to develop guidelines for review which can be used by schools independently of any local authority initiative to evaluate their curriculum and organization (McMahon, 1982). This brings us once more to the teacher, the classroom and accountability.

The teacher, the classroom and accountability

By and large, the teacher in the classroom is sacrosanct. Although headteachers may have to write reports on their teachers and while (as in Irish National Schools) principals are required to see that teachers meet the goals of the new curriculum, they do not enter classrooms for there is a strong convention against this.

According to Owens (1970) a principal cannot implement bureaucratic control because schools do not satisfy the criteria of a bureaucracy. He writes:

'In a primary school there is little differentiation of task, the principal has no control over extrinsic rewards, the professional versus bureaucratic mode of authority poses problems for control, unsettled matters in pedagogy and diffuse goals, all ensure that authority is weakened.'

But even in schools controlled by religious bodies in Ireland the ASTI would take strong action if it believed that headteachers were entering classrooms to measure the effectiveness of teachers. The most ludicrous situation of all exists in some universities in England where the performance of a new member of staff during the necessary probation period is not actually assessed, even though it is required by contract.

But there is an argument that since the teacher is a professional he or she should be responsible for what goes on in the classroom (Owens, 1970), for the professional teacher is no different from the medical doctor in this respect. An objection to this view of the autonomous professional is that teachers are inadequately trained for such responsibility. Professionals also tend to be conservative and to operate restrictive practices which are not always in the interests of their clients (see Chapter 3). In any event teachers, like engineers, are employees and so, whether they like it or not, they are not only responsible for the children they teach but are accountable to someone else for that responsibility.

'Central to the debate on accountability are the twin ideas of responsibility and answerability for actions undertaken by one party on behalf of another.'
(Sockett, 1980)

But teachers, it seems, look for a restricted notion of professionalism which is what the public would expect according to Hoyle (1973), 'a high level of classroom competence teaching skill and good relationships with pupils'. Training to achieve such competence will necessarily extend their professionalism (Collins, 1980) in a way which:

'embraces restricted professionalism, but additionally embraces other attitudes of a teacher. These include seeing his work in the wider context of community and society; ensuring that his work is informed by theory, research and current exemplars of good practice; being willing to collaborate with other teachers in teaching, curriculum development and the formation of school policy; and having a commitment to keep himself professionally informed.' (Hoyle, 1973)

Toward this end, J Elliott, who is considerably opposed to the American approach based on achievement testing, has argued that accountability should be the teacher's responsibility.

'If teacher education is to prepare students or experienced teachers for accountability then it must be concerned with developing their ability to reflect on classroom situations. By "practical reflections" I mean reflection with a view to action. This involves identifying and diagnosing those practical problems which exist for the teacher in his situation and deciding on strategies for resolving them. The view of accountability which I have outlined, with its emphasis on the right of the teacher to evaluate his own moral agency, assumes that teachers are capable of identifying and diagnosing their practical problems with some degree of objectivity. It implies that the teacher is able to identify a discrepancy between what he in fact brings about in the classroom and his responsibilities to foster and prevent certain consequences. If he cannot do this he is unable to assess whether or not he is obliged to. I believe that being plunged into a context where outsiders evaluated their moral agency without this kind of developmental preparation would be self-defeating since the anxiety generated would render the achievement of an objective attitude at any of these levels extremely difficult.' (Elliott, 1976)

If Elliott's view is acceptable, some form of in-service staff development would be integral to the education of teachers (Rushby and Richards, 1982). Initial training, as will be evident from the examples in the final chapter, can only provide a base. It is the evaluation of experience which is so essential to the development of educational criticism.

References

Assessment in Performance Unit (1977) *What it Is and How it Works* Department of Education and Science: London

Birchenough, M (1982) Keeping the college under review *Educational Management and Administration* 10 pp 189-94

Bloom, B (1964) (ed) *The Taxonomy of Educational Objectives* Vol I, Longmans Green: London

Burns, T and Stalker, G (1961) *The Management of Innovation* Tavistock: London

Callan, J (1982) Unpublished evaluation reports, Department of Education, St Patrick's College, National University of Ireland: Maynooth

Church, C H (1983) (ed) *Practice and Perspective in Validation* Society for Research into Higher Education: Guildford

Collins, H P (1980) A study of some aspects of the status of organized teachers within the education system, MEd thesis, School of Education, University of Dublin: Dublin

Cooper, K (1973) Assessment and evaluation: pamphlet. Schools Council, History Geography and Social Science Project, School of Education, University of Liverpool: Liverpool

Cox, C B and Boyson, R (1975) *Black Paper 1975* Temple Smith: London

Cox, C B and Dyson, A (1971) (eds) *The Black Papers on Education* Davis-Poynter: London

Dew-Hughes, D, Heywood, J, Mortimore, G, Montagu-Pollock, H and Oldfield, F (1966) A group study of staff and student attitudes to the distant minor. A report to the Leverhulme Foundation, Department of Higher Education, University of Lancaster: Lancaster

Donald, M (1978) *in* Becher, A and McClure, S *Accountability in Education* NFER Publishing: Windsor

Elley, W B (1972) *Strategies in Educational Assessment* New Zealand Council for Educational Research: Wellington

Elliott, G (1980) *Self Evaluation and the Teacher: An Annotated Bibliography* (three volumes) Department of Educational Studies, The University of Hull: Hull

Elliott, J (1976) Preparing teachers for classroom accountability *Education for Teaching* 100 pp 49-71

Epstein, H (1970) *A Strategy for Education* Oxford University Press: Oxford

Flood Page, C (1974) *Student Evaluation of Teaching: The American Experience* Society for Research into Higher Education: Guildford

Freeman, J and Byrne, P (1976) *The Assessment of General Practice* Society for Research into Higher Education: Guildford

Gadamer, H G (1975) *Truth and Method* Seabury Press: New York

Gaskell, S M (1982) The university validated degree: present and future imperfect *Evaluation Newsletter* No 6, Society for Research into Higher Education: Guildford

Government Publications (1970) White Paper: *Educational Development:* Dublin

Heywood, J (1972) On the development of short courses in originality *in* Gregory, S (ed) *Creativity and Innovation in Engineering* Butterworth: London

Heywood, J and Montagu-Pollock, H (1976) *Science for Arts Students: A Case Study in Curriculum Development* Society for Research into Higher Education: Guildford

Heywood, J (1977a) *Assessment in Higher Education* Wiley: London

Heywood, J (1977b) *Examining in Second Level Education* Association of Secondary School Teachers of Ireland: Dublin

Heywood, J, McGuiness, S and Murphy, D E (1981) Final Report of the Public Examinations Evaluation Project to the Minister for Education. School of Education, University of Dublin: Dublin

Higham, J (1979) How to evaluate a history department. A questionnaire approach *Teaching History* 24 pp 14-16

Her Majesty's Stationery Office (1979) *Aspects of Secondary Education* HMSO: London

Hogan, P (1980) A critique of educational research *Oxford Review of Education* 6 pp 141-55

Hopkins, D (1982) Survey feedback as an organization development intervention in educational settings: a review *Educational Management and Administration* 10 pp 203-15

Horgan, J (1978) The majority of national schools still controlled by the few *The Irish Times* 13 September

Hoyle, E (1969) How does the curriculum change? *Journal of Curriculum Studies* 1 pp 230-9

Hoyle, E (1973) Strategies of curriculum change *in* Watkins, R (ed) *Inservice Training Structure and Context* Ward Lock: London

Jones, P (1982) Evaluating a CNAA course — some suggestions for course committees *Evaluation Newsletter* No 6, Society for Research into Higher Education: Guildford

Madaus, G F, Fontes, P J, Kellaghan, T and Airasian, P W (1979) Opinions of the Irish public on the goals and adequacy of education *Irish Journal of Education* 13 p 119

McMahon, J (1976) The relationship between curricular innovation and organization structure in post-primary schools MEd thesis University of Dublin: Dublin

McMahon, A (1982) The GRIDS (Guidelines for Review of Institutional Development in Schools) project *Educational Management and Administration* 10 pp 189-94

Munro, R G (1977) *Innovation Success or Failure?* Hodder and Stoughton: Sevenoaks

Nevo, D (1979) New strategy for evaluation *Urban Education* 13 p 441

O'Rafferty, M (1984) Accountability in primary education in Ireland, MEd thesis, University of Dublin: Dublin

Owens, R C (1970) *Organizational Behaviour in Schools* Prentice Hall: Englewood Cliffs, New Jersey

Parlett, M and Hamilton, D (1972) *Evaluation as Illumination* Centre for Educational Sciences, The University of Edinburgh: Edinburgh

Robinson, M J V (1982) Schools reviews: A New Zealand experience *Educational Management and Administration* 10 pp 195-202

Rushby, T and Richards, C (1982) Staff development in primary schools: a survey of views and practice in nine schools *Educational Management and Administration* 10 pp 223-31

Scriven, M (1967) The methodology of evaluation *in Perspectives in Curriculum Evaluation* American Educational Research Association, Rand McNally: Chicago

Sizer, J (1981) Institutional performance: assessment for survival and revival. Paper for the 5th international conference on Higher Education, University of Lancaster: Lancaster

Sockett, H (1980) *Accountability in the English Educational System* Hodder and Stoughton: London

Taylor, W (1977) *A New Partnership in Schools* Report of a committee, Her Majesty's Stationery Office: London

The Times (1982) Editorial, 3 September

Trow, M (1974) Problems in the transition from elite to mass higher education *in Policies in Higher Education* Organization for Economic and Cultural Development: Paris

Chapter 9

Educational Connoisseurship

Introduction

In the previous chapter it was argued that teacher accountability begins with self-evaluation for which continuing in-service staff development is essential. Initial training can provide a base on which to build skills of self-criticism. First, it can provide the teacher with an understanding of what it is to be a professional. In this chapter Eisner's (1979) model of the teacher as an art critic (educational connoisseurship) is discussed. It is then argued that the skills of self-evaluation can be developed through an objectives approach to lesson planning which is informed by an adequate theory of instruction.

The concept of educational connoisseurship

The idea of educational connoisseurship is due to Eisner (1979), an American educationalist, and is very similar to the concept of illuminative evaluation put forward by Parlett and Hamilton (1972) although its derivation is different.

Eisner's idea develops from an attack on the scientific approach to curriculum study and evaluation by a particular version of behavioural psychology. In contrast, he argues that there is a need for educationalists to develop a technique for evaluation similar to the kind of criticism used in art which he calls educational connoisseurship. Eisner describes the relationship between educational criticism and educational connoisseurship thus:

> 'The consequence of using educational criticism to perceive educational objects and events is the development of educational connoisseurship. As one learns how to look at educational phenomena, as one ceases using stock responses to educational situations and develops habits of perceptual exploration, the ability to experience qualities and their relationships increases. This phenomenon occurs in virtually every arena in which connoisseurship has developed. The orchid grower learns to look at orchids in a way that expands his or her perception of their qualities. The makers of cabinets pay special attention to finish, to types of wood and grains, to forms of joining, to the treatment of edges. The football fan learns how to look at plays, defence patterns, and game strategies. Once one develops a perceptual foothold in an arena of activity — orchid growing, cabinet making, or football watching — the skills used in that arena, one does not need the continual expertise of the critic to negotiate new works, or games or situations. One generalizes the skills developed earlier and expands them through further application.' (Eisner, 1969)

Eisner argues that for evaluation we require a model of the teacher as an artist. I would argue that we also need a model of the teacher as an actor for too little attention is paid to the needs of the teacher in educational literature. But I would also argue that we need models of the teacher as a scientist insofar as that embraces decision-making and the management of learning. For me the best model is that of the engineering designer, not the engineering scientist with whom the engineer is too often confused (Krick, 1966) and in many respects this is akin to the model of the artist. Each of these models provides for a different perspective on the problem to be investigated and has, therefore, a role in educational evaluation.

The reaction to the scientific movement in education seems to me to have produced a response which leads educationalists to be over-subjective. Admittedly, too much has been expected from measurement in terms of objectivity but to neglect measurement at the expense of subjectivity is dangerous. On the one hand we do not have instruments sufficiently refined to explore learning in the way we would wish, while on the other, we can too easily use the argument of subjectivity to justify behaviour in ourselves which others may see to be disfunctional in terms of pupil learning.

Educational criticism is the art of looking at our work and that of others and it must be part of the professional obligation of a teacher to become an effective critic. Eisner admits that the development of such thinking is only in its infancy and has room for several models:

> 'Whether the salient model will turn out to be a literary form of ethnography, the legal adversary model or the model of art criticism is not yet clear. I believe the field has more than ample room for these three models and for scientific models, as well. For what I believe the study of education needs is not a new orthodoxy, but rather a variety of new assumptions and methods that will help us appreciate the richness of educational practice, that will be useful for revealing the subtleties of its consequences for all to see.' (Eisner, 1979)

Whether or not we shall ever have a salient theory is a matter for conjecture. At present our understanding is so limited that we have to be eclectic, for different analyses provide different perspectives. On the one hand we have to paint descriptive pictures, and on the other we have to accept that these pictures will inevitably be impressionistic. Moreover, since the personal dispositions of teachers differ so much, teachers will inevitably be biased toward one model. A literary person is likely to be attracted to the phenomenological model suggested by Eisner, whereas a mathematician may well be attracted to the science model.

In teacher training, therefore, it is important to see that there is recognition of the other's point of view and inspection of the examples on pp 168 - 173 suggests that at least on paper such an objective is achievable. While this is no measure of commitment and while essay examinations cannot evaluate the degree of commitment, pencil and paper responses ensure that respondents have faced themselves with the issue. This may be done by framing the examination questions in such a way that the student is forced to evaluate theory in his or her teaching practice and argue for or against that theory. Since supervisors also observe students while teaching, it is possible for us to gain some idea of the level of attention given to theory and its application. Eisner also points out that supervision itself is an artistic activity requiring similar skills to those used in painting (Eisner, 1982).

Skills in educational criticism require an adequate theoretical base. We have to be clear about the role of theory and Eisner clarifies this when he relates it to reflective thinking which he regards as the base for curriculum planning. He calls the reflective moments that a teacher has, 'preactive teaching', a term due to P Jackson. Such moments occur, Eisner writes:

> 'Prior to actual teaching: planning at home reflecting on what has occurred during a particular class session, and discussing in groups ways to organize a programme. Theory here sophisticates personal reflection and group deliberation. Insofar as a theory suggests consequences flowing from particular circumstances, it enables those who understand the theory to take those circumstances into account when planning.
>
> In all of this, theory is not to be regarded as prescriptive but as suggestive. It is a framework, a tool, a means through which the world can be construed. Any theory is but a part of the total picture . . . In one sense all teachers operate with theory, if we take theory to mean a general set of ideas through which we make sense of the world. All teachers, whether they are aware of it or not, use theories in their work. Tacit beliefs about the nature of human intelligence, about the factors that motivate children, and about the conditions that foster learning influence the teachers' actions in the classrooms. These ideas not only influence their actions, they also influence what they attend to in the classroom: that is, the concepts that are salient in theories concerning pedagogical matters also tend to guide perception. Thus, theory inevitably operates in the conduct of teaching as it does in other aspects of educational deliberation. The major need is to be able to view situations from the varied perspectives that different theories provide and thus to be in a position to avoid the limited vision of a single view.' (Eisner, 1979)

Eisner therefore calls for something akin to Newman's 'philosophical habit of mind' which is continually developing the skill of educational criticism and this is surely what Elliott (1976) means by practical reflection (see p 160). Inspection of the examples in this book as well as those in *Pitfalls and Planning in Student Teaching* (Heywood, 1982) suggest that our student teachers were beginning to acquire the art. Their problem was that they have relatively little experience on which to base their judgements and therefore the art of lesson planning assumes some importance in the development of the art of educational criticism, as does the requirement for regular in-service training.

In this chapter the art of lesson planning as a vehicle for development in the skill of educational criticism is considered. Because the view is taken that lesson planning mirrors the strategies for curriculum planning, implementation and evaluation and vice versa, it is argued that curriculum improvement will stem from lesson improvement. Educational connoisseurship begins in the classroom. The final chapter develops this theme more generally in relation to the curriculum.

A base for educational criticism

Criticism and evaluation depend on a person knowing what he or she is doing in a field of human endeavour. It is the understanding of the 'why' as well as the 'what'. In second-level education there is a fair amount of agreement about what should be taught in subjects, although it is clear that, as in engineering and manufacture, restructuring of the artefact or curriculum goes on all the time (see Chapter 2). It is also clear that there have been improvements even though the increments may have been small. Occasionally there are substantial changes as, for example, the effect of the objectives movement on examinations in England and Wales.

It is argued here that an 'objectives approach' has the most to offer student teachers during initial training since it provides a means of organizing and testing their work. There is a controversy among certain psychologists and sociologists about the value of objectives, and the several different 'objectives approaches' have led to many misunderstandings between proponents and opponents. It will be argued in the final chapter that curricular improvement depends on reforms in public examinations and tests which benefit from a particular approach to educational aims and objectives (see pp 195 - 196).

For the moment, let us consider the problem of trainee teachers faced with their first class. Traditionally they believe they have to get over a certain body of knowledge. They cull the textbooks for information and make a value judgement as to how it should be ordered. If they are teaching an examination class they check to establish whether their value judgement coincides with what they believe the examiner wants. Then they worry about discipline and motivation. In all these activities student teachers are working out how to cause pupils to behave in certain ways although they do not have any simple stimulus-response view of behaviour in their minds. They want children to behave as 'gentlemen', to use Newman's description of the educated person.

In this sense Newman's aims of education are behavioural, for the outcomes of learning are a set of dispositions which enable the educated person to handle ideas and people. It is in this generalized sense of behaviour that behavioural is used in this text, not primarily in the stimulus-response (S-R) sense, except insofar as it describes the small incremental changes in behaviour arising from programmed instruction or psychomotor skill learning. Narrowly constrained S-R programmes can be very helpful in learning and there are some excellent examples of their use in remedial work (Ainscow and Tweddle, 1979). It is easy to see that such an approach can become overpowering and negate good teaching.

When, for example, psychologists suggest there are motivational phases in learning and that lessons should be planned around those phases, they are expressing a form of outcome related to the normal behaviour of students. It is as much an objective of the teacher to have the pupils motivated as it is for them to learn something. It is not unreasonable to plan for this even though the outcomes might be unintended (see Chapter 1). Eisner, I think, would call these *expressive outcomes*. 'They are the consequences of curriculum activities that are intentionally planned to provide a fertile field for personal purposing and experience.' He would change the term objective to *expressive outcome* which retains the broad use of objective. Although I do not have any difficulty with this view I shall retain the term objective and use it in a number of different ways.

So far we have one set of objectives which relate to the phases of a lesson and especially to motivation. Equally the selection of concepts and principles is a selection of objectives. To obtain an understanding of Newton's First Law of Mechanics is a broad general statement of intention in non-behavioural terms. But the selection of a concept leads immediately to a question of strategy. How will pupils best obtain this understanding? Will a mathematical description on the blackboard suffice? Is there some form of experiment which would be better? Should it use a guided or pure discovery approach? The behaviour looked for in the pupils is (i) that they will be able to state the law and (ii) demonstrate that they understand it. Again there are a variety of evaluation procedures which can be used to see if the behavioural objectives have been achieved.

A lesson plan must therefore be rather complicated. One possible scheme for lesson planning which relates these different items is shown in Figure 9.1 (see p 168). The first column distinguishes between aims, non-behavioural and behavioural objectives. Even these terms are used by different authorities in different ways. Eisner would use aims only to define some very long-term outcomes of the educational process as, for example, growth. He uses goals for intermediate statements that are more specific in their direction. These it seems could be either aims or non-behavioural objectives in the terminology of Cohen and Mannion (1977) used here.

In my experience most trainee teachers find it useful at the beginning of their teacher training to formulate simple lesson plans in these terms. Although they do not continue to do this after their training it does provide them with insights helpful to the development of the skill of educational criticism during their initial training. Answers to examination questions support this view and show how teachers modify theoretical ideas to suit their own mode of operation (Heywood, 1982).

Organizing question

Distinguish between behavioural and non-behavioural objectives. Give examples of each for a single lesson in the subject you teach. Discuss the advantages and disadvantages of the behavioural objectives approach to design, implementation and evaluation of studies in the subject you teach.

Class:			
Ability range:			
Aids required:			

Aim	Lesson phases	Content	Learning strategies
	Introduction		eg
Non-behavioural objective	Presentation	Facts	Large group Small group Individualized
Behavioural objective	Application	Concepts	Discovery Guided discovery Expository
		Principles	Role-playing Case study Project work Laboratory work
(Problem to be solved)	Conclusion	(Problem to be solved)	
Questioning			

Figure 9.1 *A scheme for a lesson plan*

Examples

EXAMPLE 1. A VERY BROAD STATEMENT OF AIMS RELATING TO
THE TEACHING OF SCIENCE
'I see my aim as a teacher is to develop a scientific or observational awareness
in young people of the world about them and all its interactions. I also want
them to develop the skills that will help them secure meaningful roles in the
community. Sadly all these aims are overshadowed by getting good grades in
a very meaningless exam for most people.'

EXAMPLE 2. BEHAVIOURAL AND NON-BEHAVIOURAL OBJECTIVES
IN ENGLISH
'*Lesson in English*. Dealing with the concept of *imagery*.
Objective (non-behavioural). That the class will understand what is meant by
imagery, its purpose in the poem and its contribution to home and
atmosphere.
Behavioural objective: that the girls will *pick out* and *list in writing* all the
images in the first stanza.'

EXAMPLE 3. BEHAVIOURAL AND NON-BEHAVIOURAL OBJECTIVES
IN BIOLOGY
'This lesson is for first year students of mixed ability 23 in number.
Aim: 'To help the children to develop an awareness of the concept
"living".'
Non-behavioural objective: using the cell as an example to illustrate how
it is alive.
Behavioural objective: at the end of the class the pupils should be able to
(i) draw a cell, (ii) label its parts, (iii) say why it is a living thing.'

EXAMPLE 4. A CRITICISM FROM A TEACHER OF GEOGRAPHY
'The weakness of behavioural objectives lies in interpreting general aims in such terms. Being able to list something does not necessarily imply that one has an understanding or appreciation of what has been covered. By reducing aims to such terms one ignores the effects on the child's thoughts, beliefs, outlook etc and uses overt behaviour as a surrogate for such effects.'

EXAMPLE 5. FROM A TEACHER OF LITERATURE
'The behavioural objectives lend themselves to practical work such as the close examination of a text, and as well as forcing the teacher to be exact and precise in his plans they provide a much more reliable guide to the success of the lesson, referring to feedback from the pupils rather than output from the teacher. They are not always suitable however. Some topics are by their nature vague and open-ended (for example, a discussion of a large and open-ended topic like the nature of drama, or the difference between prose and poetry) and are better suited to non-behavioural objectives. The use of behavioural objectives in those cases could constrict exploration and discussion too much. It must always be remembered that the behaviour is not in itself the end (purpose) of the lesson, but merely an indication of the extent to which learning (the actual purpose) has taken place.'

EXAMPLE 6. AIMS AND OBJECTIVES FOR A COURSE IN ECOLOGY
'*Aims:* That pupils should develop an appreciation of the delicate balance of nature. That pupils should be aware of the position of man in relation to the biosphere.
Objectives: That pupils should develop scientific skills — observation, recording, classifying, hypothesis making, analysing data, and using statistical methods. That the pupils should be familiar with handling experimental animals, plants and apparatus. That pupils should develop a scientific attitude eg conservation or development.'

Discussion

Example 1. is a statement of aims or goals if the Eisner terminology is used. It is rather vague. What does the respondent mean by scientific awareness and how would she know that it had been achieved? Observational awareness is a little more precise and training in observation could be given.

Example 2. moves from a precise statement of intention to a fairly precise requirement from the pupils. Note that it is for a class in literature even though it is English teachers who are among the strongest objectors to the objectives approach. Compare that statement with the discussion from another teacher of English in example 5. There is no aim expressed in example 2. although there might well have been an aim for a series of lessons in this category. In contrast, example 3. shows a lesson scheme with an aim, a non-behavioural objective and a behavioural objective. Notice how the syllabus is implicit in the two statements of objectives. There are many more examples in this set of responses showing that it is possible to draw up lesson objectives in each of the subjects of the curriculum.

The fourth and fifth examples contain criticisms of this approach. One is from a geographer who draws particular attention to the danger of listing items, for lists do not imply understanding or appreciation. How can a teacher tell whether the subject matter has been understood and/or appreciated? But there is no need for objectives to be limited in this way. For example, the ability to generate alternative solutions to a problem is a high-level skill in the analysis of historical events or, for that matter, engineering design. Equally, it is of great importance in mathematics because, by and large, children are not taught to solve problems in which there is more than one answer. The teaching of problem-solving is a considerable exercise for the teacher because traditional chalk and talk procedures are unlikely to develop the skills required and much more time is needed for the kinds of exercise (eg brainstorming) which will. More than one lesson is necessary to achieve a single significant objective. Group discussions, for example, require considerable changes in the teacher's role. Objectives and personal views have to be held over to the end and not presented if they do not fit the directions of the discussion. It is then up to the teacher to decide whether or not another lesson is necessary for the derivation or presentation of those views.

Eisner puts it this way:

> 'I believe that it is perfectly appropriate for teachers and others involved in curriculum development to plan activities that have no explicit or precise objectives. In an age of accountability, this sounds like heresy. Yet surely there must be room in school for activities that promise to be fruitful, even though the teacher might not be able to say what specifically the students will learn or experience.' (Eisner, 1979)

Of course, all sorts of other things are learnt during a lesson planned by objectives. It is a part of the skill of educational criticism to understand the totality of experience in the classroom, including one's own reactions to pupil response. This is particularly important in respect of those who fail, for failure does not mean that there has been no incremental improvement and that increment of improvement may be considerable for one reason or another in a particular pupil. Thus, when questions are being asked by the teacher about his or her objectives, other things are learnt about the pupils and their dispositions. As the example in Figure 1.1 (see p 17) shows, all of these are important in the assessment of pupils.

Example 5. reminds us that sometimes we decide on a topic and do not always know where it is going to lead. This student cites open-ended topics about the nature of drama or the differences between prose and poetry. To have to include such discussions in a course is to meet an aim which can be behaviourally evaluated in terms of the development of skills in critical thinking. If a topic relates to an examination syllabus the teacher may have to ensure that certain ideas are discussed. It is very likely that the teacher has a view of the subject for there is an aim implicit in every decision. However, inspection of classroom activities and projects has led me to the view that the more vague the aim, the less successful the activity will be. The introduction of such activities requires a high level of preparation on the part of the teacher as well as self-evaluation, and the production of a work plan by objectives is an aid to such self-evaluation.

170

It may be argued that if there is so much criticism of this approach to lesson planning it should not be used, to which the response must be: can it be avoided?

First, generally speaking, we need to know where we are going and this is especially true of the student teacher. We also need to know whether we have arrived. Second, many student teachers run into difficulty because they over-prepare and try to do too much. Pupils and students have only limited powers of concentration and for this reason an objectives approach should focus on one or two well-chosen objectives. As one student wrote:

'To get beyond the facts and more on to the evaluative level in many lessons I did find that the less I did and the more they did the better off we were. However, because of the volatility and high spirit of the average 13-year-old I found that I had to plan and pace each exercise very carefully (I did not always succeed!). I found that I had to allow more time to explaining and giving instructions than I had originally assumed was necessary. I found that I had to be more rigorous in defining the aims and objectives of each lesson or exercise.'

It should force a teacher to think about what is, and what is not, important. Third, it should also force the teacher to think about the best methods of achieving an objective and to recognize that there are a variety of strategies available for learning. Fourth, it simplifies the preparation of lesson notes. Lesson schemes can be as constraining as objectives particularly if they are copied in large chunks from textbooks.

Finally, the failure to achieve objectives must lead the teacher to try to work out why they were not achieved or how they might be achieved or how they might be changed. Such questioning with the aid of theory and sometimes measurement embraces the art of educational criticism. But it is also the beginning of curriculum improvement, a point illustrated by example 6. which shows how aims and objectives are applied to a course in ecology. Objective 3. relates to the attitudinal domain and in this type of classification it is more properly an aim. It is an example which is yet another reminder of the complexity of the curriculum process. The examples which follow also illustrate these points.

The objectives approach and course design

Organizing question relating to the planning of courses

'In planning a course a teacher should ask the questions for what purpose and for which students and under what learning conditions should I employ any one method of instruction?' (De Cecco and Crawford, 1974).
Discuss. Illustrate your answer with reference to the subject you teach.

Examples

EXAMPLE 7. RELATING TO THE TEACHING OF HISTORY
'In my opinion, the history teacher does, to a certain extent, "restructure" the curriculum. Firstly, in choosing the aims. Her overall aim may be to develop a genuine love of history in the student; to develop a logical approach to the

study of history, to encourage the student to be analytical and objective; to make the student aware of the events of Europe and Ireland from X to Y; to relate the events of the past to those of the present, to enable the student to place himself in another person's position; to develop an informed love for Irish culture and heritage, etc within the confines of the examination. The teacher can have all, or none or some of these as aims. Her objectives will be more specific but equally variable.

The learning strategies she chooses will depend on her aims and objectives. If, for example, she has chosen the ability to empathize as particuarly important, she will include a lot of role-play, imaginative essays, open discussion in her class. If she has chosen the transmission of culture, she may well introduce many readings which are "off the course", encourage project work, etc. . . The teacher is free to choose her own aims and objectives, so long as she keeps in mind the requirements of the examination and ensures that her learning strategies incorporate these . . . Thus a teacher who has chosen as an aim the relation of the past to the present may concentrate on the themes and concepts of socialism, capitalism, power, democracy, facism, etc and still ensure that the student is equipped to sit the examination.'

EXAMPLE 8. RELATING TO THE TEACHING OF SCIENCE
'For instance in planning a course on light, one of the general aims would be "that the pupils would have an awareness of how light interacts with various media". Given this aim it is now possible to select specific educational objectives which in the opinion of the teacher will help to bring about this awareness. For instance the objective would be "that the pupils will be able to draw ray diagrams illustrating how the image of an object is formed by a convex lens for differing object distances". Here the teacher has picked what he considers to be a worthwhile aim and a testable objective which he hopes will help to achieve this aim. It is possible to arrive at the "worthwhileness" of aims and objectives by considering the philosophy of the subject, by task analysis of practitioners of the subject, by considering sociology and child psychology, etc.

Once one has fixed on specific objectives it is then possible to select the best method or combination of methods to achieve these objectives. For instance, in order to achieve the objective above the students will want to know what a light ray is and why light can be studied using rays. One strategy for doing this would be to show diagrams on an overhead projector. They will also need practice in forming images using lenses. The method used here would be group work working with lenses.

Selection of method will also depend to a large extent on the class one is teaching. If the class is poorly motivated then motivation will play a large part in the method used, for instance the use of filmstrips or spectacular experimental demonstrations in science in order to get students interested in the topic. If the class is highly motivated a discovery method would be used, eg after an introductory lesson the pupils may reach the objective by doing their own research.'

EXAMPLE 9. RELATING TO CURRICULUM DEVELOPMENT
'The competencies needed to design curricula are not identical with those needed to create sophisticated and useful curriculum theory. Aptitude differences exist among individuals, and the kind of experience one needs in each realm of activity differs. Theoretical training requires intensive study of relevant disciplines within philosophy and the social sciences and the critical analysis of one's written work by competent critics. The skills of curriculum development are acquired in the act of designing curricula and in experiencing first hand the problems of transforming ideas into educational materials and events. Those skills include the ability to work with others, the ability to deal with the complexities of practical deliberation, the ability to establish distance between one's work and oneself in order to see it more clearly, and the

ability to envisage the way in which activities might function within a classroom. It requires the ability to appreciate the demands that a task makes on teachers and students and to be able to judge how much guidance they might need to engage in that task. Such skills are not trivial, nor are they non-intellectual. They are demanding, they require a sense of taste and style and the ability to deal with frustration.'

Commentary

That the same general approach can apply at the level of course planning would seem to be self-evident from these examples. Contrast examples 7. and 8.: the first deals with the course while the second considers physics at the level of the lesson. Notice the considerable amount of choice available, and how each example begins with some view of the aims or goals of the course or lesson. One must ask whether the curriculum can be truly organic without self-evaluation.

Next compare any of the above with the final example which relates to curriculum and is taken from Eisner's book (Eisner, 1979). Notice how he introduces the term 'ability' and observe that it interchanges with the term 'skills'. Eisner uses these terms to define some general ability, such as the ability to generate an alternative solution or skill in designing lessons or the abilities in the middle schools programme shown in Figure 7.3 (see p 130). Now examine the examples immediately preceding Eisner's and you will see that they can be reinterpreted into a set of abilities. If you choose a goal or non-behavioural objective to cover a course, as for example 'to illustrate how a scientist (or a historian, or anyone else for that matter) solves problems' you will necessarily derive a model which is both process and product (Heywood and Montagu-Pollock, 1976). More than that you will be able to make a list of significant abilities which ought to be fostered.

I maintain that the objectives movement has failed because there has been inadequate discussion of aims in relation to an adequate theory of instruction and because its interpreters began with too restricted a view of Tyler's axioms (Tyler, 1950).

The evidence of newspaper reports and conferences suggests that much discussion among experienced teachers is not informed by theory and would be better if it were. Trainees respond to this requirement, if only in a limited way, because they are forced to by the need to respond to assessments in the classroom and in examination papers. The examples in this and the chapter which follows demonstrate that students acquire a mental framework for the development of skills in educational criticism. How then can these skills be developed in a self-monitoring situation? This and other issues will be considered in the final chapter.

References

Ainscow, M and Tweddle, D A (1979) *Preventing Classroom Failure: An Objectives Approach* Wiley: London
Cohen, L and Mannion, L (1977) *A Guide to Teaching Practice* Methuen: London

De Cecco, J P and Crawford, W R (1974) *The Psychology of Learning and Instruction* Prentice Hall: Englewood Cliffs, New Jersey

Eisner, E W (1979) *The Educational Imagination: on the Design and Evaluation of School Programs* Collier Macmillan: London

Eisner, E W (1982) An artistic approach to the supervision *in* Sergiovanni, T J (ed) *Supervision of Teaching* Association for Supervision and Curriculum Development: Washington

Elliott, J (1976) Preparing teachers for classroom accountability *Education for Teaching* 100, pp 49-71

Heywood, J and Montagu-Pollock, H (1976) *Science for Arts Students. A Case Study in Curriculum Development* Society for Research into Higher Education: Guildford

Heywood, J (1982) *Pitfalls and Planning in Student Teaching* Kogan Page: London

Krick, E V (1966) *An Introduction to Engineering Design* Wiley: New York

Parlett, M and Hamilton, D (1972) *Evaluation as Illumination* Centre for Educational Sciences The University of Edinburgh: Edinburgh

Tyler, R W (1950) *Basic Principles of Curriculum Construction* Chicago University Press: Chicago

Chapter 10
Toward Curriculum Improvement

Introduction

The real potential for innovation in the absence of centralized direction must come from a steady flow of minor improvements in the classroom. These can be strongly influenced by changes in the system of assessment and examination which a society holds to be important.

Examinations and assessment procedures may be improved by an approach which links aims and objectives, and knowledge and learning experience in such a way that the syllabus is the outcome of the curriculum development process, and assessment an integral part of continuing evaluation. In this chapter an argument is presented for this view and a model described.

Previous attempts to employ the objectives approach failed because it was trivialized. The need to design learning strategies to obtain the objectives was not understood, and assessment continued to remain apart from the learning process. The idea of screening put forward by Furst (1958) was not taken up and consequently there was much thoughtless use of objectives. Student examples relating to the use of the philosophy and sociology of education and the psychology of learning in screening objectives are given. These demonstrate the relevance of the screening process not only toward the curriculum but in initial teacher training. An example is presented which, if applied to a curriculum, would lead to substantial changes in teaching method, content and structure.

In societies where there are public systems of examination these may be reorganized to provide for much greater teaching involvement. This is an effective way of maintaining teacher performance at a high level of enthusiasm within a framework that is self-evidently accountable.

Toward curriculum improvement

All the evidence suggests that the real potential for innovation in the absence of centralized direction must come from a steady flow of minor improvements in the curriculum made by teachers in the classroom. This explains the title of the chapter and it is not without significance that two recent American books include the phrase 'curriculum improvement' in their titles (Doll, 1978; Trump and Miller, 1979). The evidence is that teachers could do much more to improve their teaching than is currently the case.

Among the authorities whose work has been discussed, and the student teachers whose illustrations have been used, there is a persistent complaint that examinations limit what they can do in the classroom. Some of them advocate the abolition of examinations which they would replace by school-based assessment, but it is hardly likely that such a global change would be allowed in our society. There may well be improvements in methods of assessing and reporting on the less able, but society will continue to demand examinations if only as a relatively dispassionate means of assessment by which it really means selection. Therefore, if there is to be curriculum improvement it has to begin with those examinations and assessment procedures which society holds to be important, not only in the techniques employed, but in the system of organization and the way it involves teachers in the work of examining. In this chapter a brief study is made of the contribution which an objectives approach can make to the development of techniques of examining and assessment to induce learning and motivate students.

Examining to some purpose

In England prior to 1960 little or no use was made of objective tests in O and A level school examinations. There is some evidence that one or two university departments, especially in the medical field, were using them (Heywood and Iliffe, 1966). By and large teachers in both schools and colleges felt they only tested recall. Moreover, the answers were easily guessed, and this is a view which is still held despite evidence to the contrary (Heywood and Youngman, 1981).

In contrast, objective tests have been widely used in America especially in the Scholastic Aptitude Tests and the tests of the American College Testing Programme for over 50 years. The higher level tests of the College Entrance Examination Board look much more like the corresponding examinations which are set in England at the Advanced level of the General Certificate of Education.

Around 1960 the Joint Matriculation Board with Professor R A C Oliver developed an A level examination in general studies (Forrest, Smith and Brown, 1970). It was intended to cause a broadening of education in sixth forms in England which was regarded as rather narrow, and at the same time test the skills in *The Taxonomy of Educational Objectives* (Bloom, 1964). Although no syllabus was published, which was itself a major change, it ranged across science, the humanities and languages and is now taken by thousands of pupils each year. It has been compared experimentally with a British equivalent of the American Scholastic Aptitude test which was tried on a very large sample in the mid-1960s and not found wanting as a predictor of future academic success (CVCP, 1966). An attractive feature of this examination was the comprehension test which required the students to read an article and then respond to short-answer questions. Of equal significance was the inclusion of objective questions (items, as they are technically called) in various sections of the paper. Nowadays very many O and A level examinations use objective items in their papers. Examiners will tell you that they are used to test knowledge (of facts, principles, etc) but it is clear that often they test higher order problem-solving skills particularly in science and technology subjects (Heywood, 1977).

Before the advent of objective tests, typical O level examination papers in the humanities in Britain might require five or six essay questions from a choice of eight or nine in two to three hours. Science papers would also require relatively long answers in response to the problems set. The norm at A level was two papers, each of three hours' duration, requiring substantive essay answers to a limited choice of questions. Similar approaches to questioning were set in universities. Part of the art of sitting examinations was, and is, to spot the question used in previous years which will occur in revised or unrevised form in the next examination, for such is the predictability of examiner behaviour.

One objection to papers of this type was that they could not cover all sections of the syllabus adequately. Consequently, there was an element of luck in the guidance given by the teachers and the revision done by the pupils. Teachers became skilled in spotting those sections of the syllabus which were omitted, and crammed the students with knowledge in the sections which were regularly tested. The same thing appears to happen in higher education where, in universities especially, teachers have control over their own syllabuses. The introduction of objective tests with 40 or so items to be tested in an hour meant that much broader coverage could be given to the syllabus. Objective tests are now widely used in higher education in Britain, especially in medicine and science subjects. Their introduction also meant that skills in essay writing could be seriously tested. But this is no argument for a wide syllabus. No syllabus can contain all the knowledge embraced by a subject, although some syllabus committees undoubtedly use a cookery book approach. The objectives movement, and more especially the authors of *The Taxonomy of Educational Objectives* (Bloom, 1964), provided an alternative approach to the construction of tests and examinations but its implications for the curriculum were never fully thought through.

The first outcome of this movement was the declaration of aims and objectives by many syllabus authors. In Ireland the Intermediate Certificates Examination Committee was greatly influenced by *The Taxonomy*, and because they believed that the examination only tested the recall of knowledge, they recommended that it should be redesigned to test higher level skills of learning to be described by behavioural objectives.

The approach adopted by some examiners in England was to choose the main categories of *The Taxonomy* and then write objectives appropriate both to the category and the subject. Sometimes the same categories as in *The Taxonomy* are used; sometimes the sub-categories are reclassified into another category. A typical example is shown in Figure 10.1 (see page 178). It will be seen that the sub-operations within the category are fairly broad and do not relate to the 350 or so specific lessons which make

up the course. This is in complete contrast to programmed instruction
in which a behavioural objective is set for each sub-problem. (Of course,
not all programmed instruction materials are designed in this way as,
for example, those in the *Science for Arts* programme referred to
previously — Heywood and Montagu-Pollock, 1976).

B. THE OBJECTIVES OF THE EXAMINATION
This statement is intended to provide a general indication of the abilities
which the examination will be designed to test in relation to the items listed
in the syllabus. It is not suggested that such clear distinctions can always be
applied in constructing examination questions, and a particular question may
test more than one skill.

1. Knowledge and abilities to be tested

(a) Knowledge. The recall of terminology, conventions, basic constructions
and engineering components.
(Example. Ability to distinguish the characteristics of multiplanar axono-
metric and oblique methods of projection.)

(b) Technique. The ways and means of using drawing instruments to achieve
good draughtsmanship, well-proportioned sketches as well as construc-
tional accuracy.
(Example. Ability to construct an accurate funicular polygon.)

(c) Visualization and interpretation. The demonstration of basic understanding
of form and function from verbal or graphical information; translation of
written information into drawings and vice versa; recognition of functional
and dimensional requirements.
(Examples. *(a)* Ability to construct a cam profile from a descriptive specification. *(b)* Ability to explain the functioning of a valve from its assembly
drawing.)

(d) Application. The thorough understanding of specified geometric and
mechanical concepts, or components, within new practical situations.
(Example. Ability to recall the graphical method ensuring constant velocity
ratio for gear teeth and to apply it to construct a conjugate profile to a
given arbitrary curve.)

(e) Analysis. The breakdown of given material into constituent parts in order
to determine their effect and relationship within the whole. This process
demands the recognition of elements essential for the application of
analytical methods.
(Example. Ability to analyse a mechanism to find the output force and
displacement, given their input values.)

(f) Synthesis. The putting together of geometric concepts and mechanical
elements in such a way as to constitute a new whole.
(Example. The ability to propose locking devices and suitable bearings to
make up a gearshaft of known function and general proportions.)

Figure 10.1 *Abilities to be tested in geometrical and engineering
drawing at A level* (reproduced by kind permission
of the Joint Matriculation Board, Manchester).

Inspection of Figure 5.1 (see p 84) which illustrates the aims and objectives
of the Intermediate Certificate Examination in history in Ireland, in
contrast to *The Taxonomy* (Volume 1 on the cognitive domain) not only
mixes up aims and objectives but places cognitive and affective dimension
alongside of each other, but not to the general detriment of the statement.
The list does not have the detail of the curriculum for geometrical and
engineering drawing shown in Figure 10.1, but it does focus on a few key

performances (behaviours) required of the pupil in the cognitive domain while, at the same time, pointing toward the development of real dispositions in the understanding of people and events. The methods by which these goals are to be achieved are left to the decision of the teacher.

A broadly based approach to aims and objectives of this kind should require no apology, provided that the examination procedures and instructional strategies go some way to obtaining those aims and objectives. However, it is by no means certain that this point is generally appreciated. The power of the example of the history examination is gained from the cultural context which it has to examine content-wise. For the last decade Anglo-Irish relations have been exceptionally tense. There has been a bloodbath in Northern Ireland; the British are accused of not understanding Irish history and at least two British Ministers have accused the Irish of distorting history. Yet in Figure 5.1 are a set of objectives developed by the Irish Inspectorate and its syllabus committee which any historian would accept. Such statements are perhaps best described (following Eisner) as expressive outcomes. It is evident that not everything can be measured and it will never be known whether pupils will acquire the responsibilities required of them. For most people, it probably does not matter that it is not possible to measure the effects on behaviour of learning strategies and assessment procedures designed to test the pupils' understanding of what it feels like to be in someone else's position. However, it will matter for most people that the course should try to do this, and a statement of expressive outcomes of this kind helps to keep the issue in focus.

It is also apparent that even if sub-tests are designed to assess specifically described skills, as for example in the evaluation of sources, other skills which contribute to performance in this area will also be assessed. Since intelligence is an important contributory factor in any such measurement of performance, the simple isolation of higher level skills at this level may be difficult if not impossible (Heywood, 1977). Yet papers clearly designed to test such skills will provide a focus for study and learning. An examination of this kind can only test whether a few objectives regarded as significant have been obtained and may force teachers to use learning strategies which focus on the attainment of these objectives. For example, role-playing can be used to try to demonstrate what it feels like to be in someone else's position and projects can be used to develop skills in the location, acquisition and recording of simple historical information (Heywood, 1977). Jackdaws (packs of historical data) can be used to train pupils in the evaluation of sources.

However, in England and Ireland the examining bodies have been content only to declare aims and objectives. Often the relationship between them and the examination is far from clear, and if the examinations do test them it is more often by accident than design. It is this as much as anything else that has brought the 'objectives' approach into disrepute, for its implications for examination design and teaching and learning have never been thought through.

The pilot 16+ syllabuses (England) which the present author has seen are accompanied by examinations which do not 'apparently' specifically test the objectives that have been stated, except in the areas of knowledge and comprehension (especially when comprehension tests are set). Their proponents argue that the questions will in any event test many objectives. It is suggested that if the examinations are factorially analysed question by question, factors will emerge to show that the objectives are being tested when the questions in the clusters are inspected item by item, but studies of this kind have yet to be undertaken. Teachers in Ireland who were asked to rate the questions in the public examinations concluded that the questions did not test the objectives stated at the beginning of the syllabus. They thought the experimental examinations' sub-tests, designed to meet specific but broadly defined objectives, were better.

The designers of the JMB A level engineering science syllabus were very much influenced by the work on general studies and by Furneaux's study of examinations in mechanical engineering which suggested that all the examinations tested only one factor (Furneaux, 1962). Such examinations did not reflect the activities of an engineer at work. Using a model of the engineering design, seven broad categories thought to be significant in the work of an engineer were selected for examination. They were:

1. *Knowledge and Basic Problem-Solving*
   One hour 40-item objective test.
2. *Comprehension*
   One hour. Article to be read. Short answer questions.
3. *Project Planning and Design*
   One hour. Short answer.
4/5. *Application of Science to Engineering Problems*
   Three hours. Part 1. 15-minute problem-solving questions.
   Part 1. 40-minute problem-solving questions.
6/7. *Coursework*
   Part 1. Two experimental investigations of 12 hours' duration (approx). Part 2. Project of 50 hours' duration.

The factorial evidence (which has been repeated yearly) indicates that there are five specific factors which are associated with the five main components and this suggests that different areas of knowledge are being tested in each of these papers. The coursework assessment procedure concentrated on six specific skill areas relating to project planning (in particular those abilities related to the recognition of the assumptions and their effects, the generation and evaluation of alternative solutions, the utilization of resources, project implementation and evaluation).

The most curious outcome was that the correlation between coursework and the project planning paper was the lowest of all the inter-correlations between the components (Heywood and Kelly, 1973). This was surprising as the project planning exercise was intended to mirror the project planning. There are a number of statistical reasons for this result but in an 'illuminative' investigation it was found that several teachers did not feel it was necessary to provide any particular instruction for the written paper since the skills would be acquired while doing the project. It was also apparent that planning under the duress of an examination might require different, but nevertheless useful, skills from those used in planning in a 50-hour project for which there was plenty of warning.

This led the present author to the view that for each significant objective there will be an appropriate set of learning strategies which will best ensure that the objective is attained. To put it simply: if examinations influence learning as we all agree they do, and if they are designed to test specified objectives, then teachers will have to provide learning strategies which will best meet those objectives. This is not to deny that all learning has a major collateral component (Hogan, 1980), or that there are many unintended and expressive outcomes to any learning experience (see pp 166 - 8). It is to argue that in all learning there must be focus which necessarily implies an objectives approach. All learning requires organization, structure and meaning.

One of the aims which the Irish teachers of history wished to test was the interpretation and evaluation of different kinds of data about the same event, as, for example, the comparison of a newspaper article with official statistics. Their paper was called Evaluation of Sources. It was found that training was required if pupils were to treat this paper adequately; they had to spend time in their courses looking at different kinds of historical data (Jackdaw packs have been designed with this kind of objective in mind). The teachers also wished to encourage essay writing which, in addition to narrative, would show some evidence of skills in analysis and evaluation and for this it was also found necessary to provide specific training.

Specific training must take time and this must be at the expense of the syllabus. We found that a quite serious weakness in our experimental assessments was that pupils were not trained to meet the objectives which the teachers had designed for the examination and assessment procedures. These studies led to a modification of the often published circular model of the curriculum shown in Figure 10.2 (see p 182). In this version the syllabus is in the centre of the circle for it is the outcome of a complex interactive process in which significant aims and objectives are selected, learning strategies (and appropriate materials) designed to obtain those objectives, and test and assessment procedures developed for their evaluation.

As things stand these relationships may or may not exist. The evidence suggests that in all probability they do not, and is in no small measure due to the lack of involvement of teachers in the examining process. The emphasis in teaching is still on the syllabus and the teacher's interpretation of it. An objectives approach of this kind is likely to require a reduction in syllabus if time is to be found for the kind of learning strategies appropriate to the attainment of skills of the type described. It is difficult to see

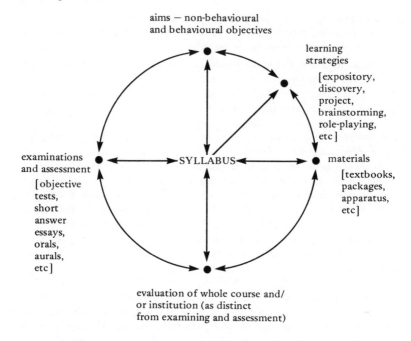

aims — non-behavioural
and behavioural objectives

learning
strategies

[expository,
discovery,
project,
brainstorming,
role-playing,
etc]

examinations
and assessment

[objective
tests,
short
answer
essays,
orals,
aurals,
etc]

SYLLABUS

materials

[textbooks,
packages,
apparatus,
etc]

evaluation of whole course and/
or institution (as distinct
from examining and assessment)

Figure 10.2 *A model of the assessment instruction process*

how there can be objections to this form of systems analysis of the curriculum and its associated learning and assessment procedures.

Murphy (1976), after a study of the attitudes of teachers involved in the experimental projects in Ireland, argued that unless the teachers internalized the objectives in such a way that they became committed to them, the objectives were unlikely to be obtained. Therefore, teachers have to be actively involved in the construction of the curriculum. The objectives approach has never really been tried; if anything it has been trivialized, something which would not have happened had the ideas of Furst (1958) on screening been taken up (Heywood, 1981).

Screening is the activity of selecting significant aims and objectives using the philosophy of education (and the subject), the sociology of education and the psychology of learning. It is with this aspect of curriculum design that initial training should be concerned. That it can be undertaken at this stage is well illustrated by the student responses to the question on screening below.

Aims and objectives in course planning

First organizing question

Briefly describe the contribution of philosophy, psychology and sociology to the selection of aims and objectives for the school curriculum. Illustrate your answer with reference to the subject you teach.

Second organizing question

Discuss the role of sociology in the screening of aims and objectives.

From responses to the first organizing question

EXAMPLE 1. RELATING TO THE IDEA OF SCREENING

'A careful and systematic approach is essential in the planning of a curriculum, and steps must be taken in an ordered and organized way if effective planning is to be achieved. The first step involves the *who* and *what* of the curriculum. Who is it being designed for and what do you want it to achieve or in other words what are your aims and objectives? Philosophy, psychology and sociology all have an important role in the screening of aims and objectives in curriculum design. Philosophy applied to aims and objectives forces you to consider the nature of the person or persons for whom you are designing your curriculum and the relative values of your objectives. In an English curriculum why should we have the aims of enabling pupils to think critically and not just have knowledge or comprehension? This is a philosophical value judgement — critical ability is more highly valued than skill in comprehension . . .

Psychology in education deals with the nature of the learner and the theory of instruction, in other words, how the learner learns. An understanding of psychology will therefore enable the curriculum designer to devise the best possible learning strategies in order to achieve the aims and objectives. In an English class if one wishes to convey the mastery of Keats in describing the moods of Autumn will it best be achieved by reading the poem aloud, showing pictures of Autumn scenes or asking pupils to describe Autumn themselves in verse or prose? These are the questions relating to aims and objectives which a knowledge of educational psychology will help you solve and determine.'

EXAMPLE 2. RELATING TO THE MANY SOURCES OF OBJECTIVES

'Aims and objectives for a school curriculum are obtained from many sources. One such source is studies of the learners themselves. These studies would determine the interest areas of the students. Progressives would argue that we should incorporate into the curriculum topics that are of interest to students. Although these areas may not comprise the whole curriculum they can act as starting points. Essentialists on the other hand would argue that the curriculum has come down through the generations relatively unchanged and we should not be too concerned with student interests which are transitory. They call this concern the "cult of presentism".

Another source of objectives is studies of contemporary life outside school. What are the needs of students outside of school? Needs are used in two senses, one is what does the student need to survive in the world? This would include training needed to obtain employment and the ability to care for oneself physically. These needs would differ from culture to culture and from age to age. The other type of need is a psychological need. Students need to be given a feeling of self-worth; they need to feel that they are wanted and belong.

A third-level source of objectives is the subject specialists. They define objectives in terms of their own subjects. A mathematician for instance would define the utilitarian, cultural, social and personal objectives for having mathematics on the curriculum.

With all these objectives available curriculum designers have to be able to select some and eliminate other objectives. This process is called screening. They do this with the use of philosophy, psychology and sociology.'

EXAMPLE 3. RELATING TO ENGLISH AND METHOD

'Philosophy puts much emphasis on the value of freedom and choice in education. I based some of my objectives on this. I gave the pupils the

opportunity of writing weekly English essays on any topic they wanted —
I never prescribed. Theirs was the only choice. Similarly we planned the
English courses together — I did not impose my will but let the students decide
for themselves with my help what we should do. So I used the philosophy
course which always put great emphasis on freedom and choice to help me in
narrowing aims.'

EXAMPLE 4. RELATING TO THE TEACHING OF RELIGION
'Philosophy: Many people would question whether religion should in fact be a
school subject. Indeed I was asked that very question at a recent interview for
a job — I got it! Obviously this is a vital question and philosophy does provide
answers; granted you find contradictory answers but one has to judge the value
of each.

Lonergan in his discussion of knowledge divides it into three:
(i) experiential, (ii) rational and (iii) para-rational. Under para-rational he
includes art, co-natural ethics and religion. Lonergan would argue that since
religion is an experience of man, and a special one at that, it must be studied.
This is not a surprising statement from a priest!'

EXAMPLE 5. RELATING TO THE TEACHING OF POLITICS IN SCHOOLS
'Philosophy is concerned with the values we should have in society and how
to live a full and happy life . . . If one has a philosophy of education for
democracy then one would try to strengthen the pupils' confidence and
faith in the democratic system of government.

Aim: To give the pupils an awareness of the value of democracy in
upholding the rights of the individual.

Objective: To demonstrate how the individual was subordinate to the
state in Hitler's Germany and Fascist Italy. To outline the discrimination and
persecution of the Jewish community. To list the civil liberties which were
withdrawn.'

EXAMPLE 6. RELATING TO THE TEACHING OF THE IRISH LANGUAGE
'As regards teaching the Irish language philosophy has an important role to play
for the screening of aims. Presuming that one has already made a value
judgement on the inclusion of Irish on the curriculum, one must then try
to decide what importance it has. Should one concentrate on the language
itself or on the cultural or historical aspects of it? As we have learned from
philosophy, language is uniquely human insofar as human language is
propositional and reflects a desire on the part of any human to communicate
with his companions, not simply for the passing on of information but for
discussing ideas and opinions which show the richness of the human being.
Thus language must play an important role and its primary aim should be to
enable the person to communicate effectively. Language should be taught
not simply for its grammatical aspect but to facilitate communication.

We also learn from philosophy that a human being must learn to live in
his own society and so an important aim of education is to enculture the pupil.
Thus another aim in teaching Irish could be to give the pupil a better
understanding of the Irish culture, traditions, art, songs, legends etc. Philosophy
also shows the importance of values in society and education should make
pupils aware of the values of their own society. In this respect the aim of
teaching the historical aspect of the Irish language would be to provide an
understanding of the fortunes of the language throughout the ages and to
show pupils how these have affected the values and attitudes of the Irish
people. The historical perspective can provide the understanding upon which
the pupil can make his own judgements as to whether or not he will accept
those values.'

EXAMPLE 7. RELATING TO THE TEACHING OF ENGLISH LITERATURE
'Any discussion of philosophy of education with particular regard to the teaching of English must take account of the work of David Holbrook, a celebrated authority, in this area. His contributions to this subject including *English for Maturity, English for the Rejected, Children's Writing*, etc have joined the list of essential reading for any teacher of English.

His method is unequivocally based on a philosophy of life which holds the teaching of English as a fundamental and essential area of the education of children. His philosophy of education, if one were to attempt to categorize it, would fall under the heading of the Romantic Tradition (as distinct from the Classical or Progressive types). It is child-centred, intended for the development of the child as an imaginative, intelligent individual.

Holbrook decries the moral decline of contemporary society (for which he blames the impoverishment of our lives by the mass media, particularly television) and laments the fact that adolescents in their formative years of development and personal conflict have no touchstone, no symbols, no suitable objects of emulation. The "pop" and football culture of today is an impoverishing one and a poor substitute for the folk culture of pre-twentieth century days.

Holbrook sees in the English class enormous potential for the enrichment of children's lives. Drama, music and religion are all incorporated into his curriculum along with poetry, novels and short stories. The children are encouraged to write their own work and read it aloud in class. His philosophy not merely "screens" his educational aims and objectives, it is their very foundation, and pervades them at all levels. If his aims are wide-ranging and ambitious, his objectives are equally generalized.

As to behavioural objectives — they merit little in Holbrook's estimation, abhorrent as he is of standardization and measured limits which fail to take account of the human potential.

Critics of Holbrook maintain that his particular brand of philosophy has little relevance in today's multi-racial, multi-denominational comprehensive. His ideas are based on English literature, music and drama as the basis from which to work with children. What of the thousands of immigrants, and the non-Christians for whom much of this heritage has little relevance?

This criticism is a valid one and points out the danger of educationalists showing too strong a bias towards one aspect, in this case philosophy, to the practical exclusion of other areas of consideration, psychology, sociology, etc. For an adequate standpoint from which to 'screen' aims and objectives, all the above-mentioned areas must come into play.'

EXAMPLE 8. RELATING SOCIOLOGY TO THE CURRICULUM IN THE COMPLEX RACIAL SITUATION TO BE FOUND IN TRINIDAD
'Trinidad being such a complex country in terms of races, cultures and creeds, it was necessary to consider sociological issues with regard to the plan. For example, East Indian parents expected their daughters to be docile and passive (in the main, there were of course exceptions especially in upper income groups, but we had few of those). Students were to be encouraged then to have opinions and to state them. Small discussion groups were to be used at first to enable the girls to get used to having their say on matters of religion and morality. Again there was a social problem involving antagonism between Negroes and East Indians. Here philosophy and sociology merge for the idea was to inculcate and encourage the development of respect for the human being and not for the lightness of skin or straightness of hair. Role-playing and short dramatized situations were seen as one way of dealing with this, especially since Trinidadians are natural actors and very, very witty. Another social issue was the status of the dialect. In the past the dialect had been treated as "bad English" and had been vigorously discouraged. It is though

highly expressive and the language of the students' homes. Various studies had been made by linguistic experts and the status has risen in academic circles. It was necessary to bring it to grass roots level. The role-play and drama included dialect, if appropriate, and it was hoped that students would come to respect themselves more, from the respect accorded in school to their language.'

EXAMPLE 9. RELATING TO SOCIOLOGY AND THE TEACHING OF FRENCH
'I know a particular teacher who began teaching French in a working class school in Dublin, and he met with considerable opposition when he tried to attain his objectives of teaching about France, and French people, as well as the language. The pupils couldn't see any relevance of French to their lives — when would they get a chance to go to France? This teacher was so enthusiastic and determined that he encouraged and helped the pupils earn money toward a school trip to France, showed them films, brought them in posters of pop stars in France etc. Since then he has raised French to a high status for working class children. The sociology screen would have predicted for him the opposite.'

EXAMPLE 10. ISSUES IN THE TEACHING OF MODERN LANGUAGES

' "Traditional" methods	"New" methods
Purposes: to study the forms and structures of the foreign language.	To be able to use the language creatively, meaningfully in real-life situations.
Content: the structures and forms of the language.	Evolved between teachers and pupils — interests and needs of pupils — emphasis is on what is said not on forms or structures used to say it.
Methods: Decided by teacher — same for all pupils.	Evolved through teacher-pupil interaction — can be varied according to individual pupil needs.
Teacher role: To instruct and receive appropriate responses — all learning occurs in classroom.	To fulfil pupil needs — act as a resource centre. Make decisions about methods, content of course,
Pupils' role: To recall and deliver expected responses.	make demands of the teacher.'

and

'If one decides that one's non-behavioural objective will be for the pupils to be able to speak a certain amount of French (this amount would be more precisely defined), with reasonable pronunciation, one might then consider using an audio-visual method to achieve this, as this would expose the students to the spoken language and provide opportunity to use it. If, on the other hand, one's objective concerned accuracy of grammar, one would perhaps use a method of instruction more comparable to that eg with great emphasis on the use of a textbook.'

Screening

Screening as indicated above is a term which appears to be due to E J Furst. In his book *Constructing Evaluation Instruments* (Furst, 1958) he quotes numerous sources for aims and objectives. Among them, but only as one of a number of sources, is *The Taxonomy of Educational Objectives* (Bloom, 1964). Furst argues that there are many more goals available than any school could hope to obtain and some will be inconsistent with others. Therefore, schools have an obligation to sort out the significant goals and objectives which they feel should be met. This process he calls screening. To do this schools must work out their educational and social philosophy. A school programme designed to encourage young people to accept the present social order will be different from one which encourages pupils to try to improve the present social order. His questions tend to emphasize social philosophy rather than the epistemology. Clearly we have to be sure about the reasons for the particular stance we take toward the knowledge we believe should be taught. Screening of this kind may for example suggest that we achieve very little in terms of the general aims of education as Furst shows. The present author has been particularly concerned with screening as it applies to the development of the curriculum within individual subjects (Heywood, 1968; 1981).

Of course, the activity of educational research is screening, and in-depth studies go on all the time (eg Lawton, 1973; 1978), for example, a philosophical treatise like that presented by Brent (1978) or more recently by Brumbagh (1982) on Whitehead, or Mulcahy's argument that the position taken by Newman on liberal education is inconsistent with his philosophical position, expressed more especially in the *Essay in Aid of a Grammar of Assent* (Mulcahy, 1973). The debate about the merit of determining aims of education is itself an exercise in screening as is the discussion about the influence of environment and heredity on IQ (Eysenck and Kamin, 1981; Evans and Waites, 1981). In arriving at a list (or no list) the participants and individual teachers come to a clear understanding of the learning theory they wish to defend and this is an essential professional obligation for every teacher.

Questions relating to the structure of knowledge and modes of thinking are clearly important, not least because, as Shulman (1970) shows, all psychological theories have an epistemological foundation. However, Furst argues that schools and teachers are also obliged to understand the learning theory they wish to defend and the evidence of the student examples suggests not only that they can do this but that, had those who advocated the objectives approach subjected their objectives to philosophical, sociological and psychological analysis, less trivial examples would have occurred and there would have been fewer arguments against system approaches to curriculum design and evaluation (Stenhouse, 1975).

Furst wrote his book before recent developments in the sociology of knowledge, so while he refers to psychology as the 'second screen' he does not refer at all to sociology, which is a considerable weakness. Nowadays, we would look at the curriculum in terms of Eggleston's (1977) five factors, that is, in terms of:

'1. the definition of what shall be regarded as knowledge, understanding, values and skills;
2. the evaluation of this knowledge — into areas of greater or lesser importance and status;
3. the principles on which such knowledge shall be distributed: to whom and at what time various kinds of knowledge shall be made available and from

whom they shall be withheld;
4. the identity of the groups whose definitions prevail in these matters;
5. the legitimacy of these groups to act in these ways.'

It is fairly easy to see how psychology can be used as a screen, for it asks such questions as: Can a learning objective be readily attained at a given level of maturity? Will this particular concept be understood if that particular method of teaching is used? At what pace should the content of a syllabus be presented? At the level of lesson planning students have little difficulty in relating the ideas of Piaget to their work, as their examples show, but the idea that a particular psychological theory can have a major bearing on the structure of a curriculum is seldom discussed in educational circles (Duckworth, 1979; Kuhn, 1979). This particular point is no better illustrated than in the application of Perry's model of intellectual development (Perry, 1968) to the engineering curriculum by Culver and Hackos (1982).

Illustrating the application of a development theory to the design of a curriculum in higher education

As a result of a longitudinal study to determine what happened to students during their four years in liberal arts education, W G Perry formulated an empirical model for the sequence of intellectual development in which there are nine stages or positions. In this theory a student progresses from a simple dualistic view of life and knowledge in which absolute answers exist for everything, to relativism in which knowledge and value judgements are seen as contextual and relativistic (position five). Following this, an adjustment is made to the relativistic world and in the last three stages students begin to experience the need for commitment and make an 'initial commitment in some area such as career selection, values, religious belief, etc'. In the ninth position commitment becomes 'an ongoing, unfolding activity through which their life styles are expressed'.

Culver and Hackos (1982) argue that the traditional lecture method reinforces the dualism of the first two positions. The professor is the authority and the Bible the textbook. The curriculum is received and is reinforced both by the structure of the timetable and the organization of knowledge within the traditional disciplines. This, Culver and Hackos say, leads the students to a restricted view of problem-solving. 'They do not realize that real life problems are a smorgasbord of several "subjects".' Students do not learn how to define problems or work through to an open-ended solution. Even at positions three and four of the model students have only a limited ability to evaluate evidence. The solution of real life problems requires that students operate at the higher order positions.

To overcome the effects of the traditional system in which students respond to authority Culver and Hackos proposed a four-year programme which, beginning with the initial stages of intellectual development, would support the students as they grew to the sixth position. Thus they proposed to challenge the students with open-ended problem-solving within the highly structured and secure setting of the traditional course. They show their model as a tree (Figure 10.3, see p 190).The traditional subjects provide the tools for problem-solving which is the main activity of the professional. The mode of instruction is intended to support an inquiring approach to education rather than the presentation of new facts even at position one where, in Piagetian terms, students have difficulty in understanding an abstract concept. Culver and Hackos describe how Knefflekamp (1974) related learning strategies to course content for positions one and two (freshman years) by means of the diagram in Figure 10.4 (see p 191). In his experiment students on a humanities course and an English composition course were taught by a traditional method and a Perry-based scheme. It is claimed that those who were taught on the Perry-based scheme achieved more intellectual growth than those on the traditional scheme and that this was significant.

Culver and Hackos note that when students are challenged to perform at higher intellectual levels at the lower position of development they become confused and suffer cognitive dissonance because the new ways of looking at the problem may be too unrelated to the highly structured content of the normal curriculum. Therefore, they argue, the specification of behavioural objectives is important for course design since it should ensure that complexity is in the subject matter and not the course organization. The students who provided the examples in this book will be aware of this problem since the lecture programme in the applied psychology of instruction set out to achieve similar goals in respect of teaching. Traditional lectures were not given: instead of the usual textbook approach the students discussed problems arising from their classroom experience. Many students found this experience difficult to handle which has suggested to the present author that learning in any subject involves the learner in a staged or positioned development even in Piagetian terms. It will be of some importance to follow up these studies to see if the attitudes to study generated by such schemes 'persist' and also whether the students transfer them to the other subjects they study. In the Culver and Hackos model they embrace the whole of the technical curriculum.

It is not always necessary to predicate a psychological model of the curriculum to arrive at a similar conclusion about the curriculum if the initial question is: 'What does a student need to prepare him or her to handle the problems with which he or she will be faced in life?' An engineering curriculum based on a model of what engineers did at work led to a curriculum structure in the first year of a four-year course which was radically different from the traditional one. Its intention was to draw out the principles and concepts of engineering science and design from the solution of practical problems set as carefully selected projects so that the range of principles and concepts would be illustrated.

The general idea was presented in matrix form as the example in Figure 10.5 (see p 192) shows. Along one axis are the resources available to engineers for the solution of the problem. Along the other axis are the

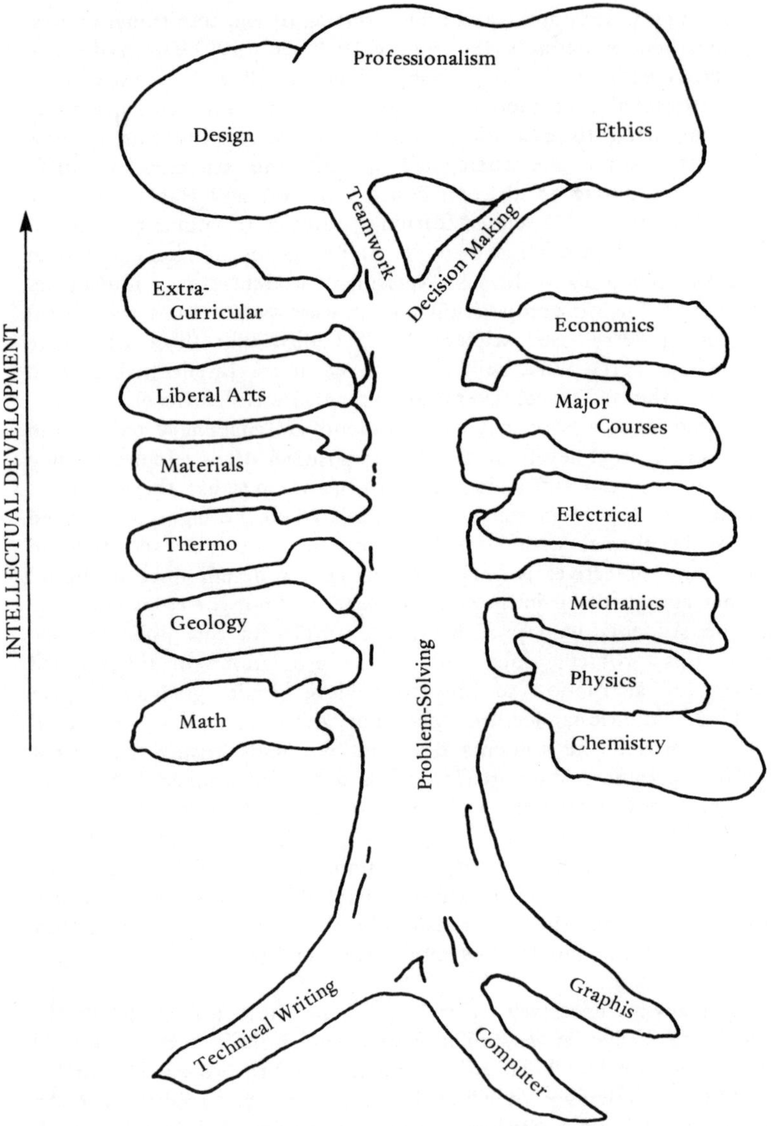

Figure 10.3 *An alternative model of technical education described by R S Culver and J T Hackos (reproduced by kind permission of the authors and the editors of the Journal of Engineering Education)*

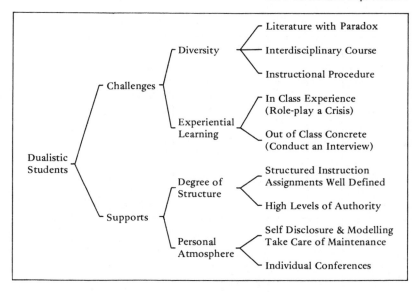

Figure 10.4 *A representation of Knefflekamp's model (Knefflekamp, 1974) of course design as described by R S Culver and J T Hackos* (reproduced by kind permission of the authors and the editors of the *Journal of Engineering Education*)

operations used in the utilization of these resources. The authors Heywood *et al*, 1966) argued that a series of projects would not only illustrate how engineers went about their tasks but also the applications of engineering science in design and manufacture. The projects would have to be chosen to ensure that a range of different activities was covered as well as the essential principles of engineering science (Woodson, 1966). In one example, the relation of the matrix to the problem of ventilating an aircraft is shown and two of the lines — columns two and three — are expanded to show more detail in Figure 10.6 (see p 193). Further details of the compressor would be obtained from a detailed analysis of the different types of aerodynamic and displacement compressors. In a course structured on these lines it would be important to ensure that knowledge could be transferred to unseen problems and an examination would probably help students integrate their knowledge for such transfer. Subsequently, Lewis (1966) included vegetation and animals in the resource columns and he subdivided a human being into energy and ideas. Using a matrix he devised a complete programme for a college of technology which is shown in Figure 10.7 (see p 194). Notice how this is an expansion of the tree suggested by Culver and Hackos (1982) (Figure 10.3, on p 190). The British students for whom such a programme was suggested would be a year in advance of their American counterparts.

Both Perry and the Piagetian psychologies suggest that students might

The problem is the provision of clean air in aircraft

Resources / Operations	Energy (a)	Space (b)	Force (c)	Materials (d)	Men (e)
1. Forms and Properties	Heat: CO2: Effective Temperature				
2. Location and Acquisition	In Wings — Off Main Power Units (see Figure 10.6)				
3. Measurement			Compressor Characteristic Pressure/Flow/Temp (see Figure 10.6)		
4. Control		Navigators, Pilots, Passenger, Steward, Compartments			
5. Transformation and Conversion	Cooling: Heat Removal From Fluid			Filters in order to remove dust, etc	Number of passengers and crew
6. Transmission		Recirculated air for heat balance	Method of recirculation	What has to be recirculated? What has to be lost?	

Figure 10.5 *An example of the application of the matrix approach based on the problem of ventilating an aircraft* (Based on *High Altitude Passenger Flying with Special Reference to Air Treatment* by B T Turner, JIInstE, 68 p 219, 1958).

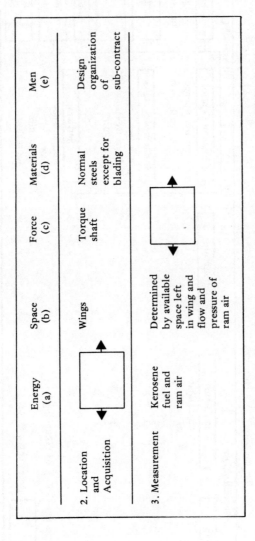

	Energy (a)	Space (b)	Force (c)	Materials (d)	Men (e)
2. Location and Acquisition		Wings	Torque shaft	Normal steels except for blading	Design organization of sub-contract
3. Measurement	Kerosene fuel and ram air	Determined by available space left in wing and flow and pressure of ram air			

Figure 10.6 *Shows the first expansion of columns two and three in the matrix of Figure 10.5*

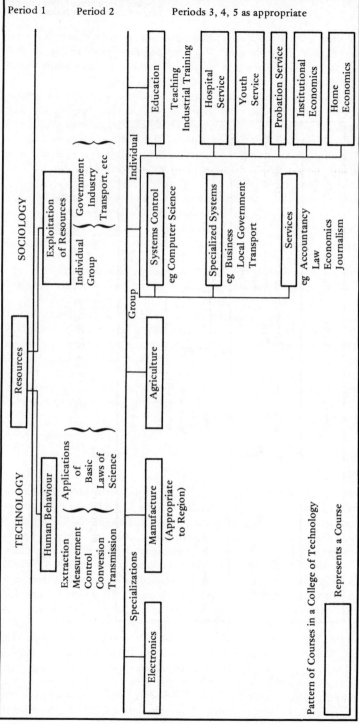

Figure 10.7 *A development of the matrix idea for a subject (Figure 10.5) to the curriculum for a college of technology by E R L Lewis (1966).*

have difficulties with this approach since it is not related to the traditional structures of their expectations. But the authors were aware of *The Taxonomy* and thought that they would be able to give coherence to the course through the application of behavioural objectives.

There are numerous issues which ought to be subjected to this kind of scrutiny. For example, does the fixed school leaving age prevent the achievement of socially acceptable goals? What implications would the introduction of graded tests in mathematics have for the structure of the curriculum? Moral education raises all sorts of issues: should it, or should it not, be associated with religious education? What implications does the development of a multi-cultural society have for the curriculum? Is it a good example of the way in which answers will be shaped by the particular culture in which the question is put? (Batelaan and Hofmans, 1982; Hobbs, 1982; Hogbin and Palmer, 1982; Lynch, 1983.) Views of English authors in this field are unlikely to be acceptable in Ireland, and vice versa.

The idea of screening reminds the teacher that education is the outcome of a complex set of interactions in which his or her personal philosophy and psychology of learning play an important role and he or she cannot enter this curriculum debate without understanding their role in his or her thinking. How then can teachers be trained in screening? One approach is to require teachers to undertake a practical curriculum study during their initial training. But projects do not ensure that teachers can either implement their ideas or retain their enthusiasm during the long years of professional practice. One way of achieving these goals would be to involve every teacher in the process of examining and assessment, as is done by some examinations boards.

The organization of examinations, curriculum and self-improvement

Various proposals have been made for improving the school examination system in societies where there are public systems of examination. First, there has been the demand that examinations should be replaced by a system of school-based assessment and profile reporting. It seems likely that there will be substantial experiments with profiles, particularly for the less able. These are likely to be based on criterion-referenced groupings of objectives (abilities). School-based assessment has not been taken up, although many teachers operate mode III examinations for which the syllabuses and examinations are teacher-designed to the approval of the examining authority. Some employers view mode III examinations with suspicion and do not believe that their standards can be judged. The Irish Committee on the Intermediate Certificate Examination proposed a nationally normed objective test to get round this problem. Teachers would do two assessments: one would be related to the subject taken and the other to a school report so that comment could be made on all those non-examinable things thought to be of educational value. A third score would be the nationally normed test. The Committee's research unit opposed these proposals on the grounds that study for the national test would dominate learning. It proposed instead a system similar to that operated by the Southern Regional Examinations Board (SREB) in England because:

1. Not every teacher wants to design his or her own syllabuses and set his or her own examinations. Those who wish to do this should be allowed this facility.
2. The assessment of coursework within an examination is now a common feature of assessment.
3. Improvement is more likely to occur when teachers continually discuss their ideas and problems together.
4. The subject committees of examination boards do not provide teachers with sufficient involvement except for the few.

The SREB system gets round these issues thus:

1. It offers all three modes of examination.
2. It involves every teacher in his or her subject area through regionally-based consortia.
3. Independently of the mode of examination the teacher is the first marker of his or her children's scripts.
4. The scripts are then moderated by the teachers acting together in consortia.

One modification suggested by the Irish Committee was that field officers should be appointed with responsibility for subject improvement and training and that the consortia should be the sources of curriculum improvement. Recently Barnes (1982) has described and exemplified systematic strategies for thinking about the curriculum both in initial training and workshops. This approach seems to be similar to the group activities which led to the teacher design of the experimental 15+ examinations in Ireland (Heywood, McGuinness and Murphy, 1981). The consortia approach to the structure of an examinations board provides for workshops in which curriculum and examinations can be critically considered together. Here the Board combines the functions of examining and curriculum development. It has the advantage of being a relatively cheap and effective way of maintaining teacher performance at a high level of enthusiasm within a framework that is self-evidently accountable.

References

Barnes, D (1982) *Practical Curriculum Study* Routledge and Kegan Paul: London

Batelaan, P and Hofmans, T (1982) Multicultural education in the Dutch educational system *European Journal of Teacher Education* 5 pp 45-54

Bloom, B (1964) (ed) *The Taxonomy of Educational Objectives* Vol I, Longmans Green: London

Brent, A (1978) *Philosophical Foundations of the Curriculum* Unwin: London

Brumbaugh, R S (1982) *Whitehead, Process, Philosophy and Education* State University of New York Press: Albany

Committee of Vice Chancellors and Principals (1966) *The Test of Academic Aptitude: Introductory Booklet* CVCP: London

Culver, R S and Hackos, J T (1982) Perry's model of intellectual development *Journal of Engineering Education* 73 (2) pp 221-6

Doll, R C (1978) Curriculum improvement *Decision-Making and Process* Allyn and Bacon: Boston

Duckworth, E (1979) Either we're too early and they can't learn it or we're too late and they know it already: the dilemma of 'applying Piaget' *Harvard Educational Review* 49 (3) pp 297-312

Eggleston, S J (1977) *The Sociology of the School Curriculum* Routledge and Kegan Paul: London

Evans, B and Waites, B (1981) *IQ and Mental Testing. An Unnatural Science and its Social History* Macmillan: London

Eysenck, H J and Kamin, L (1981) *Intelligence, the Battle for the Mind* Macmillan: London

Forrest, G M, Smith, G A and Brown, M H (1970) *General Studies (Advanced) and Academic Aptitude* Joint Matriculation Board: Manchester

Furneaux, W D (1962) The psychologist and the university *Universities Quarterly* 17 pp 33-47

Furst, E J (1958) *Constructing Evaluation Instruments* David McKay: New York

Heywood, J (1968) Social studies and technology in the sixth form: some implications for the study of the curriculum *Studies in Education and Craft* 1 pp 12-18

Heywood, J (1977) *Examining in Second Level Education* Association of Secondary Teachers Ireland: Dublin

Heywood, J (1981) The academic versus practical debate: a case study in screening *Institution of Electrical Engineers Proceedings* 128A pp 511-19

Heywood, J and Iliffe, A (1966) *Some Aspects of Testing for Academic Performance* Bulletin No 1, Dept of Higher Education, University of Lancaster: Lancaster

Heywood, J and Kelly, D T (1973) The evaluation of coursework: a study of engineering science in schools in England and Wales, Proceedings of the Third Frontiers in Education Conference, IEEE: New York

Heywood, J, Lee, L S, Monk, J D, Moon, J, Rowley, B G H, Turner, B T and Vogler, J (1966) The education of professional mechanical engineers for design and manufacture (a model curriculum) *Lancaster Studies in Higher Education* No 1 pp 3-15

Heywood, J, McGuinness, S and Murphy, D E (1981) *Final Report of the Public Examinations Evaluation Project to the Minister for Education* School of Education, University of Dublin: Dublin

Heywood, J and Montagu-Pollock, H (1976) *Science for Arts Students: A Case Study in Curriculum Development* Society for Research into Higher Education: Guildford

Heywood, J and Youngman, M B (1982) Pupils reactions to multiple choice items in mathematics *Educational Research* 23 pp 228-9

Hobbs, M (1982) Teacher education for a pluralist society. The British Case *European Journal of Teacher Education* 5 pp 28-44

Hogan, P (1980) A critique of educational research *Oxford Review of Education* 6 (2) pp 141-55

Hogbin, J and Palmer, M (1982) Education, the city and migrant communities *European Journal of Teacher Education* 5 pp 55-64

Knefflekamp, L L (1974) Developmental instruction: fostering intellectual and personal growth of college students. Unpublished doctoral dissertation, University of Minnesota: USA

Kuhn, D (1979) The application of Piaget's theory of cognitive development to education *Harvard Educational Review* 49 (3) pp 340-60

Lawton, D (1973) *Social Change, Educational Theory and Curriculum Planning* University of London Press: London

Lawton, D *et al* (1978) *Theory and Practice of Curriculum Studies* Routledge and Kegan Paul: London

Lewis, E R L (1966) *Higher Education and the National Need* Report of the 1966 Annual Conference of the East Anglian Regional Advisory Council for Further Education: Norwich

Lynch, J (1983) *The Multicultural Curriculum* Batsford: London

Mulcahy, D G (1973) Newman's retreat from a liberal education *Irish Journal of Education* 7 (1) pp 11-22

Murphy, D E (1976) Problems associated with the implementation of a new national system of educational assessment in Ireland, MEd thesis, University of Dublin: Dublin

Perry, W (1968) *Intellectual and Ethical Development in the College Years* Holt Rinehart and Winston: New York

Shulman, L S (1970) Psychology and mathematics *in* Begle, E (ed) *Mathematics Education* 69th Year Book of the National Study for Education, University of Chicago Press: Chicago

Stenhouse, L (1975) *An Introduction to Curriculum Research and Development* Heinemann: London

Trump, J L and Miller, D F (1979) *Secondary School Curriculum Improvement: Meeting Challenges of the Times* Allyn and Bacon: Boston

Woodson, T T (1966) *An Introduction to Engineering Design* McGraw Hill: New York

Appendix

A Student Curriculum Project

by Nancy Bates

This appendix serves to illustrate first the idea of curriculum design and evaluation suggested in Chapter 10 and second a student's response to that idea. Nancy Bates is an American graduate who undertook her initial teacher training in our course and her teaching practice in a Dublin comprehensive school. The project which is presented below was undertaken as part of the coursework and as such, while informed by her teaching experience, remained as a design. Her evaluation and conclusions relating to practice and potential are of special interest. Another approach to curriculum design (in geography) by one of our students, Gina Plunkett, is given in the appendix in *Pitfalls and Planning in Student Teaching* (1982) Kogan Page: London.

Readers should be aware that in the Republic of Ireland there are no examinations in religious education and that outside of the vocational and comprehensive school system, which is administered by the State, religious studies in schools are denominationally controlled. An agreed syllabus is being developed for the Leaving Certificate Examination at the present time.

The junior second-level cycle is of three years' duration and begins at the age of 12. The project title refers to the first two years of this programme.

John Heywood

Introduction

Curriculum development is a complex and difficult process (Sockett, 1976). These difficulties are compounded when one is dealing with the highly sensitive subject of religious education.

My own attempt to develop a curriculum for first- and second-year religious education at an Irish Comprehensive School telescopes many decades of research into curriculum design. Beginning with a tidy syllabus drawn up in the comfortable isolation of my study, undistracted by knowledge of the students, I have subsequently been forced to draw up one provisional plan after another, *ad lib* in class, frequently deal with topics I had not expected to arise and jettison many topics I would dearly love to have taught.

This challenging process can now be structured in the light of both hindsight and recent curriculum development research. I found that the most satisfactory model of curriculum design is that proposed by

Heywood (1977) in *Examining in Second-Level Education* which is succinctly summarized by the diagram:

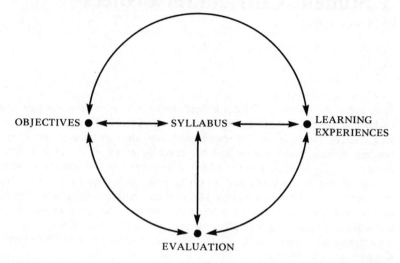

That is, the curriculum is developed by an organic process in which aims, objectives, learning strategies, syllabuses and evaluation are interdependent.

Because this is an organic process, the description of curriculum development in a linear sequence can be misleading. That the proposed curriculum begins with aims and objectives should not imply that these aims and objectives appeared, heaven-sent, fully expounded on the third of September. They are, in fact, the outcome of a rather fortuitous interplay between original aims, further theoretical study, trial learning strategies and practical evaluation.

However, for the sake of clarity, this curriculum is presented as a series of four basic steps: 1. the determination of aims and objectives; 2. the selection of learning experiences; 3. the formulation of a syllabus; 4. the formulation of evaluative procedures (Heywood, 1977). It must be emphasized again at the beginning of this paper that this linear structure is useful theoretically, but does not pretend to describe the lived experience of curriculum development which is, in fact, extraordinarily complex. For example, the phrasing of a test question can clarify an aim; the natural bent of a specific group of students can indicate a fertile learning strategy; an unforeseen event in world affairs can provoke a change in the syllabus, etc. However, all of these variables can be structured if — and only if — one's aims and objectives are clearly defined. I find the analogy of a circus juggler useful: without a clear statement of aims and objectives, the juggler is blindfolded; many, many teachers have developed, perforce, the skill of being able to juggle blindfolded. However, with a clear statement of aims and objectives the juggler can see the objects she is juggling — she can evaluate their relative weights and speeds;

the teacher in this position must continue to juggle (teaching does not suddenly become a simple leisurely pursuit!), but she can see what she is doing and plan at least one step ahead!

Aims and objectives

Thus I begin with the determination of my aims and objectives for first- and second-year religious education. The screening of aims and objectives is the most fundamental aspect of curriculum development and, particularly in the subject of religious education, it is a never ending process (Smart and Horder, 1975). I hope that my reading and experience will stimulate me to rethink and 'fine-tune' my aims and objectives as long as I am teaching.

This screening begins, as does any pursuit, with hypotheses and questions. The hypotheses are based on my past experience and education. My central hypothesis was — and still is — that non-denominational, non-catechetical religious education can be an interesting, stimulating subject that can promote an inquiring, respectful attitude to religious belief. This attitude is the foundation both of an informed religious stance and of genuine tolerance of other religions. It is my further hypothesis that this study is most profitably undertaken during adolescence when the natural scepticism of the developing child can be deepened into intelligent questioning through intellectual study.

This set of hypotheses was based on my own experience as a student and human being. It was informed by neither educational theory nor experience as a teacher. Therefore it needed to be generalized and structured. In order to articulate my aims I began not only with hypotheses but also with a series of questions (Heywood, 1977). On the most general level — determining aims — are the questions:

1. What do students need to know?
2. What do students need to think?
3. What attitudes do students need to have?

On a more specific level — determining objectives — are the questions:

1. What major insights will develop as a result of this course?
2. What change will there be in the students as a result of this course?
3. How will the pupil apply knowledge from this course?

In order to support my hypotheses and answer these questions, I investigated four current theories of, or approaches to, religious education.

The first approach is phenomenological. Championed in England by Ninian Smart and in the USA by Mircea Eliade, this is essentially comparative religions with a theoretical twist (Eliade, 1963; Smart, 1968). Different religions are studied through the lens of several invariant 'dimensions', concepts and key concepts of religion: mythical, ritual, experiential, ethical, social and doctrinal. This approach 'takes "religion" as its field of study and seeks to show what is distinctive and unique about religion as a [unique] 'mode of thought and awareness' (Grimmett, 1978).

This is a useful approach: it imposes order on a confusing jumble of information; it facilitates comparison; it provides an extremely useful theoretical 'handle' with which to conceptualize religion. The six dimensions or concepts of religion can be taught in a simple way even to first-year students (Bruner, 1960). Both as a student and as a teacher I have found it to be a successful approach.

A second approach is 'experiential'. This approach treats religion as a self-awakening; it de-emphasizes the factual information about religions in order to stress the personal, emotional and numinous aspects of religion. As with the dimensions of the phenomenological approach, this approach introduces key concepts, especially the concept of the holy in Rudolf Otto's sense (Otto, 1950). The rationale behind this approach is well stated by Grimmett:

> 'If we can help the child to learn to look into his own existential experiences at depth and then, at the appropriate time, bring religious concepts within the ambit of these experiences, not only will we assist his development of mature, creative religious concepts but also give him the opportunity of assessing their relevance or irrelevance to him.' (Grimmett, 1978)

This relevance to the student's own inner life is crucial, and it presents an extraordinary challenge to the teacher. If the student's understanding of religion is purely intellectual, then it is impoverished: it must also include emotional understanding (Grimmett, 1978).

This is a difficult, long-term task: only the foundations of this intellectual-cum-personal, emotional understanding of religion can be established at this early stage of secondary school (Hulmes, 1979).

A third approach overlaps and structures much of the content of the first two approaches. It draws on psychological theories about the moral development of the child (De Cecco and Crawford, 1974; Duska and Whelan, 1977; Grimmett, 1978). There is vigorous debate as to the relationship of religious education to moral education. Frankly, I fail to accept that there is a legitimate conflict. If religious education is taught along the lines thus far outlined it necessarily would include both a discussion of the ethical dimension of religion and a discussion of the basis of the student's own moral sense. In this scheme, therefore, moral education appears to be legitimately and properly a part of religious education.

Furthermore, the research on moral development is most helpful and illuminating to the religious education teacher. For example, Kohlberg has outlined six stages (divided into three levels) of moral development (Duska and Whelan, 1977). Like Piaget's developmental theory, Kohlberg asserts that the order of progression through these stages is invariant but may occur at different ages and that development may be arrested at any stage. However, he suggests age gradings for each level and provides tests whereby the teacher can determine the level, or entering behaviour, of each student. The crucial point to the curriculum planner is that a person is only interested in discussing moral issues at one level beyond his or her present level. To present material at a higher or lower level is at best a waste of time and at worst positively confusing (Duska and Whelan, 1977). An impression of Kohlberg's scheme may be ascertained in this radically condensed summary. An individual determines what is right and what is wrong in six developmental stages: 1. according to its physical consequences; 2. according to its self-gratification; 3. according to its conformity with perceived norms; 4. according to its strict conformity with rigid rules; 5. according to its relationship to general, theoretical standards; 6. according to the individual's own wise conscience. Stages 1. and 2. are roughly pre-adolescent, 3. and 4. are early adolescent, and 5. and 6. are late adolescent or later, if achieved at all! It is probable that students in first and second years are in stages 3. or 4. and therefore are interested in stages 4. or 5. Kohlberg's research is only one example of developmental psychology being of assistance to religious education curriculum planners. The research of Piaget (De Cecco and Crawford, 1974) and Goldman (Duska and Whelan, 1977) also helps to structure the religious education course. Their research is particularly relevant in its demonstration that students in first and second years are becoming interested in abstract and symbolic thought. This reassures the teacher that it is not too early to treat difficult concepts such as symbol, myth and justice.

The final approach to religious education to be used in the proposed curriculum is its incorporation into an integrated studies programme (Brown, 1975). This is a practical educational technique. Religious education is unlike other subjects: it cannot be thoroughly evaluated through tests, it is more personal than other subjects and, in Ireland, it is a non-exam subject. This creates many problems: students may perceive religious education classes as easy rest periods; even interested students may lose continuity with so few classes and minimal homework. Therefore, it makes sense to ally religious education with integrated studies, ie English, history and geography. It can benefit by association with these 'serious' subjects; it can enrich topics handled factually in integrated studies; it can shed its isolation and fragmentation. It would be foolish to be a slave to such a linkage, but when it seems appropriate, it should be of benefit to everyone.

The study of these four approaches to religious education, together with the study of the psychology and philosophy of education in general, and the experience of teaching religious education for a year, have served to clarify and particularize my aims. I am now ready to answer the initial question posed at the outset of the screening process.

What do students need to know? The students need to know what religion is, what role it plays in their lives and what role it plays in society. They need to know certain key concepts of religion, especially myth, ritual, the sacred and symbol. They need to know about Christianity and, to a lesser extent, about other world religions.

What do students need to think? They need to think about fundamental philsophical questions such as 'Why am I here?' and 'Who am I?' and 'What is Justice?'

What attitudes do the students need to have? They need to develop an attitude of conscious reflexivity (Teilhard de Chardin, 1959) and, therefore, self-knowledge. They need to develop a questioning, respectful attitude to the various ways people impose meaning on existence. They need to develop a conscious, articulate morality.

Thus I can state the general aims of religious education in secondary schools in the following terms:

Knowledge and comprehension

1. The student should have a clear knowledge of many aspects of Christianity: the life and teaching of Jesus, the history of the Bible and of Christianity, the different branches of Christianity;
2. The student should have a clear knowledge of the key concepts of other world religions;
3. The student should understand the key concepts of religion in general.

Skills

1. The student should be able to evaluate and comprehend any set of religious data according to the key concepts that have been learned;
2. The student should be able to apply knowledge about religions to other fields;
3. The student should be able to interpret and weigh any evangelization directed at him or her.

Attitudes

1. The student should know and be able to articulate his or her own stance to religion;
2. The student should know and be able to articulate his or her own stance to moral issues;
3. The student should develop an attitude of informed respect and tolerance to other religious traditions;
4. The student should be curious about the philosophical questions dealt with in religion.

These general aims lead to particular objectives for each year. Obviously all the aims cannot be incorporated into every year, but there should be a balance in each year between the cognitive and the affective domains.

Thus one can particularize and structure the course for the first year by first answering the questions posed at the beginning of the search for objectives.

The major insight of this first-year course will show that religion is not simply an 'irrelevant' exercise on Sundays; it relates to one's own way of life and it sheds light on human culture.

As a result of this course the student will be more 'reflexive', have a firmer knowledge of the life and teachings of Jesus and of the religion of the Celts, and have the rudiments of a theoretical understanding of religion.

The student will apply these changes in three domains: 1. in his or her own way of life, 2. in academic studies and 3. in future religious education courses.

Thus, stated simply, the main objectives of the first-year religious education course are:

Specific

1. Knowledge of the life and message of Jesus as portrayed in the Gospels;
2. Knowledge of three basic religious concepts: myth, symbol and ritual as they relate to Celtic religion.

General

1. Initial reflection on own life and own religious stance;
2. Initial reflection on own moral stance;
3. Appreciation and respect for others' viewpoints.

Repeating this process for the second year, I can state that the major insight of the course will be that religion is a complex phenomenon embracing a people's way of life, morality and history.

As a result of this course the student will have a broad concept of religion that will enable him or her to structure information about diverse religions; the student will have rudimentary knowledge of some aspects of the history of Christianity; and the student will have thought deeply about one of Dublin's social problems.

The student will apply these changes to his or her personal life, to academic study and to future religious education classes.

We can now state boldly the aims of the second year:

Specific

1. Knowledge of several key events in Christian history;
2. Basic knowledge of role of Christianity in Ireland today;
3. Basic knowledge of the sociology of religion as it applies to urban/rural contrast;
4. 'Spiralwise' reinforcement and expansion of understanding of key concepts: myth, symbol, ritual, the sacred, etc.

General

1. Awareness of the significance of their adolescent stage of life as conceived by religions of many cultures;
2. Deep thought about one of Dublin's social problems;
3. Deeper respect and appreciation of others' points of view.

The justification and reasoning behind these specific objectives should become clearer as learning strategies, the syllabuses and evaluative procedures are described. It should be clear at this stage that they particularize the general aims of religious education, that they lay the groundwork for further study of religion along phenomenological and experiential lines and that they begin to develop a critical moral sense in a psychologically sound manner.

Learning strategies

Given these general aims and particular objectives, the curriculum designer must determine the best possible way to achieve his or her objectives.

It is useful at this point to take the specific school situation and entering behaviour of the students into account. My school is an unusual school in the Irish context. A Protestant comprehensive, it has an inter-denominational staff and student body. Both staff and students (and their parents) tend to be liberal in their religious beliefs; they are undogmatic and eager not to give offence. Religious education seems not to have been given top priority. Last academic year it was only scheduled for one 35-minute lesson each week to each class of approximately 30 students. (This year there will be two lessons a week for the first three forms.) It is a non-exam subject and very little homework is assigned. There are few available class sets of textbooks. However, to counteract these difficulties, the school offers the teacher of religious education several significant advantages: the staff, particularly the chaplain, is supportive of serious innovation, and the students and their parents are sufficiently liberal to enable experimentation to occur, which, I suspect, would be anathema in many Irish schools.

The entering behaviour of the students is varied. The catchment area of the school is broad, and students from diverse backgrounds are present in every class. However, in terms of religious education it seems fair to generalize that a minority of students have undergone a rigorous training in religion, either in primary school catechetics religion classes, regular church attendance or Sunday school. The majority appears to be quite poorly informed about all things religious and, furthermore, not highly motivated to be better informed! Indeed it may be postulated that their very eagerness not to give offence has dampened their natural curiosity. Of course, in order to determine entering behaviour, several simple tests could be given along the lines, 'Are you a Christian? If so, of what denomination? When did you last attend a religious service? Of what kind? Why did you attend?' etc. However, such a survey would have its drawbacks – it could be construed as an invasion of privacy and it could mislead students as to the aims of the religious education course. A more sensitive and useful test would be one along the lines of Piaget's tests of moral judgement (Duska and Whelan, 1977). These would provide both useful information to the curriculum planner and a standard with which to assess one aspect of the year's work. It is my intention to administer this type of test this year.

The aims of the religious education course must be seen in the light of this particular school situation. It colours many aspects of the curriculum: due to the interdenominational and liberal nature of the school, it does not pursue any catechetical line of argument; due to the students' general lack of knowledge the curriculum begins with the basics of Christianity — the life and message of Jesus.

The lack of emphasis placed on religious education in the general curriculum has moulded, of necessity, several learning strategies of the religious education curriculum. The best way to overcome the lack of time, resources, and examinations of religious education is to integrate it with other more 'serious' subjects, particularly with the well-developed integrated studies course in the Junior cycle.

Given these initial considerations, it is possible to diagram the objectives and learning strategies for first and second years.

First-year objectives and learning strategies

Objective	Learning strategy
(a)1. Knowledge of life and message of Jesus	— Link life of Jesus with their own lives, being investigated in the Integrated Studies unit on 'autobiography'. — Read original sources (four gospels). — Filmstrips. — Role-play exercises.
2. Knowledge of three concepts: symbol, myth, ritual	— Link this with a study of Celtic religion to be allied with Integrated Studies unit on 'The Celts'. — Visits to Newgrange and Craganoen. — Role-play — acting myths and rituals. — Many supplementary examples of myths, symbols, rituals presented by teacher to class.
(b)1. Reflection on own life	— Supplement Integrated Studies unit on 'autobiography' particularly stressing philosophical question of identity. — Extensive discussion.
2. Reflection on morality	— In conjunction with 'autobiography' stress practical moral questions. — Role-play is especially useful here.
3. Development of respect and tolerance	— Discussion and listening. — Role-play.

Second-year objectives and learning strategies

Objective	Learning strategy
(a) 1. Knowledge of Christian history	— Link with Integrated Studies projects on 'Dublin' and 'Aran'. — Visits to Dublin and to Aran. — Independent project work. — Filmstrips.
2. Knowledge of role of Christianity in Ireland today	— Natural stage of 'Dublin' and 'Aran' projects, dealing with modern times. — Visits to Dublin and Aran. — Independent project work especially 'My Local Church'.
3. Sociology of urban/ rural contrast	— Final, comparative stage of 'Dublin' and 'Aran' projects. — Discussion and essay.
4. Reinforcement of key concepts	— Study of simple, alien religions, especially the Hopi Indians. — Lectures, reading. — Slides.
(b) 1. Adolescent initiation	— Link with study of Hopis. — Independent research. — Discussion.
2. Social problems	— Independent project as part of 'Dublin' project. — Role-play. — Outside speaker.
3. Broaden respect and tolerance	— Discussion and listening.

Syllabus

With the articulation of objectives and learning strategies, a syllabus is almost an afterthought or, as Heywood has stated, the outcome of the curriculum process. Far from being the backbone of the curriculum, it is its outgrowth. This is advantageous because it means that the syllabus can be very flexible whilst the curriculum need not essentially change.

Perhaps an analogy would clarify the radical difference between the old and new procedures of curriculum design. The old way — syllabus first — is like an invertebrate. The rigid outer skeleton of the syllabus restricts the development of the aims, learning strategies and evaluations of the inner organism. The new way — aims first — is like a vertebrate. The aims present a flexible yet strong spinal cord from which emanate learning strategies and evaluations. The syllabus, to extend the metaphor, is like the shape of the body: it is dependent on the bone structure but, within limits, it can be modified.

The syllabus is simply the organization and elaboration of learning strategies. Thus, in outline form, the syllabuses are:

Syllabus for first year

SECTION 1

(20 weeks) Autobiography and Life of Jesus. Each week there are two lessons: (a) and (b). These two lessons follow parallel but distinct routes. (a) relates closely to the Integrated Studies unit on 'autobiography' and will use the IS textbook *Families and Friends* (CDVEC, 1978). (b) is linked in content with (a) and will use the *New Testament* as its text.

The rationale behind this split approach is that two different teachers are timetabled to teach the two RE classes each week.

Week 1:   (a) and (b): Introductory sessions.
Week 2:   (a) Birth: discussion of own birth; celebrations and rituals of birth.
          (b) Birth of Jesus.
Weeks 3   (a) Socialization; discussion; lecture on extreme examples of
and 4:   socialization, eg wolf child.
          (b) Society in Palestine in Jesus' day.
Weeks 5   (a) Significant events in one's own life: turning points,
and 6:   moments of joy, moments of confusion.
          (b) Significant events in Jesus' life: in the temple, the temptation (role-play).
Week 7:   (a) Growing up – discussion, short essay, brief lecture on initiation.
          (b) The ministry of Jesus, music from Jesus Christ Superstar.
Week 8:   (a) Future goals – discussion.
          (b) Jesus' death.
Week 9:   (a) Whatever cannot be described in words; discussion of symbol; bring in music, art, dance, etc.
          (b) The Resurrection.
Week 10: (a) Review.
          (b) Filmstrip.
Week 11: (a) Families in other cultures: Celtic fosterage, Israeli Kibbutz.
          (b) Jesus' attitude to the family.
Week 12: (a) People without families and families in need; visit to old people's home; work of Simon and Samaritans; work of Concern; collect rose-hips.
          (b) The Christian concept of the poor and social justice.
Week 13: (a) Rules needed in a family; role-play.
          (b) The 10 Commandments and Jesus' attitude to the law.
Week 14: (a) Discussion about what one can do to help one's family.
          (b) The Christian emphasis on love.

Week 15: (a) Friends: who they are, what influence they have, etc;
                discussion and role-play.
          (b) The Disciples.
Week 16: (a) Gangs and bullies and scapegoats.
          (b) The persecution of Jesus.
Week 17: (a) The 'rules' of friendship.
          (b) Christian 'rules' or ideals of behaviour.
Week 18: (a) Role models and heroes. The influence of media: crushes.
          (b) Different types of love.
Week 19: (a) The influence of school.
          (b) The influence of the Church.
Week 20: Review.

SECTION 2
(10 weeks) The Religion of the Celts. In this section there will be no
division between the two lessons each week. Both will deal in a straightforward manner with the religion of the Celts. This will be closely linked
with the Integrated Studies section on 'The Celts'. It will use the two
texts, *The Celtic Way of Life* and *The Ulster Cycle* (CDVEC, 1976).

Week 1:   (a) What is a symbol?
          (b) Symbols in everyday life; symbols in religious life.
Week 2:   (a) Investigation of Celtic spirals.
          (b) Visit to Newgrange.
Week 3:   (a) Link need for symbols to inadequacy of language to
                describe everything about oneself, discussed earlier.
          (b) Rituals as a type of symbol. Examples of rituals.
Week 4:   (a) Celtic sacrifices.
          (b) The meaning of sacrifice.
Week 5:   (a) Celtic calendric rituals: Samain, Bealtaine, Lughnasa.
                Lughnasa.
          (b) Primitive and modern ideas of time.
Week 6:   (a) Celtic magic and druids.
          (b) Celtic burial rites.
Week 7:   (a) Myth: read *The Children of Lir*.
          (b) Contrast with heroic tale in *The Ulster Cycle*.
Week 8:   (a) Examples of myths.
          (b) Myth as a type of symbol.
Week 9:   (a) Myths in our own culture.
          (b) Is science a myth?
Week 10: (a) Review.

Syllabus for second year

Note: Each week there are two lessons (a) and (b). These two lessons
follow distinct routes. (a) closely relates to integrated studies projects
and will use the texts associated with it: *Viking Settlement* to *Medieval
Dublin*, *World of Stone*, *Field and Shore*, *Island Stories* and *Aran*
(CDVEC, 1977; 1978; Daly, 1975). (b) is independent and will use *From*

Fear to Faith (Wigley, 1970) and handouts. Because (a) and (b) are not related to each other, and because they are taught by different teachers, they will be listed separately.

CURRICULUM (a)

Section One: Religion in Dublin (10 weeks)

Week 1:   Introduction to Dublin Project.
Week 2:   Church architecture
          –   sharpen observation
          –   slides and vocabulary.
Weeks 3   History of church in Dublin very briefly
and 4:   –   reading *Viking and Medieval Settlement* pp 84-96.
Week 5:   Dublin churches
          –   prepare for class trip to Dublin
            cf A Guide to Historic Dublin (MacLoughlin, 1979).
Week 6:   Social problems in Dublin
          –   discussion of causes and role of church
          –   poverty, read *Janey Mary* by James Plunkett.
Weeks 7,   Project on social problems in Dublin, including
8 and 9:   1. questions on worksheet on Dublin trip
           2. outside speaker
           3. short story
           4. writing of educational leaflet.
Week 10: Review.

Section Two: Religion in Aran (10 weeks)

Week 1:   Monasticism: brief historical background: origins in Egypt
          –   lecture with slides.
Week 2:   Spread to the West and development of orders
Week 3:   Daily life.
Week 4:   Celtic religion and society: review of first year
           cf World p 25, *Aran* pp 8-9.
Week 5:   Conversion to Christianity
           cf World pp 35-43, *Aran* p 9.
Week 6:   Island of saints and scholars: Aran as a Christian monastic
           settlement
           cf Aran pp 9-10.
Week 7:   Devotions
           cf Aran pp 34-5, *Field* pp 97-135.
Week 8:   Impact of Reformation
           cf World pp 46-8, *Aran* pp 11-14.
Week 9:   Religion on Aran today
          –   discuss students' impressions of their trip.
Week 10: Review.

Section Three: A comparison of religion in Dublin and in Aran (10 weeks)

Week 1:	Overview and review of previous two sections.

Weeks 2 and 3:	Survey of historical differences and similarities
	  — pre-Christian religion
	  — method and date conversion
	  — development of monasticism
	  — impact of reformation.

Week 4:	Comparison of role of Church in society.
Week 5:	— in education.
Week 6:	— in health care.
Week 7:	— pluralism.
Week 8:	— secularization.
Week 9:	— discussion about the future for both.
Week 10:	Review.

CURRICULUM (b)

Section One

Week 1: Introduction: reasons for studying primitive religions; importance of studying religion as it works in a culture, therefore an emphasis on Hopi Indians.
cf Living Tribal Religions (Turner, 1971) and handout.

Week 2: Introduction to the Hopis: geography, history, way of life.
cf Four Ways of Being Human (Lisitzky, 1956) and handout.

Weeks 3 and 4: Gods and spirits — Mana, 'animism', supreme beings, ancestral spirits, totemic spirits
— reading
— discussion about reading and general questions, eg What is God? How would you describe God?
— possible link with art department, eg make totem poles
cf From Fear to Faith pp 6-9, 20-2, *Living* pp 10-16, handout on Hopi gods, with pictures of Kachinas.

Week 5: Revelation and hierophany through special experiences
— discussion of students' experiences
— reading of others' experiences
cf Living pp 17-19, *From Primitives to Zen* (Eliade, 1967) pp 16-18, *Sunchief* (Simmons, 1942) pp 47-9 for Hopi experience.

Week 6: In special places and at special times — concept of sacred space and sacred time
— discussion of special places and times
— readings
cf Living pp 19-21, *Book of the Hopi* (Waters, 1963) pp 126-31 for discussion of Hopi Kivas.

Week 7: By use of symbols
— discussion of symbols

Weeks 8
and 9:

Week 10:

— reading and drawing
cf Fear pp 71-5, *Living* pp 21-4, *Book* pp 131-6 for
Hopi symbols.

Response in prayer and offering
— discussion of prayers
cf Primitives pp 268-82, *Living* pp 28-30, *Four* p 256 for
Hopi prayer, discussion of offering and sacrifice
cf Fear pp 39-47, *Primitives* pp 201-29.

Review.

Section Two: Ritual

Week 1:

Week 2:

Weeks 3,
4 and 5:

Weeks 6
and 7:

Weeks 8
and 9:

Week 10:

Response in ritual: calendric rituals
— discussion of seasonal and calendric rituals in our culture
cf Four pp 256-73 for Hopi rituals, especially the Snake
Dance.

Life-crisis rituals: the cycle of life
(a) Birth
— discussion of our birth rituals
— reading
cf Fear pp 52-4, *Four* pp 274-6 for Hopi birth rites.

(b) Initiation
— discussion of initiation in our culture: adolescence,
confirmation, bar mitzvah, tribal rituals of initiation,
emphasis on symbolism of death and rebirth. Mention
episode in 'Roots'
— vision quest
cf Four pp 276-80 for Hopi initiation, *Rites and Symbols
of Initiation* (Eliade, 1958), *Primitives* pp 287-97.

(c) Marriage
— discussion and reading
cf Fear p 55, *Four* pp 280-2 for Hopi marriage.

(d) Death
— discussion and reading, death of pets might be easiest
'ice-breaking' discussion topic. Emphasize need to express
grief beyond talking — need to 'ritualize'
cf Fear pp 56-9, *Primitives* pp 359-71, *Four* pp 282-4
for Hopi death rituals (if time, could discuss ghosts).

Review.

Section Three: Specialists, myth, magic

Weeks 1
and 2:

Specialists: Shamans and medicine men. Discussion of 'holy
people' — What makes them holy? Why do we need
intermediaries?
cf Fear pp 30-6 and 10-11, *Living* pp 33-6, *Primitives*
pp 423-46, *Four* p 253 for Hopi specialists.

Weeks 3,	Myths: creation myths, theory of myth
4 and 5:	— discussion what is a myth?
	— brief lecture: theories of mythology
	cf Fear pp 17-19, *Primitives* pp 83-117, *Living* pp 24-5,
	Book pp 3-23 for Hopi creation myth, handout on
	theories of myth.
Weeks 6	Magic and religion and witchcraft
and 7:	— discussion: What is relationship, what is difference?
	— reading: types of magic
	cf Living pp 8-9, *The Heathens* (Howells, 1962)
	pp 46-65, 104-24.
Weeks 8	Morals and religion: an ethical response
and 9:	— discussion
	cf Living p 31.
Week 10:	Review: emphasis on definition of religion.

Evaluation

Evaluation will be complex and multi-faceted. In part this is due to the fact that all assessment should encompass a variety of techniques (Heywood, 1977), but it is more particularly due to the fact that religious education must 'transcend the informative' (Smart, 1968). In other words, in religious education non-behavioural aims and objectives are stressed to a degree unknown in other subjects. These non-behavioural objectives are, by definition, very hard, if not impossible, to test adequately.

One can certainly test the 'informative' aspects of religious education by objective tests, short 'modified essay' tests and extended essays. The attitudinal aspects of religious education can be evaluated both in class discussions and in personal essays. However, this assessment will rest essentially on the intuition and judgement of the teacher; I see no way to overcome this subjectivity. It is important to note that it would be ludicrous — indeed, presumptuous — to assess attitudinal objectives were this traditional catechesis. I certainly would be unwilling to cast myself in a role determining the 'saintliness' of any pupil! However, with the non-behavioural objectives of this curriculum the situation for assessment is ameliorated: the teacher need here note personal development, deepening of thought, articulateness and awareness of others.

The primary challenge in testing religious education is to maintain a balance between behavioural and non-behavioural objectives and to communicate this balance effectively to the students. There is a danger that, because they are easily tested, behavioural objectives will overshadow non-behavioural objectives. This is very undesirable. One way to guard against this might be to have a tripartite assessment procedure: one third the testing of behavioural aims, one third the testing of those non-behavioural aims that can be assessed in an essay, and one third the assessment of contributions in class.

In this way we can devise an outline of assessment for first and second years.

Assessment for first year

SECTION ONE (NON-BEHAVIOURAL OBJECTIVES)
The first section of the assessment is based on the teacher's evaluation of the student's participation in class discussion. This section should be scored individually; that is, each student is judged according to his or her own abilities, not comparatively. Each category is marked on a scale of 1 - 5. They are here expressed in their highest form (5):

(a) This student listened attentively.
(b) This student joined constructively in class discussions.
(c) This student made articulate and thoughtful contributions.
(d) The contributions and demeanour of this student showed a development of tolerance.
(e) The contributions and demeanour of this student showed an effort to grapple with philosophical questions.
(f) The contributions and demeanour of this student showed an effort to grapple with moral problems.

SECTION TWO (BEHAVIOURAL OBJECTIVES)

(a) Objective test about life and teaching of Jesus (5 points)
    — tests knowledge.
(b) Objective test about the religion of the Celts (5 points)
    — tests knowledge.
(c) Short answer test about the basic concepts of Christianity (15 points)
    — tests comprehension.
(d) Short answer test about the key concepts of religion — myth, symbol, ritual (15 points)
    — tests comprehension and analysis.

SECTION THREE (BOTH BEHAVIOURAL AND NON-BEHAVIOURAL OBJECTIVES)

(a) Autobiography coursework (10 points)
    — short essay in conjunction with IS project
    — reflection being tested.
(b) Essay test in two sections (20 points)
    — tests analysis and judgement.
    1. Think back over all the work you did this year on your autobiography. Can you think of any ways in which this increased knowledge of yourself will affect your life?
    2. Describe an occasion when you felt you were treated unfairly. Describe your argument to a judge to prove that you were wronged.

Assessment for second year

SECTION ONE (NON-BEHAVIOURAL OBJECTIVES) 30 points

As for first year.

SECTION TWO (BEHAVIOURAL OBJECTIVES)

(a) Objective test on Christian knowledge: church architecture, monasticism, reformation, etc
  — tests knowledge (15 points).
(b) Objective test on role of church in Ireland today, both in Dublin and Aran (10 points).
(c) Objective test on basic concepts of religion (15 points).

SECTION THREE (BEHAVIOURAL AND NON-BEHAVIOURAL OBJECTIVES)

(a) Project on social problems (10 points)
  — tests comprehension and analysis.
(b) Essay test on basic concepts of religion (20 points)
  — tests comprehension and analysis.:
  1. Imagine that a Hopi student came to this school. In what ways would he or she be different from you? In what ways would he or she be the same?
  2. Imagine that you are an anthropologist studying the religion of a primitive tribe. What types of things might you look for to include in your description of their religion?
  3. (a) Bearing in mind your answer to question 2, how would you define religion?
     (b) Do you think it is possible to have a human group without any religious beliefs? Give examples to support your answer.

Conclusion

With the determination of evaluative procedures we are brought back full circle to our aims and objectives. Curriculum development is a continuous spiral in which one is always building on past experience and adapting to new conditions. This proposed curriculum is, therefore, provisional. Even as I commit it to paper I can envisage further changes and emendations. This investigation caused great frustration but, at the same time, was both creative and challenging.

References

Brown, M (1975) Religious education in integrated studies *in* Smart, N and Horder, D (eds) *New Movements in Religious Education* Temple Smith: London

Bruner, J (1960) *The Process of Education* Harvard University Press, Cambridge: Massachusetts

City of Dublin Vocational Education Committee Curriculum Development Unit (1976) *The Celtic Way of Life: The Ulster Cycle* O'Brien Educational: Dublin

City of Dublin Vocational Education Committee Curriculum Development Unit (1977) *Island Life Series: A World of Stone; Field and Shore: Island Stories* O'Brien Educational: Dublin

City of Dublin Vocational Education Committee Curriculum Development Unit (1978) *Families and Friends* O'Brien Educational: Dublin

Daly, L (1975) *Aran* Albertine Kennedy: Swinford

De Cecco, J P and Crawford, W R (1974) *The Psychology of Learning and Instruction* Second Edition, Prentice Hall Inc: New Jersey

Duska, R and Whelan, M (1977) *Moral Development* Gill and Macmillan: Dublin

Eliade, M (1958) *Rites and Symbols of Initiation* Harper and Row: New York

Eliade, M (1963) *Patterns in Comparative Religion* World: New York

Eliade, M (1967) *From Primitives to Zen* Harper and Row: New York

Grimmitt, M (1978) *What Can I Do in RE?* Second Edition, Mahew McCrimmon: Great Wakering

Heywood, J (1977) *Examining in Second Level Education* Association of Secondary School Teachers of Ireland: Dublin

Heywood, J (1982) *Pitfalls and Planning in Student Teaching* Kogan Page: London

Howells, W W (1962) *The Heathens* Anchor: New York

Hulmes, E (1979) *Commitment and Neutrality in Religious Education* Geoffrey Chapman: London

Lisitzky, G (1956) *Four Ways of Being Human* Viking: New York

MacLoughlin, A (1979) *Guide to Historic Dublin* Gill and MacMillan: Dublin

Otto, R (1950) *The Idea of the Holy* Oxford University Press: London

Simmons, L (ed) (1942) *Sun Chief* Yale University Press: New Haven

Smart, N (1968) *Secular Education and the Logic of Religion* Faber: London

Smart, N and Horder, D (eds) (1975) *New Movements in Religious Education* Temple Smith: London

Sockett, H (1976) *Designing the Curriculum* Open Books: London

Teilhard de Chardin, P (1959) *The Phenomenon of Man* Harper and Row: New York

Turner, H (1971) *Living Tribal Religions* Ward Lock Educational: London

Waters, F (1963) *Book of the Hopi* Penguin: Harmondsworth

Wigley, B (1970) *From Fear to Faith* Longman: London

Name Index

Subject Index